THE NEW KEY
TO ...
Thir...

D0763324

"This guide's unself-righteous ecoconscious slant is a plus, and Ritz has clearly done her homework regarding outdoor activities. . . . Her coverage of outdoor pastimes is worth the price of admission."

—*Escape Magazine*

"This guide is dedicated to the preservation of Belize's rare and endangered species, architecture and archaeology, and is based on thousands of miles of field research. It highlights the intriguing contributions of the nation's conservationist pioneers and is as much fun for the armchair traveler as the ardent explorer."

—*Milwaukee Journal*

"Because of its complete attention to the overall picture as well to practical details, I recommend *The New Key to Belize* as a great way to unlock the door to Belize's paradise."

—*The Edmonton Sun*

"There is little doubt that guide-writing veteran Stacy Ritz has spent a fair share of time in Belize. Ritz's flowing writing style makes devouring her book easy reading, even for the person who doesn't plan a Belize trip but wonders what's there."

—*Birmingham News*

THE NEW KEY TO BELIZE
Third Edition

STACY RITZ

GLENN KIM
Illustrator

Ulysses Press

Published by: Ulysses Press
                  3286 Adeline Street, Suite 1
                  Berkeley, CA 94703

Library of Congress Catalog Card Number 97-60638
ISBN 1-56975-085-8

Printed in Canada by Best Book Manufacturers

10 9 8 7 6 5 4 3

Executive Editor: Leslie Henriques
Managing Editor: Claire Chun
Copy Editor: David Sweet
Editorial Associates: Natasha Lay, Lily Chou, Kim Suina
Cartography: Lee Micheaux, Phil Gardner, Claire Chun
Cover Illustration: Deidre Hyde
Cover Design: Leslie Henriques
Indexer: Sayre Van Young
Contributing writers: Nicole O'Hay, Richard Harris

Distributed in the United States by Publishers Group West, in Canada by Raincoast Books, and in Great Britain and Europe by World Leisure Marketing

In memory of Judith Kahn, who I deeply miss

Acknowledgments

As *The New Key to Belize* enters its third edition, I must first thank Nicole O'Hay who spent five weeks in Belize and Guatemala, exploring the cayes and probing the jungle, checking out ruins and reserves, lodges and eateries to update this book. Also at Ulysses, I offer sincere thanks to copy editor David Sweet and proofreaders Natasha Lay, Lily Chou and Kim Suina for jobs well done. And I can't imagine this project without Managing Editor Claire Chun at the helm. Her thoroughness, attention to detail, and unwavering professionalism are why things always run smoothly.

Glenn Kim is responsible for the compelling illustrations. Richard Harris, my co-author on *The Maya Route*, is responsible for Chapter Eleven, an enthusiastic and beautiful passage to the Peten in Guatemala and the Copán region of Honduras. Thanks Richard—you're the best.

For their hospitality and insights into Belize, I owe thanks to George and Corol Bevier, Tom and Josie Harding, Mick and Lucy Fleming, Rosita Arvigo and Sharon Matola, who also extended friendship. Special recognition goes to Eneida Verde at the Belize Tourist Board, and to Joan Medhurst and Christine Pressimone at Medhurst & Associates for answering the thousandth question.

And last but foremost, I am indebted to David Ritz, my number one traveling companion who also happens to be my husband. His unfailing patience and objectivity during the creation of this book will never be forgotten.

The New Key to Belize Green Rating

It is unlikely that you will encounter a place so conscious of the environment as Belize. No matter who you meet—taxi drivers, restaurant cooks, bank tellers—they will have some opinion on how their country can be preserved, especially now in the face of increasing tourism.

Among those who deserve special recognition for environmental efforts are lodge owners, who every day must weigh the immediate value of guest receipts against the value and future of their surroundings. *The New Key To Belize* recognizes and recommends those lodges that strive to follow the principles of ecotourism, including protecting local habitats and wildlife, conserving energy and employing local residents. Throughout the text, these lodges are distinguished by a special Green Rating (✪).

To obtain information about Belize lodges, researchers visited each one, interviewing owners and staff as well as guests and former guests. I also mailed an Ecotourism Questionnaire to most of the lodges highlighted in *The New Key To Belize* (those that I observed violating ecotourism principles were omitted), inquiring about numerous issues such as water and sewage disposal, use of biodegradable soap, conservation training for employees and guests, support for local environmental organizations, and what impact the lodge had on the environment during construction.

More than 30 lodges received the Green Rating, and many go well beyond the call to ecotourism. One dive lodge, for instance, prints a special brochure warning guests about damaging the precious coral reef. A jungle lodge uses local Maya talent for everything from employee uniforms and nightly dinners to room furnishings and guided tours. And a fishing lodge forbids anglers to hold their fish vertically when posing for pictures, since it may injure the fish before it is released.

This is all good news for Belize, and for travelers seeking to experience a *real* place taking pains to protect its natural treasures. At these lodges, guests can immerse themselves in the beauty and history of the region. And they can get to know Belizeans and their wonderfully diverse culture.

When booking a room, remember that these lodges, by their very nature, are not fancy but rather comfortably charming and altogether Belizean. Some are beachside bungalows whose windward architecture catches lots of sea breezes, while others are jungle huts with wild monkeys just outside the thatched door. Of course, no matter where you stay in Belize, remember to be an ecotourist.

LODGES RECEIVING GREEN RATINGS

THE CAYES

Ambergris Caye: Victoria House (pages 83–84); Caribbean Villas (page 84); El Pescador (page 86)

Caye Caulker: Chocolate's (page 93); Vega Inn and Gardens (page 94)

St. George's Caye: Cottage Colony (page 96)

The Atolls: Turneffe Island Lodge (page 99); Manta Resort (page 100)

BELIZE CITY

Colton House (page 108)

WESTERN BELIZE

Belmopan: Warrie Head Ranch and Lodge (page 134)

Cayo Country: Caesar's Place (page 138); Mida's Resort (page 139); Maya Mountain Lodge (page 139); Chaa Creek (page 140); duPlooy's (page 140); Windy Hill Cottages (pages 140–41); Black Rock Jungle River Lodge (page 141)

Mountain Pine Ridge and Caracol: Hidden Valley Inn (page 152); Pine Ridge Lodge (pages 152–53); Blancaneaux Lodge (page 153)

Chan Chich: Chan Chich Lodge (page 155)

SOUTHERN BELIZE

Dangriga: Pelican Beach Resort (pages 164–65); Jaguar Reef Lodge (page 165)

Placencia: Rum Point Inn (page 168)

SIDE TRIPS FROM BELIZE

Western Side Trips: Tikal Inn (page 188); El Gringo Perdido (page 189); Hotel Maya Internacional (page 189)

Southern Side Trips: Hotel La Casa Rosada (page 194); Hotel Catamaran (page 194); El Tortugal Resort (page 194); Hacienda El Jaral (page 200)

Spiny anteater

"The land is one great wild, untidy luxuriant hothouse, made by nature for herself."
— Charles Darwin, *Voyage of the Beagle*

Introduction

THE ADVENTURE COAST

There are places in Belize where no human has ever laid foot, at least not in the last 1000 years, not since the time when the ancient Maya ruled these jungles from their lofty pyramids. Most regions that have been explored are still wild and rugged, possessed by beautiful beasts and birds, by silky green seas overflowing with life and palm-speckled shores reveling in seclusion, by mountains wrapped in colossal trees and forests carpeted with flamboyant flowers and emerald greenery, luxuriating, as it were, in nature's own hothouse.

How nature has reigned so long here, and how Belize has come to be so undiscovered, is due at least in part to its secret location. Indeed, the tiny country is but a blink on the map of Central America, wedged between formidable Guatemala and Mexico's vast Yucatán Peninsula, a mite-sized piece of jungle confronting two giants. Facing the Caribbean, Belize seems ready to break from land and fling itself out to sea.

But packed into this country the size of Massachusetts is an array of natural wonders, including the world's second-longest barrier reef (behind Australia's), where a thread of unspoiled isles are washed by the Caribbean Sea. Here also is the world's only jaguar preserve, the longest chain of caves in the Western Hemisphere, and the seventh-highest waterfall in the world.

Wild animals come in a splendorous array of shapes, sizes and names, from spiny anteaters, spider monkeys and red-eyed tree frogs to kinkajou bears, hawksbill turtles and bare-throated tiger herons. Fishing and scuba diving are so outstanding, their praises are whispered so as not to spoil their secrets.

Beyond the natural wonders is a lost manmade world slowly waking from its jungle slumber. Entire Maya cities, some only discovered in the last 45 years, are being resurrected by teams of archaeologists. Each day's excavations reveal marvels offering few explanations and many mysteries, beckoning outsiders to come ponder Belize's ancient treasures. Toothy pyramids loom on mountain ridges, and three-story-high masks stare out from jungle haunts. Elaborate networks of reservoirs, causeways and *sacbes*, or ancient roads, link age-old cities sprinkled down the length of this Adventure Coast.

Here are five distinct regions—the Cayes, Belize City, northern Belize, western Belize and southern Belize. Of course, the Cayes actually extend off the coast, forming a thread of islands trimmed in coral rock and mangroves. Only about two dozen of the islands are inhabited and only two, Ambergris Caye and Caye Caulker, possess villages. Right on the coast, covering a finger of land, is Belize City. Belize's only real city, it is the country's center of business.

North of Belize City, northern Belize presents a lush, lonely landscape harboring the powerful ancient ceremonial center of Lamanai and the peaceful Altun Ha, where fantastic jade artifacts have been found. Here, too, are vast sanctuaries for birds, butterflies and baboons, the Belizean name for howler monkeys. Western Belize attracts chic adventurers who stay in charming jungle lodges and explore Maya medicine trails, the popular ruins at Xunantunich and the cool, shady depths of the Mountain Pine Ridge forest. The west is also home to the great Caracol, a Maya city swallowed in jungle, hours from civilization, and home to the tallest building in Belize.

Southern Belize is a far-flung outback where hard-core explorers go to see what few travelers have seen: primitive Maya and Garifuna villages and the profound ruins at Lubaantun and Nim Li Punit. Along the southern coast is an anomaly called Placencia, whose pure white beaches and sun-dappled waters are attracting a coterie of young travelers and fueling tourism and development. Inland, impermeable cloud forests cover much of the region, protecting an extraordinary web of life, including the world's densest population of jaguars, who reside at Cockscomb Basin Wildlife Sanctuary.

For those who would adventure beyond Belize's borders, thrilling side trips await to the west and south. Guatemala's Petén, North America's largest rainforest, sprawls across Belize's western border, thrilling travelers with the exquisite and daunting Maya city of Tikal. Southward from Belize is Guatemala's Río Dulce, the picturesque "Sweet River" that leads to relaxing, time-locked villages. And then there is Copán, just across the Honduras border and enveloped in banana plantations, the site of unequaled Maya stone sculpture and hieroglyphic carvings.

Throughout these regions, travelers will find few creature comforts. Instead, they will discover a land that still belongs to the rainforest and to the sea, not to the frills of tourism. For unlike the money-driven throngs of "developed" countries, the residents of Belize have chosen to stay undeveloped, preferring the old, natural ways to the new, glitzy ones, opting to build a simple thatched lodge instead of a seaside highrise, to make nature and culture, not some contrived theme park, the big attractions.

And therein lies the reason for Belize's decided allure, and for the traveler's compulsion to go back once she has returned home, an affliction known as the "Belize Factor." Belize holds boundless opportunities for adventure, beckoning around every turn of a wornout jungle road, calling from every mountaintop washed in sun-dappled haze, waiting deep in a sea set with brilliant coral.

There is a certain innocence in Belize, a simple existence where the rigors of life have not yet slipped in. Events here often seem surreal: rabbits hop around a restaurant floor, a monkey joins you for breakfast, and toucans fill the garden where you're having a jungle massage. Women wash their clothes in the rivers and cook iguanas on their wood-fired stoves. No one wears shoes on the islands, but why should they, since the streets are made of sand.

After awhile, when you begin thinking Belize might be a little too primitive, too far out there, something Belizean happens. Like a destitute farmer donating his land to save the animals. Or a Maya villager taking time to show a stranger how to grind corn. Or a wild dolphin taking you for a swim off an isolated island. And then you fall in love with Belize all over again.

Belize is just like that. In no time, it burrows deep into your consciousness. And before you know it, you find yourself humming a Garifuna tune, listening for the howl of a monkey, searching the horizon for the familiar site of a Maya village.

Table of Contents

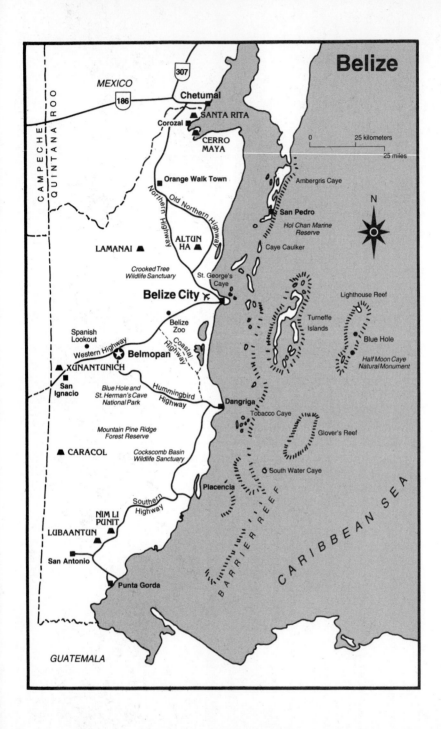

Belize

MEXICO

307

186

Chetumal

CAMPECHE

QUINTANA ROO

Corozal

SANTA RITA

CERRO MAYA

Orange Walk Town

0   25 kilometers

25 miles

Ambergris Caye

San Pedro

Northern Highway

Old Northern Highway

LAMANAI

ALTUN HA

Hol Chan Marine Reserve

Caye Caulker

N

Crooked Tree Wildlife Sanctuary

St. George's Caye

Belize City

Lighthouse Reef

Belize Zoo

Turneffe Islands

Blue Hole

Spanish Lookout

Western Highway

Coastal Highway

Belmopan

Half Moon Caye Natural Monument

XUNANTUNICH

San Ignacio

Blue Hole and St. Herman's Cave National Park

Hummingbird Highway

Dangriga

Tobacco Caye

Mountain Pine Ridge Forest Reserve

Glover's Reef

CARACOL

Cockscomb Basin Wildlife Sanctuary

South Water Caye

Placencia

Southern Highway

NIM LI PUNIT

LUBAANTUN

San Antonio

Punta Gorda

BARRIER REEF

CARIBBEAN SEA

GUATEMALA

ONE

Belize: History and Culture

Three thousand years ago, in the verdant, sun-drenched land that is now Belize, the Maya created a civilization that knew no equal. Appearing mysteriously like early-morning fog, they built magnificent cities, developed extensive trade routes and fashioned ceremonial centers that arched toward the heavens. Today, two of their temples remain the tallest buildings in Belize. For a traveler searching for historical truth, their lofty limestone summits are a haunting reminder of a civilization far grander than anything before or since in Belize history.

In fact, some legends tell that local human history began with the Maya. According to stories of the Quiché Maya, the great gods Tepeu and Gucumatz first made men from mud, but the rains came and washed them away. Then they honed them from trees, but the wooden men were mindless, so they made them of flesh and blood. These were the worst men, filled with cunning and wickedness, and had to be destroyed in a flood. Finally, Tepeu and Gucumatz pulled out some maize dough and molded the first "real men" of the world— Quiché Maya men.

Archaeologists' stories are just as vague and not nearly as entertaining, since there is little evidence of human life here before the Maya. Some speculate that primal hunters roamed the area from Mexico south through Central and South America about 13,000 years ago until the Pleistocene, or Ice Age, in 7500 B.C. Sometime during the next 3500 years, it is believed that Asians set out across the Bering Straits, perhaps even boatloads of Asians over several generations, all ending up on this part of the continent. In Belize, they probably subdued patches of swamp and jungle to grow rice, hunted the bounteous hot forests, caught plenty of fish in the rivers and seas, and laid the foundation for a society that would become the mighty Maya.

How the Maya became so mighty and so sophisticated over the next 2000 years, paralleling and even surpassing the other great thinkers of their time, is truly a mystery. What is known for sure is that it all started in the earliest, Preclassic days, from about 2000 B.C. to 250 A.D., when the Maya borrowed a calendar

1

from neighboring Olmec tribes and learned how to calculate time. They planted fields of maize and tomatoes and cacao beans, and fashioned temples for the gods of sun and rain. And they spoke a language that became the root for all modern Maya dialects.

But it was the Classic Period, from 250 to 900 A.D., when Maya life skyrocketed into a golden age of exquisitely painted and ornamented temples and palaces and pyramids, fantastic works of art, astonishing achievements in math, science and astronomy, and a writing system more sophisticated than any other ever conceived in the Western Hemisphere. Colossal stelae, or carved stone monuments, were inscribed with fanciful text and dramatic stories of war and peace and just everyday life. Belize's greatest ceremonial centers—Caracol, Xunantunich, Altun Ha, Lamanai—were built during the Classic Period, though Lamanai's architecture extends well before and after this time, amazingly spanning some 3000 years.

And though the Maya world stretched from Mexico's Yucatán Peninsula all the way south to El Salvador, recent findings point to Belize as the heart of that world, the crossroads of economic and cultural exchange, the "in" place to live. Part of it was Belize's coveted locale: a subtropical seacoast whose waters were speckled with lovely coral isles and whose interior was covered in flourishing rainforest, majestic mountains and fertile valleys. Discoveries in 1993 even revealed a rich mineral belt in southern Belize where the Maya were likely mining hematite, pyrite, granite and other valuables crucial to their economy.

Like the Morocco of the Western Hemisphere, Classic Period Belize overflowed with sophisticated trade and profound culture, mystical religions and mighty kingdoms. Great rulers and priests lived here, and so did artists, writers and aristocrats. There were peasants and farmers and also middle-class families, whose spacious thousand-year-old homes boasted big "king-size" bed slabs and ornate burial tombs, and a location convenient to reservoirs and "downtown" shopping areas. From the downtown, *sacbes*, or ancient limestone roads, ran out for miles around like spokes on a wheel, to Belize's first—and only—suburbs. (Today's sparsely populated Belize has no real suburbs, unless you count Hattieville, which grew from a temporary hurricane camp to a primitive village outside Belize City.) In fact, it is hard to imagine that one single ancient Maya city, the jungle-veiled Caracol, boasted nearly 190,000 residents—as many as live in all of Belize today. In 562 A.D., Caracol crushed its big neighbor, Tikal, Guatemala, and ruled the Maya world for more than 100 years.

And then something happened. Just as the Maya empire had mysteriously blossomed beyond belief, it mysteriously collapsed. The beginning of the end was around 900 A.D., when the Maya suddenly started abandoning their cities. This Postclassic Period of decline lasted over 600 years, during which time archaeologists theorize there may have been earthquakes, wars, famines, disease and massive peasant uprising. Any or all of these could have caused the Maya downfall, or perhaps the Maya simply evolved away from an elite society into a farming one. For the Maya are by no means gone; indeed, some four million Maya still thrive throughout Belize and the surrounding countries in an area known today as *La Ruta Maya*, or The Maya Route.

This 1500-mile-long Maya Route runs down the length of Mexico's Yucatán Peninsula, crosses the jungles and mountains of Guatemala, Honduras and El Salvador, and loops through lush Belize—a perfect place for today's travelers to begin a *La Ruta Maya* odyssey. Along the way, there are hulking temples and steep pyramids that rise above the jungle canopies, thousands of stone dwellings and *sacbes*, intricate Maya sculptures and stelae and, greatest of all, a fascinating society of proud Maya people who live much as their Classic ancestors did. From thatched-hut villages stashed deep in the jungle, tucked along rushing rivers and parked atop hills, they grow their maize and beans and rice on *milpa* farms, in an ancient endless cycle inspired by gods of sun and rain and by the beasts of the jungle. In the heat of the day, Belize's Maya women squat for hours over wood set ablaze on their dirt floors, grilling corn tortillas on a *comal*, or griddle stone, for tortillas are the staple of modern Maya life, much as they were 2000 years ago.

The Maya were no doubt tending their corn fields when the Spanish arrived in the early 1500s. Explorers Vicente Yáñez Pinzón and Juan Díaz de Solís sailed up the coast from Honduras to Yucatán around 1506 and claimed everything they saw, including Belize, for the Spanish empire. Soon missionaries made their way down from Yucatán to Lamanai in northern Belize. The Maya at Lamanai were friendly to their uninvited guests until the guests built a church and told the Maya they had to attend. Angry, the Maya burned the church. Several years later, more missionaries fashioned a second, sturdier church at Lamanai, but the Maya burned it down, too.

Other than the Lamanai incidents, the Spanish strangely did little to bother the Maya in Belize. Instead, they concentrated their efforts in neighboring Guatemala and in Yucatán, where Hernando Cortez and a small army combed the land for slaves.

While on the outs with the Spanish government, Cortez and his 11 ships and 600 troops snuck away from Cuba to the Mexican shore in 1519 and over the next few years slaughtered thousands of Maya who refused to be enslaved. Cortez' tyranny laid the groundwork for nearly 400 years of Maya oppression in the Yucatán Peninsula, during which a stream of Maya and *Mestizo* (Spanish-Maya) refugees flowed into neighboring Belize. The most profound Yucatán war was the War of the Castes, from 1848 to 1858, when the Maya slaves rose against their Spanish masters. It was a bloody decade, and those who could escaped south to Belize. Many settled on Ambergris Caye and Caye Caulker, just south of the Yucatán border, and today those islands are thriving *Mestizo* communities.

Just as refugees and former slaves helped give today's Belize its frontier veneer, so did the pirates and loggers who latched on to its shores in the early 1600s.

The pirates found Belize's sheltered cayes a prime vantage point for raiding and plundering Spanish galleons gorged with gold and silver. Belize's treacherous barrier reef helped out, too, laying open the bowels of many a ship carrying treasure. The pirates particularly loved tiny St. George's Caye, where they would catch large sea turtles and smoke their meat over mangrove fires on large racks called "boucans"—hence the name buccaneers. They sold the meat to passing loggers, privateers and other pirates, and began what would become Belize's most lucrative fishing business through the late 1800s.

As for the loggers, many were driven south from Yucatán and north from Honduras by Spanish harassment, and they, too, settled on the Belize shores, building meager thatched huts on a muddy bank near the mouth of what is now the Belize River. By the mid-1600s, as logwood became prized in Europe for its black, blue and purple dyes, many pirates made a career change to logwood cutting. They soon became known as the Baymen, for they would haul the logs across the Bay of Honduras, though it was too romantic a name for such a disgraceful lot who regularly drank themselves to the bottom of rum bottles and tormented the Puritans who had migrated from Nicaragua and Honduras. One 1705 report to the British Trade Council called the Belize settlement a "River of Bullys." In fact it is said that ship's captains used to mark the spot on their maps with an "obelize" to signify a place of corruption, and then the word itself

Margay

was eventually corrupted into "Belize." Others say Belize got its name from Scottish buccaneer Peter Wallace, who established a community at the river's mouth in 1638, and whose name was pronounced Wal-EEZ. Still others claim the roots of the word go deeper in history, back to the ancient Maya word *belikin*, meaning "toward the east," as Belize faces east out to sea. No one can tell you the real truth, but most everyone in Belize can tell you that Belikin is the name of their good-tasting national beer.

By the 18th century, the logwood and mahogany business was flourishing and so was the lawless society of British Baymen, who hacked away at the forests and fought off frequent attacks by the Spanish. Spain still claimed the land, despite a 1763 agreement in which it gave England the "right" to cut logwood. Of course, it wasn't the English who did the actual cutting, but slaves who were imported by the Baymen. Most slaves were West Africans brought over via Jamaica and Bermuda, or Indian slaves from the Mosquito Tribes of Nicaragua. Many were women forced to care for the Baymen, primarily as sex slaves, though a number of Baymen did free their commonlaw wives—a custom that set the tone for a future ethnic-rich Belize. In fact, the beautiful, tan-skinned children of the Baymen and slaves would be the first of many generations of Creoles, who are today Belize's foremost ethnic group. The West African slaves also fused the growing settlement with their pulsing dances, drum-driven music—the first "goombay" sounds in Belize—and obeah black magic; their celebrations in the swamps outside their huts lasted all night, with the obeah man or woman appealing to dead ancestors to free them from the shackles of their white masters.

It was not obeah but the British government that finally freed the slaves in 1807, though many Belizean landowners refused to give up their free labor. In 1812, slaves laid the cornerstone for Belize's first church, St. John's in Belize City, then spent 14 grueling years building the cathedral brick by brick. A few years after the church was finished, church fathers held a little ceremony for the slaves to celebrate their "emancipation."

While the 19th century heralded the beginnings of freedom for slaves, it also ended the pesky attacks by the Spanish. The attack that ended it all was in 1798, near St. George's Caye, then the capital of the colony. Recorded history recalls a great cannon battle between Spanish and British ships, though many say it was no more than a few Spanish galleons retreating after being threatened by a ragtag band of Baymen. Whatever the truth, the Battle of St. George's Caye officially ended Spanish claims and secured British dominion, though it was not until 1862 that the colony formally became British Honduras. Today, a national holiday commemorates St. George's Caye Day, though some political and cultural independents do not join the festivities, believing that the day commemorates British rule and not Belizean freedom.

Freedom was the reason thousands of new immigrants arrived during the 1800s. From the north came the Maya and *Mestizos* escaping Yucatán's Caste War and settling in northern Belize and on outlying cayes. In northern areas, where the terrain had been stripped by logging, they planted sugar cane—and thus began the industry now number-one in Belize. They also flavored this northern area with Spanish-Maya culture, and travelers today who drive through the towns of Corozal, Santa Clara and Santa Elena Concepción will be met by pueblo and mission architecture.

The 1800s also saw a stream of new residents from Honduras in the south. The Garifuna, oddly enough, came to Belize to escape British oppression. Their story is one of great intrigue and mystery, as their history is woven with both true and questionable tales. What is certain is that in the 1600s, a ship carrying West African slaves ran aground on the Caribbean island of St. Vincent. The survivors either became slaves or citizens, or perhaps both, and eventually intermarried with the native Carib Indians and created the Garifuna. From these haphazard beginnings, they founded a culture on freedom—freedom to play their driving, soulful music now known as *punta rock*; freedom to farm their simple plots of earth; freedom to practice their obscure religion, which revolves around the *dugu* ceremony of calling to dead ancestors; and, most importantly, freedom of self-rule. But the British wouldn't allow it, and drove the Garifuna from St. Vincent when they refused to colonize. Most were banished to the deserted but paradisaic island of Roatan in the Bay of Honduras. From there, they made their way to mainland Honduras, Guatemala and Belize.

In southern Belize the Garifuna established outposts along the coast and began reviving their close-knit society. Over the years, the colonial government sought to suppress their religion and force the Garifuna into Catholicism, but the Garifuna simply pacified the British by adding a few Catholic practices to their own ceremonies. As late as the 1950s and 1960s, *dugus* were held in secret so as not to incite local magistrates. Today, however, Belize's 15,000 Garifuna worship freely and in recent years have even begun allowing outside observers. In the southern Belize towns of Dangriga and Punta Gorda, artists' canvases dramatically recreate scenes from dugus and from the Garifunas' voyage from St. Vincent to Honduras and Belize.

While the colony broadened culturally during the 1800s, it struggled economically. The logging industry went boom and bust several times, and by the late 19th century large accessible forests were nearly wiped out. Sugar cane did reasonably well in northern Belize and bananas were planted in southern regions. By the turn of the century, sapodilla trees were surrendering their precious sap for the chicle business, which peaked at the height of World War II with Chiclets chewing gum.

But the 1900s brought many setbacks, not the least of which was a nameless 1931 hurricane that nearly blew away Belize City, killing 10 percent of the capital's 15,000 residents. In 1949, when colonial magistrates devalued local currency and raised the cost of living, British Hondurans formed a People's Committee to protest. A year later, the grassroots committee had strengthened and, changing its name to the People's United Party (or PUP, as it's called today), began rallying for Belize independence.

In 1950, Belizeans elected five party members to the Belize City Council to form a majority, and over the next decade worked toward national democracy. In 1965, Great Britain gave its blessing to the new nation but Belize stopped short of declaring independence because of Guatemala. Like Spanish conquerors of earlier centuries, big-neighbor Guatemala had long laid claim to the colony. And since Belizeans had been pushing for independence, Guatemala had begun pushing to take over Belize. So Belize waited 16 more years, until 1981, to officially become Belize. At the time, Belize struck a deal whereby British troops could train in the Belize jungles if they'd keep a show of force against Guatemala.

The soldiers stayed until 1994, when the majority were withdrawn, and today the British have only a token presence in Belize.

And while the British returned home, thousands of Guatemalans, Hondurans and El Salvadorans have streamed into Belize during recent years, searching, like so many immigrants of centuries past, for a better way of life. Today, Belize's 222,000 residents are a truly diverse phenomenon, an improbable blend of Creoles and Maya, Mennonites and Chinese, Arabs and *Mestizos*, Germans and Garifuna, and of course, British. English is the country's official language, but Spanish is nearly as pervasive, and Maya, Garifuna and Creole comprise the other three major languages.

It is this kaleidoscope of humanity, of music and art and dress, of triumphs and defeats and expectations, all joined by a determination to exist free, that makes Belize so unusual. Born of Maya brilliance, baptized by raucous pirates and Spanish outlaws, ignited by African rhythms and only slightly refined by British gentility, Belize is branded with a tenacious pioneer mentality. That same mentality is what ensures travelers of a great adventure on this tropical coast.

WHITE IBIS

TWO

The Ecological Picture

ECOTOURISM

It is hard to imagine that in just two centuries, more than 80 percent of Latin America's tropical forests have been erased from the planet. Population explosions, frenetic development, widespread logging and slash-and-burn farming—where forests are burned to grow crops and raise cattle—are mainly to blame. Much has been written about the destruction, but little has been done until recently, with the advent of a concept called ecotourism. The basic idea behind ecotourism is that visitors to a place can contribute to the environment and support the people who live in that environment. If villagers can make a living from tourism, it is reasoned, then there's no need to burn off the forest for food or hunt endangered animals for the price of their skins.

But ecotourism means much more than that. In fact, this catchword of the '90s has come to mean setting aside vast forests as sanctuaries and preserves and controlling tourism to those areas. It means fighting destruction of virgin lands planned for resorts, and encouraging reforestation in decimated areas. It means giving someone tempted to loot a Maya ruin a job as a tour guide to those ruins. It means convincing a family who doesn't know where their next meal is coming from to preserve the forest that provides that meal. And for a traveler, it means safeguarding the areas you visit as if they were your own backyard. If you must leave something behind, let it be footprints.

Among Central American countries, Belize is a paradigm of ecotourism. Indeed, this tiny country, where the per capita income is only US$2330 a year, is waging an intense campaign to save its environment. More than 25 wildlife and archaeological preserves have been set aside, including the 100,000-acre Cockscomb Basin, the world's only jaguar sanctuary. Jaguars have been wiped out of other parts of Central America, where rainforests are ravaged every day. Belizeans point to this devastation, as well as to overdevelopment in Florida and the Caribbean, in the crusade to save their country. Bumper stickers proclaim Belizeans' love for wild animals, and local gossip is laced with the latest ecotourism news.

Every day, new ecotourism programs are being created. Numerous environmental organizations, as well as the Belize government, are working together to promote ecotourism. In 1992, Belize welcomed countries from around the world to an ecotourism "congress," which addressed the earth's environmental problems and needs. Environmentalists, government officials, developers, tour operators, hoteliers and others in the tourist industry met for intense discussions. The congress included field seminars where participants learned about such subjects as recycling and eco-sensitive diving and sportfishing.

Of course, ecotourism can only work if it is supported by tourists. To help visitors better enjoy and contribute to the environment of Belize, we've compiled a short environmental code of ethics:

1. **Do not disturb wildlife and natural habitats.** Stay on the trails and avoid using machetes and collecting plants or wildlife. Coral reefs are especially sensitive, and should never be touched. Even a slight brush with your fin can cause disease in the reef. Bird nests should be viewed from a safe distance with binoculars, and nesting sea turtles should be observed only with a trained guide. Do not feed monkeys and other wild animals, because it alters their diets and behaviors. Raccoons, who normally live alone, become pack animals when fed and spread diseases that kill them.

2. **Do not litter.** If you'll be in remote areas, take along a sack to carry out your garbage.

3. **Be conscious of helping local communities.** Use native tour guides—they *are* the best—and patronize locally owned inns and restaurants. Buy souvenirs from native crafts people; the Maya villagers make marvelous handicrafts.

4. **Be culturally sensitive.** Remember that you are a guest in a country. Make an effort to learn basic local customs and follow them. Don't judge Belize by your hometown. On one jungle tour, two travelers from Texas constantly compared everything to "how it is back home." Somehow, I couldn't imagine the Maya guide being interested in a four-hour litany on how things are done in Texas.

ECOSYSTEMS

GEOGRAPHY

Few regions as small as Belize are so physically diverse. Where else, in a space the size of Massachusetts, do you find cool pine forests and saunalike jungle, luscious green islands and parched brown savannah, majestic mountains and flat muddy swamps? There are hushed coastal lagoons and fizzing streams, thundering waterfalls and shadowy rivers cocooned in jungle. And then there is the emerald sea, which stretches to the horizon where it blends into sky. Everywhere there is wild landscape, but few people. Offshore, many of the untamed and mostly uninhabited cayes are actually peaks of the Maya Mountain Range. These coral rock islets peek up from a shallow underwater valley, called the Inner Channel, that runs from the Belize coast out to a great barrier reef. The reef, in turn, stretches some 180 miles from the Gulf of Honduras to the Bay of Chetumal in southern Yucatán. Formed over thousands of years, and second in scope only to Australia's Great Barrier Reef, Belize's reef system is complex beyond imagination: millions of life forms interacting and interdepending, yet so fragile that humans could obliterate them in a few years.

If coral rock defines the reef, then limestone is the trademark of northern Belize. In fact, the northern region is the end of a great limestone shelf that reaches down from the Yucatán Peninsula. From the air, you can see the vast flat shelf poking out into the frothy green Caribbean Sea. A thin layer of soil covers much of the limestone, and is fertile enough to support a healthy sugar business. In the winter, farmers burn underbrush from the cane fields, and dark smoke clings to the skies.

But most of northern Belize still belongs to the forests—mangrove along the coast, pine and palmetto along a central plain, and luxurious broadleaf rainforests in the west. Ponds, lagoons and swamps decorate the forests, as do abandoned logging camps—testaments to centuries when mowing down trees was the biggest business in Belize. Today, many camps lie within reserves where selective logging is practiced.

The land across central and western Belize is rippled with hills and valleys and terraced fields, and spidery rivers that nourish the fields. Out in the district known as Cayo, broadleaf jungle is interspersed with great forests of slash pines, where the soil is a mix of sand and clay, and waterfalls and bubbling streams create vistas of stunning beauty. The limestone here is ancient, probably of the Cretaceous Age, and eons of percolating water have created vast sinkholes and caves and underground streams.

The Maya Mountains form a spine of granite down southern Belize. Most prominent of all Belize's natural features, they are marked by deep canyons and shallow valleys, snaking rivers and ebbing ridges, which eventually rise to Victoria Peak, Belize's highest at 3675 feet. But mostly the area is solid jungle, with areas so dense and remote they have yet to be visited by modern-day humans. Southern Belize boasts true "cloud forests," tropical rainforests high enough to enjoy thick mists and rains most every day. Here there are double canopies of trees, with cohune palms that reach five stories high, and deep webs of bromeliads and mosses that thrive in perpetual dampness.

FLORA

Seeing the jungle for the first time is exhilarating, indeed overwhelming. Take just one tree. Soaring like an ancient column, its limbs drip with perfumed orchids and lacy mosses, its branches offer refuge to both a hawk's nest and a nest of yellow wasps, its trunk bears the scrapings of a jaguar along with the scars of a human machete. Vines and epiphytes—aerial roots—creep and curl around the tree in orderly fashion, then slither away on the jungle floor. Wildly colored fungi cling to its wood and leaves, and ferns blanket its feet. On this, a single tree, the intricate web of life is nearly beyond comprehension.

Yet this one tree is but a blink in the Belizean florascape. In fact, it would take volumes of books to do justice to the flora of Belize. Within this fabulously diverse region are more than 4000 species of flowering plants, including 250 different orchids and 700 types of trees. There are heart-shaped anthuriums and paddle-shaped heliconia, flaming bromeliads and purple passion flowers. And there is much beauty that does not bloom—water-gorged jungle plants and cathedrals of pine trees, island palms burdened with coconuts and grand old cedar and mahogany trees that somehow eluded the logger's axe. There are strangler figs that can fell a 100-foot oak tree, and vines that will wound with their thorns and then heal that wound with their leaves. And there are jungles so unimaginably dense they have buried whole cities for thousands of years.

Here, in Eden-like settings, bromeliads and orchids grow as big as tree trunks and trees grow as tall as skyscrapers. Guanacaste trees, which can reach

Ocelot

400 feet high, are decorated with flowering air plants—making them nature's own Christmas trees. The bookut also grows tall and wide, with a canopy spanning about 40 feet. Howler monkeys love to eat its seed pods, though the pods' musky smell gives the tree its nickname of "stinking toe." The black oozing sap from the poisonwood tree inflicts angry blisters that last up to two weeks. The antidote, used since the time of the Maya, is to apply sap from the gumbo limbo. Near every poisonwood tree there's always a gumbo limbo tree.

The sap from the sapodilla tree fueled the country's largest industry during the first half of this century. Chicling, or the harvest of sapodilla sap, was accomplished by *chicleros*, rugged bushmen who would climb 40 to 60 feet up a sapodilla tree, then, working their way back down, use a machete to slash deep zigzags along the trunk. Chicle was used as a base for chewing gum (remember Chiclets?). Today, Belize forests are filled with sapodilla trees, though rare is the one that does not bear the scars of a *chiclero*.

But it is the cohune palm, with its thick trunk and elegant plumed fronds, that has come to symbolize Belize's jungles. Preferring to grow in deep, rich, well-drained soil, cohunes have been an integral part of local life since the time of the Maya. Virtually every part of this exquisite tree can be used—the sturdy fronds for making thatched roofs; the tender hearts, as a culinary delicacy; the tiny, coconutlike nuts, for making charcoal and oil. During World War II, the U.S. Air Force used the husks of cohune palms to make charcoal filter masks for its pilots. Today, Maya villagers boil the nuts to extract their oil, which is bottled in a glass jar, corked with a corn cob and sold at the markets. Surely no Belize sight is more mystical than that of cohune palms dripping in the foggy aftermath of a forest rain, looking like wispy giants of the jungle.

Riverbanks play host to dense webs of spiny bamboo, whose love of water makes it amenable to floods. The bamboo protects the banks from erosion, and protects itself with sharp barbs that can reach four inches long. Few trees can protect themselves from the strangler fig, which slowly and methodically kills its prey. The strangler wraps its roots around a tree trunk until, after a few years, the roots grow and fuse and choke the tree to death. The trunk falls and becomes hollow, providing shelter for a variety of animals. Bats particularly love the damp, dark space where they can escape the light of day.

The jungles are also thick with tropical fungi that bloom with brilliant color and take on exotic shapes. Ferns cool the forest with their double ceiling canopies and provide food for many animals. In less dense areas, ferns also form soft green carpets that make openings in the forest.

Out of the jungle and along the Caribbean coast, the flora resembles many people's idea of tropical paradise: shade-giving papaya, mango and breadfruit trees; rambling bougainvillea and hibiscus bursting with brilliant color;

and wind-blown palms, heavy with coconuts. Exotic flowers, such as red ginger and birds of paradise, grow wild. Here, too, are the mangroves, propped along the shore, looking like bushes on stilts. Mangroves are crucial to the environment, as they provide nurseries for birds and animals and protect the shore from erosion.

FAUNA

It is a feat of nature that a place as small as Belize should possess such a mind-boggling array of exotic animals. Here among the Maya mysteries live mysterious creatures like spiny anteaters and kinkajou bears, long-nosed bats and portly tapirs, scaly iguanas and gangly Jesus Christ lizards—who actually *can* walk on water.

These enchanting animals thrive in Belize's amazing range of environments, from pine forests, dry savannahs and moist jungle and rainforest to offshore islands, low coastal plains and swamplands. However, as their homes quickly succumb to farming and development, many face extinction. During recent years, Belize has set aside protected sanctuaries where animals can flourish and people can view their worlds. With a little time and patience, one soon learns how easy it is to witness this wonderful wildlife.

JAGUARS   "God decided to make man because the jaguar already existed," begins a Maya folktale, related in the book *Jaguar*. The jaguar was in fact a god to the ancient Maya, steeped in mystery and worshipped from a distance. Today's Maya still revere, and fear, this king of carnivores they call *balum*.

Jaguars are brooding creatures who prefer a solitary life and lots of room—a male will roam over a 100-square-mile area. They are massive, weighing as much as 300 pounds, and cloaked in downy soft coats with spots that are sometimes shaped like flowers and butterflies. Despite their reputation for aggression, jaguars rarely attack people unless provoked. A caged jaguar, however, will hypnotize you with his eyes; one flinch and he will charge his fence.

The jaguar is a night lover, using the cool blackness of the jungle underbrush to pursue its favorite meal—prickly, piglike peccaries. When a jaguar attacks, it is lightning-fast: one swipe to the neck with its massive paw, then a head-crushing blow with knifelike teeth. But he is not a picky eater, and will feast on whatever mammals come around: monkeys, deer, otters, birds, and even iguana and fish. During the day, he dozes on a bed of leaves or on fallen tree trunks.

Jaguars are rare throughout their range—Mexico to Argentina—though thanks to recent conservation efforts, Belize is thought to have the world's greatest concentration of the hulking spotted cats. The world's only jaguar preserve, the Cockscomb Basin Wildlife Sanctuary, lies in southern Belize, the very area where just ten years ago it was common for wealthy, rifle-toting Americans to hunt for "trophy jaguar." Poaching still occurs in Belize and perhaps will until people no longer feel compelled to display the animals' stuffed skulls and skins.

OTHER CATS   The Belize jungles are also home to other exotic cats—pumas, ocelots, margays and jaguarundis—who, like the jaguar, are threatened by poaching. Pumas are in fact quite rare, having been nearly obliterated by hunters, and it is doubtful you will see one in the wild. Known also as cougars or mountain lions, they love the mountains as well as low forests and savannah. Pumas are slightly smaller than jaguars, weighing up to 200 pounds, and have wild, piercing eyes and fur the color of honey.

Ocelots are much smaller, less than 35 pounds, and margays are the size of big housecats. Both are slender and dainty, and exquisitely garbed in velvety coats with spots and stripes that run together like watercolors. Sadly, it is their gorgeous coats that make them more valuable dead than alive.

Jaguarundis do not look like cats as much as weasels, with long, barrel-shaped bodies, stumpy legs and snaking tails. Most common of all wild cats, with coats that are dark brown to black, they prefer to live in savannahs and scrub forests, foraging the ground for small prey.

TAPIRS   Belize's national animal may also be its homeliest, growing as large as 650 pounds, sporting a long upper lip and splayed toes, covered with hairless ashen skin, and boasting characteristics of both the pig and cow. It is, in fact, a relative of the rhinoceros and the horse, though its nickname is mountain cow. Tapirs will live anywhere there are tasty plants and fruit, from dry savannah to swampy mangroves to dense rainforest, but they never pass up a chance to wallow in a mudhole.

Belize's most famous tapir, April, lives at the Belize Zoo. Every April, school children from around the country gather to celebrate her birthday and watch April gulp down a two-foot-tall cake of horse chow, bananas and carrots. Don't miss a chance to visit April; it will probably be your only encounter with a tapir. The bright animals are shy, having been hunted to near extinction in every Latin American country but Belize. Though they are not particularly good to eat, tapirs are thought to be cattle killers (which they're not), and local myths say they cast spells on people. Baby tapirs, which have spots and stripes, are especially feared. Unfortunately, some people shoot tapirs just for the sport of it, leaving them to die in the forest with bullet wounds.

MONKEYS   Two types of monkeys live in Belize: the spider monkey and the black howler. It takes a watchful eye to spy either species scrambling through the treetops, though if you spend even a few days in the Belize jungle, you will likely see many monkeys.

Spider monkeys are found only in Belize and Mexico's Yucatán Peninsula; they were nearly wiped out by yellow fever in the mid-1900s. They have lanky arms and legs and tails as long as their body. Their hands are thumb-less—all the better for zipping gracefully from branch to branch.

Nearly twice as big as spider monkeys, weighing up to 22 pounds, black howlers have a slightly wider range that includes Guatemala. Called baboons in Belize, they have faces that are hauntingly human, and a male and female will hold hands while resting. When they are ready to mate, the pair will lock eyes, then flick their tongues at each other and lick tails, before the male approaches from behind, clinging with his tail to a tree limb for support.

Howlers howl to defend a troop's territory, or sometimes before a rain or if frightened. If you are ever awakened by the jackhammer scream of a howler at night, you may well think an angry lion is bearing down on your door.

OTHER MAMMALS   Few jungle inhabitants seem so well equipped as the anteater, whose long slithery tongue is fitted with tiny prongs that keep the ants marching in the right direction—toward its stomach, where a special muscle crushes insect exoskeletons. An anteater spends its waking hours poking its uninvited nose into termite nests, where ants inhabit the outer compartments. Its front claws are curled and strong, useful for digging deep into nests. Anteaters are common, though their telltale signs—raided termite nests—are commoner still.

Like the anteater, a kinkajou makes its home in a hollow tree, preferring to snooze during the day. At night, it emerges to feed, flicking its long tongue in the honey pot of a bee's nest or the nectar pouch of a flower. Chestnut colored and rippled with soft fur, it is also called honey bear or nightwalker, although it is a relative of the raccoon. Kinkajous are so appealing they are frequently stolen from the jungle and turned into pets, though they make lousy ones, refusing to be housebroken and staying up all night wrecking one's house.

Coatimundis, also known as coatis or quash, look even more like their relative the raccoon, with their snouty masked face and tail of black rings. Found throughout the Belize forests, they have a wide diet, feasting on everything from lizards and snakes to mice and fruit. Tayras, or bushdogs, are lean and mean creatures a little smaller than coatimundis, but with the same culinary penchants. A member of the weasel family, the tayra isn't particularly dangerous but extremely territorial, and will snarl at anyone who encroaches on its homestead.

You will know a peccary is near even before you see him, since the odor that precedes him is not unlike that of a dairy farm. The smell radiates from the animal's back and actually entices other peccaries, who will rub their head in it, though it would seem painful, since peccaries are covered with bristly spines.

Peccaries look and taste a lot like wild pigs, and are the favorite meal of jaguars and many other jungle predators. There are two types of peccaries in Belize: collared, who have bands of white hair around their necks; and white-lipped, with white whiskers. Both move in herds, and a herd of 100 or more white-lipped peccaries has been known to charge people who stumble upon them in the rainforest. Researcher John C. Kricher advises that "climbing a tree is the best escape route, though the peccaries may wait around beneath the tree for a while."

Rare is the visitor who encounters a paca, a handsome, intensely shy little rodent who leaves his hole only at night. Hunters, however, chase the furry creatures from their holes and shoot them, for their white flesh is prized throughout Belize. Paca is also known as gibnut and royal rat, the latter name being bestowed upon it several years ago when the queen of England ate stewed paca in Belize. Less tasty but still killed for its meat, agouti is another common rodent that's smaller and furrier than the paca.

White-tailed deer and brocket deer have been hunted incessantly, though sightings in Belize are more frequent now that reserves provide some protection. White-tailed deer grow to 200 pounds, though they average about 60 pounds in Belize. They have an elegant, lustrous body sheathed in peppery brown to whitish brown fur, and a fluffy white tail, which they hide when attempting to elude a predator. Brocket deer are diminutive, usually weighing less than 40 pounds, and have a silky auburn coat that blends nicely into the rainforest.

FROGS, LIZARDS AND TURTLES   Belize has numerous frogs and also toads, but the most dazzling is the red-eyed tree frog, whose ruby gelatinous eyes are like night beacons of the jungle. As the frog perches on an emerald leaf, attached firmly by rubbery, neon-orange hands and feet, its eyes bulge out from its metallic green body, which is splashed with white dots and blue patches. All in all, it makes quite a spectacle.

Green turtle

Not nearly as resplendent as the tree frog but immensely entertaining, the basilisk lizard sprints on two hind legs right across the top of a river. Nicknamed the Jesus Christ lizard, he's a comical sight, really, a miniature dinosaur constantly on the run with nothing chasing him and nowhere in particular to go. The basilisk's lizard opposite is the iguana, who prefers to bask lethargically all day on a riverbank. Iguanas seem to be everywhere—including restaurant menus, where they're often listed as "bamboo chicken."

Hickatees have all but disappeared from the rivers, victims of relentless hunting and pollution and their inability to lay many eggs. Unlike sea turtles, who lay over 100 eggs at a time, these Central American river turtles may lay as few as a dozen eggs, depositing them under a canopy of floating vegetation or along a sheltered riverbank. If an egg is not snatched by a wood rail or otter, it will become a baby turtle hunted by crocodiles and raccoons. If it survives to adulthood, it will probably meet its fate at the end of an oar—the preferred weapon of human hunters, who whack the brownish green turtles as they float along the river's surface, snoozing the day away.

Amazingly, hickatee hunting is still legal in Belize, as is sea turtle hunting. Belize's three types of sea turtles—the green, the loggerhead and the hawksbill—are all endangered for countless reasons, including hunting, coastal development (which eliminates the turtles' eating and nesting grounds) and fishing nets that entangle and drown them.

Green turtles graze on sea grass, which turns their fat green and gives them their name. Unfortunately, as more seabeds are dredged, the turtles have fewer places to feed. Green turtles used to grow as large as four feet and weigh over 600 pounds, but thanks to humans, they no longer make it to such a ripe old age.

Loggerhead turtles have big heads, stocky necks and reddish shells shaped like hearts. The female returns each year to the same beach to lay her eggs, abandoning the safety of her sea home and swimming through dark waters toward a familiar shore, hauling her 300-pound body awkwardly across the sand and digging a giant pit, laboring for hours in the moonlight. Then, one by one, she painfully deposits her eggs—up to 100 of them—covers them with sand, and lumbers back to sea before dawn. For all her hard work, poachers will soon come and steal most of her eggs. The few they leave will hatch and wait for night, then scurry toward the surf, only to be picked off by birds, lizards and crabs. Today, fewer than five percent of baby loggerheads will grow to become adults, when they become eligible to be hunted. And which is why tomorrow there may be no more loggerheads.

Hawksbill turtles have peculiar-looking, sharp-hooked beaks, but are also gloriously adorned with shells of golden brown and orange shingles. Their shells have been their doom, fetching big bucks in markets around the world for many years now.

POISONOUS SNAKES   When you walk in the jungle, your thoughts (and possibly fears) will eventually turn to poisonous snakes. Travelers worry more about snakes than they should, since the vast majority are neither aggressive nor poisonous. Those few that are venomous fall into two categories: rear-fanged and front-fanged. Venom from rear-fanged snakes is dangerous only to the snakes' small prey, such as lizards and toads, but is *not harmful to humans.*

Front-fanged snakes are a different story. The coral snake, also called a bead-and-coral snake, is a front-fanged snake whose venom attacks the nervous system, causing paralysis and sometimes death. Fortunately, the coral snake is rarely aggressive and an excellent coral snake antivenin is widely available.

The front-fanged snake Belizeans fear most is the fer-de-lance, a pit viper also known as a yellow-jawed tommygoff for the yellow jaws and throat that accentuate its brown body. The most poisonous snake in Central America and one of the most common, it has unusually long, spiked fangs that resemble inverted tusks. Mice are its main prey, so the fer-de-lance spends much of its time on the ground and around barns and wells and other places mice enjoy. It has a reputation for aggressiveness, but truth is it would rather flee than strike a human, if given the chance. Even when it does strike, the bite is not always fatal, since the snake rarely disgorges all its venom on something too large to eat.

If you encounter any snake, retreat as quietly as possible. If you are bitten by a poisonous snake, go immediately to a hospital or other emergency facility. Every public hospital and clinic in Belize stocks antivenin. Contrary to local bush practice, you should not cut the wound to make it bleed (you might cut a blood vessel or nerve, causing more harm than the snakebite) nor drink alcohol, which only speeds the flow of blood and therefore venom.

BIRDS   Belize's islands and coastal marshes are filled with beautiful and bizarre birds such as the red-footed booby, which has golden white feathers and outlandish red webbed feet. Its name comes from a lack of fear—sailors to the New World used to walk right up and strike it on the head. Much less friendly is the frigate bird, whose gaunt, black silhouette gives it an ominous appearance. Despite its penchant for fish, the frigate refuses to get wet, and so has become adept at swiping flying fish in midair from other birds. The cinnamon-colored jacana bird, which lives in marshes, ponds and rivers, is nicknamed the lily pad trotter—it gracefully hops across each pad with pencil-thin legs.

But the most famous of all Belize water birds is the jabiru stork. The largest flying bird in the Western Hemisphere, it reaches human proportions, growing as tall as five feet with an astounding wing span of up to ten feet. Unfortunately, it is greatly endangered, as fewer than 300 birds are thought to still be alive.

Inland, birds are flamboyantly colorful. The tiny hummingbird shimmers in iridescent colors as it hovers motionless sucking out flower nectar. Its incredibly high metabolism forces it to feed from dawn to dusk. The turkey-like curassow, who mates for life, boasts lacy crests and lustrous black or crimson feathers. Male curassows are extremely protective of females, and will risk their lives to keep others from getting near their mates.

The bird probably most associated with the Belize jungle is the keel-billed toucan, who sports a crayola-yellow bib and a fantastic, rainbow-hued bill fashioned like a capsized boat. It flies with the bill up and out, as if trying to keep up with the huge apparatus, though in fact the beak is quite light. The national bird of Belize, toucans are best seen in deep rainforest, far away from the people who want to trap them to sell as pets.

Woodpeckers are the jackhammers of the forest, spending hours drilling into tree trunks at unimaginable speeds. The hammering is so constant and tire-less that one wonders how the bird's pointy little beak manages not to be mangled by day's end. There are many species of woodpeckers, ranging in color from black to red to green and richly embellished with stripes or streaks. All woodpeckers have tough-as-nails tails to prop them against trees while they do their jackhammering.

Oftentimes, woodpeckers will drill their nest holes only to have them stolen by woodcreepers. Though similar in appearance, woodpeckers and wood-creepers are not closely related, and woodcreepers do not drill holes but probe them. The most intriguing woodcreeper is the scythebill, whose beak resembles a long, sharp upside-down scythe.

One reason birdwatchers come to Belize is for a glimpse of a blue-crowned motmot, distinguished by a tiara of shimmering blue feathers and a racquet-shaped, blue-green tail that's half as long as its body. There's no mistaking its call, either, a series of delicate *hoot-hoots* that echo through the forest. Montezuma oropendolas are also sought by bird lovers, though it is their nests, draped from trees like elaborate baskets, that are most fascinating. Montezuma oropendolas are blackish-brown and have the silhouette of a crow, their close relative.

INSECTS   Some of the jungle's most ingenious and industrious creatures are not much bigger than a pinhead. Take leaf cutter ants, who work all day and all night chopping leaves and shuttling them in perfect lines to piles that reach six feet high. Each leaf is lifted by a tiny ant who seems to have the strength of Hercules. Another ant pilots the leaf, sending codes to ants in the back of the parade to watch out for that stump, rock—or anteater.

The ants' leaf piles turn into deep, rich soil that trees love. In fact, it's not uncommon to see a cohune palm towering ten feet above surrounding co-hune palms that were not lucky enough to grow in leaf cutter compost. What do the ants get out of it? They crave a fungus that grows on the cut leaves, kind of like ant caviar.

Termites are everywhere, as evidenced by their gray spun nests fastened to trees of all varieties. The nests, many larger than basketballs, are made of a papery glue formed by digested wood and termite feces. The obese queen, burdened by a yellow, pouchlike abdomen and hardly able to move, is hidden deep in the nest and is tended to (and impregnated) by zillions of worker termites. The workers are blind, making their way around the nest by sniffing chemical trails laid by other workers. Soldier termites defend the nest from invaders by discharging a sticky, musky liquid.

When termites eat wood, they expel chemical gases. Considering the size of a termite, this would seem inconsequential until you consider how many termites there are in the world. Some researchers believe the gases may contribute to global warming. John C. Kricher, quoting the studies of P. R. Zimmerman, suggests that the termites' "combined digestive abilities produce significant quantities of atmospheric methane, carbon dioxide and molecular hydrogen."

The forest-floor millipede spews its own chemicals, though they are harmless to humans and used strictly for self-defense. At the first hint of danger, the yellow-orange, many-legged creatures tuck themselves into a tight ball and squirt a liquid up to a foot away.

Above the forest floor, butterflies color the air with extraordinary poise and beauty. Most elusive and naturally most sought after by butterfly collectors is the blue morpho, or in Belize, the Belizean Blue. For several years, British naturalist Charles Wright has been living in the deep jungles of southern Belize studying blue morphos. About his subject, he writes that "this butterfly cruises the light and shadow pattern along a forest trail, electric flashes of turquoise blue accompany its passage. It is indeed something to remember."

Similarly fascinating, and cloaked in many Maya myths, is the lantern fly. Looking like a miniature crocodile with wings, it soars through the air toting a toothy, woody-brown snout, resembling some shrunken beast escaped from a Japanese horror movie.

Actually, the tiny creatures are quite benign; indeed they spend most of their time eluding predators. However, Maya folktales say they glow in the dark, which they don't, and that if a girl is bitten by a lantern fly, she must have sex with her boyfriend within 24 hours or she will perish. No doubt the tale was concocted by someone's frustrated boyfriend.

MEDICINAL PLANTS AND NATURAL HEALING

For thousands of years, Belize's rainforests have yielded plants, trees and shrubs prized for their medicinal value. These "healing" plants and their uses are carefully guarded secrets, passed down through generations of Maya bush doctors, though today many Maya villagers use the jungle as their backyard medicine cabinets. The leaves of the wild pineapple plant, for instance, can be heated and formed into a cast to set injured bones. The seeds from the custard apple are a sure cure for head lice, and the sinewy, water-gorged grapevine supplies water so pure the Maya used it to cleanse newborn babies—a practice that continues today. The prickly "give and take" vine stabs with its spikes, then stops the blood flow with its leaves. And the gnarly bullhoof vine, when boiled and consumed as a liquid, will stop internal bleeding.

One tree, the negrito, is nicknamed the dysentery bark tree for its ability to cure the oft-fatal disease. In the days of New World exploration, the tree's bark saved European sailors suffering from severe cases of dysentery and diarrhea. They promptly named it dysentery bark, and began shipping it to Europe, where it was worth its weight in gold for over 200 years.

For stomach problems experienced by many of today's travelers, there is jackass bitters, also known as *tres puntas*. The boiled leaves, turned into a tea or wine tincture, are a powerful antidote to parasites, amoebas, giardia and even malaria. The taste is so bitter, however, that some have trouble keeping it down.

Of course, there are hundreds, perhaps thousands, of other healing plants residing in the jungle. It is impossible to recognize them without some training. Several places around Belize offer jungle tours that explain basic medicinal plants. The best is the Rainforest Medicine Trail (formerly called the Panti Maya Medicine Trail) near San Ignacio, where Americans Rosita Arvigo and Gregory Shropshire are conducting research on natural cures for cancer, AIDS and other diseases. Grants from several U.S. organizations are funding their work, including the National Cancer Research Institute and U.S. A.I.D.

Bottled herbal treatments, labeled Rainforest Remedies, and herb packets are available at the trail, or by mail by writing to Dr. Rosita Arvigo, Ix Chel Tropical Research Foundation, San Ignacio, Cayo, Belize, Central America. Among the potions are:

Belly Be Good, a mild sedative for indigestion, gastritis and constipation. Made with man vine.

Blood Tonic, for anemia, rheumatism, arthritis and fatigue. High in iron and minerals, and made with wild yams and China root.

Female Tonic, for menstrual cramps or irregularities. Made with man vine, contribo, guaco and copalchi.

Flu Away, for colds and flu. Made with garlic, cane, jackass bitters and alcohol.

Jackass Bitters Tea, a bitter-tasting brew for internal parasites, amoebas, malaria, ringworm and yeast infections.

Male Tonic, for impotence and kidney and bladder problems. Made with balsam bark, corn silk, man vine root and cane alcohol water.

Sunburn Ointment, made of beeswax, aloe, herbs and vegetable shortening.

Travelers Tonic, for that pesky *turista*. Made with guava leaf and jackass bitters.

ENVIRONMENTAL EXPEDITIONS

Many tour companies specialize in environment-oriented expeditions across Belize. A few of the best include:

Chaa Creek Inland Expeditions, P.O. Box 53, San Ignacio, Cayo, Belize; 92-2037, fax: 92-2501.

Close Encounters, P.O. Box 1320, Detroit Lakes, MN 56502; 218-847-4441, 888-875-1822, fax: 218-847-4442.

Discovery Expeditions Belize, 126 Freetown Road, P.O. Box 1217, Belize City, Belize; 2-31063, fax 2-30750.

Native Guide Systems, P.O. Box 1045, Belize City, Belize; 2-75819, fax: 2-74007.

Sea and Explore, 1809 Carol Sue Avenue, Suite E, Gretna, LA 70056; 504-366-9985, 800-345-9786, fax 504-366-9986.

HOW TO HELP

For information on environmental programs, contact one of these organizations:

Belize Audubon Society, 12 Fort Street, P.O. Box 1001, Belize City, Belize; 2-35004, fax: 2-34985.

Belize Center for Environmental Studies, P.O. Box 666, Belize City, Belize; 2-34397.

Belize Zoo & Tropical Education Center, P.O. Box 1787, Belize City, Belize; phone/fax: 8-13004.

Programme for Belize, 2 South Park Street, P.O. Box 749, Belize City, Belize; 2-75616, fax: 2-75635.

Iguana

THREE

Planning Your Trip

WHEN TO GO

CLIMATE AND SEASONS

Located in a subtropical rainforest region, Belize has just two seasons: rainy and dry. Generally, rain falls and temperatures rise during summer and autumn months, from June through October. Daily rains can soak inland jungle roads, creating sludge trails that are impassable without four-wheel-drive vehicles.

Summer rains increase dramatically in Belize as you head from north to south. Northern Corozal, for instance, averages 50 inches of annual rain, while Punta Gorda, only 200 miles to the south, gets an incredible 170 inches a year. During the rainy season, afternoon showers give life to the forests and a welcome drop in temperatures for those who reside there. Temperatures along the coast and inland rainforests, however, often reach 95 degrees by midday during summer months.

Late summer and early fall can also mean hurricane season, particularly along the Caribbean coast. It's not likely that you'll encounter one—they blow in every decade or so—but if you should, take it seriously: hurricanes are monsters that take lives and leave paths of destruction. In October, "northers" usually set in, bringing persistent winds from the north of 15 to 25 knots. Northers are the lower fringe of cold fronts that swirl down from North America.

During the dry season, from November through March, the thermometer registers in the comfortable low 80s. In the mountains of inland Belize, the mercury drops into the 50s at night during winter, with perfect daytime weather in the 70s. During winter, some lodges, particularly in the cayes, raise their prices as much as 30 percent in response to visitors arriving to enjoy the idyllic weather.

Springtime creates crystalline waters in the offshore cayes, with visibility reaching an amazing 100 feet in some dive spots. However, the months of April and May enjoy neither winter trade winds nor cooling afternoon rains, and can be intensely hot—in the 100s—and suffocatingly humid. May is when many Belizeans living inland head to the cayes for heat relief. This author, despite being a native Floridian accustomed to the tropics, finds an air-conditioned room a necessity in Belize during April and May.

All that said, visitors should know that those who follow Belize's weather say it is entirely unpredictable. For instance, during the "rainy" season, there may be many days with overcast skies but little rain. And in the dry season, there may be several days of drizzling or even torrential rains. George Bevier, an American entomologist living in southern Belize, has recorded the daily weather for more than 20 years, only to find that there are absolutely no consistent patterns!

HOLIDAYS

You may want to plan your Belize visit around a certain holiday or festival and join in the local spirit. Make your reservations at least three to four months in advance, because hotels fill up fast during special events.

During major holidays, rum and island music flow freely through towns and villages, and locals celebrate with jumpup street dances that can last until sunup. Remember that because of the festivities, everything else practically shuts down, including government agencies, businesses and professional offices. In other words, if there's a holiday, forget about business and join the party!

Here are the most important events in Belize:

JANUARY–FEBRUARY

New Year's Day is celebrated on January 1 as a national holiday, complete with parades and fireworks.

MARCH–APRIL

Holy Week—the week leading up to Easter—rivals the Christmas season as the biggest holiday of the year. Businesses close for **Good Friday**, **Holy Saturday**, **Easter Sunday** and the following Monday so locals can celebrate at home. On March 9, **Baron Bliss Day** pays homage to the man who left his $2 million fortune to the tiny country. Belizeans remember him with a day of fishing and sailing, an apt remembrance since the baron was devoted to both pursuits.

MAY

Belizeans take a break from work every May 1, which is **Labour Day**. Kite contests, bicycling and horse races, and a harbor regatta are featured. On May 24, they pay respects to the British Commonwealth on **Commonwealth Day**. Also in May, the residents of Crooked Tree Village in northern Belize celebrate the cashew harvest season. Their **Crooked Tree Cashew Festival** features storytelling and Caribbean folklore performances, Belizean cuisine, nature walks, river trips and expeditions to local Maya ruins.

JUNE

June 29 is the **Feast Day of Saint Peter**, patron saint of San Pedro, Ambergris Caye. Residents celebrate the 1848 founding of their village with merrymaking and a parade of fishing boats that are blessed in the town harbor.

JULY–AUGUST

Mexico, Guatemala, El Salvador and Honduras join Belize in the **International Sea & Air Festival**, held the third week of July in San Pedro, Ambergris Caye. Showcasing myriads of ethnic dances and cuisines, costumes and crafts, the festival is a celebration of the countries' cooperation and work together on the Mundo Maya (Maya World) tourism project.

SEPTEMBER

September means virtual nonstop celebrating in Belize. One of the biggest, most joyous national holidays, **St. George's Caye Day** remembers the September 10, 1798, victory of the British over the Spanish. Every town joins in with a week of parades, jumpup street dancing and community-wide feasting. The British eventually gave Belize its independence on September 21, 1981, and Belizeans celebrate with **National Independence Day**. The whole country is like a carnival, and streets are filled with artisans, musicians, dancers, actors and delicious local food.

OCTOBER

A double holiday can mean twice as much celebrating. October 12 brings **Columbus Day**, *and* **Pan American Day**. Big events are horse races, boat racing and cross-country cycling competitions.

NOVEMBER

Pulsing drums and punta rock music signal the start of **Garifuna Settlement Day** in southern Belize. The November 19 festivities, centered in the Toledo District, mark the 1823 arrival of the Garifunas (African Indians).

DECEMBER

Christmas festivities begin on Christmas Eve, when Belizeans light the yule log and exchange presents. December 26 marks **Boxing Day**, a national holiday.

COMING AND GOING

ENTRY REQUIREMENTS

All visitors to Belize must have valid passports. Besides clearing immigration, you will need to show your passport when renting a car, cashing traveler's checks or, in some cases, checking into a hotel.

Belize does not require visas (except for visitors from Cuba, Colombia, Peru, Hong Kong, Taiwan, China, India and parts of Africa and the Middle East). Visitors who plan to stay longer than 30 days in Belize, however, should obtain an extension from the Belize Immigration Office (Mahogany Street, Belize City; 2-24620). Visa extensions cost US$12.50.

U.S. citizens who wish to cross over into Guatemala by land must have a visa, available free, in advance, from any Guatemalan consulate in the United States or Mexico, or from the Guatemalan embassy in Belize City. Those flying into Guatemala will need only a tourist card (US$5, issued upon entry into the country). Citizens of certain foreign nations will need a visa no matter how they enter Guatemala.

To cross over to the great Maya ruins at Copán in Honduras, you need only your passport. A tourist card (approximately US$10) will be issued at the Honduras border.

If you want to travel deeper into Honduras or El Salvador, where there are a few minor Maya ruins, entry requirements can range from a visa to a tourist card to just a passport, depending on who you ask. If you are flying there directly, check with the nearest consulate at least two weeks before your departure and obtain either a visa or an official letter waiving any visa requirement. Many airlines require one or the other.

CUSTOMS REGULATIONS

Belize customs regulations are liberal to tourists. However, they are notoriously slow at the Belize City international airport. This is especially true on Monday mornings, when Belizeans returning from weekend shopping sprees in Miami must itemize their purchases and pay duties. Customs officials literally check every corner of every suitcase. Twice, I waited nearly two hours in the boiling heat to clear customs. If you find yourself in this waiting-forever situation, slow down and remember—this is the tropics!

If you take your boat to Belize, the following documents must be presented to the customs officer who will board your vessel upon its arrival: (1) the boat's certificate of registration; (2) proof of clearance from your last port of call; (3) four copies of your crew and passenger list; (4) four copies of your stores list; and finally, (5) four copies of your cargo manifest, if you are transporting cargo.

Guatemala's customs regulations, as they apply to tourists, are minimal and somewhat vague. As a practical matter, instead of physically inspecting your luggage, Guatemalan *Aduana* officials prefer to charge a small fee per bag for a tag certifying that they have inspected it.

U.S. CUSTOMS REGULATIONS

Even if you live there, the United States can be harder to enter than Central American countries. When returning home, United States residents may bring $400 worth of purchases duty-free. Anything over this amount is subject to a 10 percent tax on the next $1000 worth of items. Certain items, such as unset stones, jewelry and handicrafts, are tax-exempt. In case customs officials question the values you declare, save the purchase receipts for goods you buy in retail stores and record your marketplace and street vendor purchases neatly in a notebook. Persons over 21 years of age are allowed one liter (or quart) of liquor duty-free.

Fruits, vegetables and many other fresh foods are not allowed into the U.S. and will be confiscated. Fish, shrimp and any seafood that can be legally caught in Belize can be brought across the border. However, conservation-minded travelers will catch only what they can eat in Belize. There's nothing more embarrassing than an American tourist lugging a cooler full of lobsters from a country where many children don't get enough to eat.

All items made from any part of an endangered species—such as the sea turtle, crocodile, black coral or ocelot—are prohibited in the United States and will be confiscated. Vendors of such items usually will not warn you that you can't take them home.

Ancient relics, such as Maya artifacts or pre-Colombian art, cannot be taken from their country of origin and will be confiscated if found in your possession. All archaeological finds are considered national treasures and the property of the country in which they were found.

For more details, write **U.S. Customs** (P.O. Box 7407, Washington, DC 20044; 202-927-6724); the **U.S. Fish and Wildlife Service** (Department of the Interior, Mailstop 430, Arlington Square, 1849 C Street Northwest, Washington, DC 20240; 202-208-5634); and **World Wildlife Fund and the Conservation Foundation** (1250 24th Street Northwest, Washington, DC 20037; 202-293-4800).

To avoid confiscation of prescribed drugs, label them carefully and bring along a doctor's certificate of prescription. As for contraband drugs, there's a war on. Smart travelers remain neutral.

Customs checks at the U.S. border can be stringent or swift, depending on how suspicious you look. To avoid any problems, dress neatly and declare your purchases.

TRANSPORTATION

AIRLINES SERVING BELIZE

By far the best way to get to Belize is to fly. Commercial airlines fly daily between the United States and Canada and the international airport in Belize City. **TACA** and **Continental** offer daily service from major U.S. cities to Belize City. American Airlines alternates between daily and thrice-weekly service, depending on the time of the year.

Baggage allowances on international flights are generally the same as on U.S. domestic flights—two carry-on items small enough to fit under the seat or in an overhead rack, plus two pieces of check-through luggage. In addition, some Latin American airlines have a weight limitation—typically 40 kilograms (88 pounds)—on check-through luggage. All airlines allow considerably more baggage than you would want to carry around on this trip.

During special events, holidays and the November-to-April high season, make flight reservations at least a month in advance. Air delays are common. So are flight cancellations—be sure to confirm your flight 72 hours before departure, and allow the same amount of time when confirming your return flight. Canceled flights seem to be a particular problem between Belize City and Flores (the airport for Guatemala's Tikal National Park), where the next flight out may not be for several days.

Visitors leaving Belize are required to pay a travel tax of US$10, a conservation fee of US$3.75 and a security screening fee of US$1.25.

When booking your international airline tickets, if you will be taking a connecting flight on your return trip, be sure to allow plenty of time. At the hub airport where you first land in the United States—probably Miami, New Orleans or Houston—you will have to wait for and claim your baggage, clear U.S. Customs, and recheck your bags before boarding your onward flight. Allow one-and-a-half to two hours.

DRIVING TO BELIZE

Traveling from the United States to Belize by car is a challenging and time-consuming adventure. Not that it's particularly dangerous—just demanding. The drive to Belize from Brownsville, Texas, through Mexico, is almost 1400 miles. It can be done in roughly 55 hours of actual driving time. To make the journey comfortably, without arriving in Belize exhausted, allow at least a week. Most Mexican highways are two-lane roads, not limited-access freeways, and driving takes longer than you would expect.

If you are driving to Belize from the U.S. border, plan well ahead for re-fueling and evening stops. Gas stations in Mexico are a government monopoly, and in much of the country they are few and far between. Never pass up an opportunity to fill your vehicle's tank. Driving after dark can be dangerous (the most common hazards are vehicles stopped in the traffic lane without lights and vehicles traveling without lights well after dusk—sometimes considered a display of Mexican machismo).

Note: One of the most important things you should know is that unleaded gas is not available in Belize. But then, there are not many cars in Belize. Leaded fuel is sold by the gallon at about twice the price of gas in the United States.

MOTOR VEHICLE REQUIREMENTS   For driving in Belize, your current driver's license is valid. If you're bringing your own car via Mexico, you'll need a Mexican car permit and Mexican auto insurance. To obtain a car permit (a special stamp on the owner's tourist card, issued for up to 180 days), you need proof of ownership—a current registration certificate and title. If the title shows a lien against the vehicle or if it is registered in another person's name or a company name, you need a notarized letter from the lienholder or owner authorizing you to take the vehicle to Mexico for a specified time. The owner or driver who has the car permit stamp on his or her tourist card must be in the car whenever it is being driven.

Anyone bringing a motor vehicle into Mexico must show either a major credit card or a collision/comprehensive insurance policy valid for the duration of the stay. Otherwise, the owner can be required to post a cash bond guaranteeing that he or she will return with the vehicle to the United States. At the same time, the Mexican government has promised to simplify procedures for temporarily importing vehicles. For current requirements, contact a Mexican consulate in the United States.

Auto insurance policies issued in the United States are not valid in Belize or Mexico. Purchase motor vehicle liability insurance (and, if you wish, collision/comprehensive) before crossing into Mexico. Insurance is sold by agencies on the U.S. side at all border crossings. Causing an auto accident is a crime under Mexican law, which presumes defendants guilty until proven innocent. This means that if you are involved in an accident that causes property damage, your vehicle will be impounded until you pay the damage and a fine. If any person is injured in the accident, you will go to jail.

The documentation you need to take your vehicle into Mexico is more than sufficient to bring it into Belize. However, Belize requires local liability insurance, which can be fairly expensive.

PACKING

Pack light! A camera plus whatever else you can fit in a large duffel bag and a backpack would be perfect. For a two-week trip, I carry a canvas

French Army backpack and a sturdy, woven Guatemalan bag (available in Belize for about US$30–$35) packed light enough to tote on successive boat and commuter plane trips. There is nothing like lugging 75 pounds of suitcases around the jungle to make one feel absurdly materialistic.

When choosing your clothing, remember that Belize is far from fashion conscious. In fact, both women and men dress in a practical, unpretentious manner. Flaunting a new pair of Nike Air Jordans around Belize City is not only in poor taste, it's an invitation to petty thieves. Keep your clothing modest and sensible, as befitting a country where wildlife and forests are held in higher regard than the latest styles.

Bring along a minimum of sporty, summery clothing, T-shirts, shorts and a swimsuit, as well as a rain poncho and a pair of polarized sunglasses (essential for spotting fish). Cotton shirts breathe better and wick away perspiration. For treks to the Maya ruins and wildlife reserves, you'll need a sturdy but lightweight pair of hiking boots, a comfortable pair of slacks—I like loose-fitting cotton fatigues—and socks to protect your ankles from insects. A long-sleeve cotton shirt protects against bugs and brambly bush, while a light jacket will keep you warm on winter nights. Leave your blue jeans at home. Not only are they extremely hot, they get heavy when wet.

Blue-crowned Motmot

A walk in the jungle is like a walk in the dark, unless you take a good pair of binoculars. Binoculars help you find the hundreds of tiny critters that hide out in the dense foliage all around. The best binoculars are those with high magnification that let in plenty of light—all the better for seeing in the dim, shadowy forest. Many birdwatchers recommend Zeiss or Leitz 10 x 40 lenses.

A flashlight with extra batteries is a must for exploring caves and for those nights when hotel generators shut down early. I take a lighter and a couple of votive candles for reading at night. And don't forget to take a roll of toilet paper for the long forays into the jungle.

You should definitely pack a first-aid kit. Include a good insect repellent, aspirin, band-aids, cold capsules, vitamins, motion sickness tablets, prescription drugs you use, iodine or alcohol for disinfecting wounds, antibiotic ointment, water purification tablets, sunscreen with at least a 15 SPF, lip balm and diarrhea medicine. For insect bites and jellyfish stings, carry a bottle of calamine lotion, a tube of Benadryl ointment or bottle of Benadryl spray, and a bottle of Benadryl pills. When you're covered with itchy red welts that keep you up all night, nothing gives relief like Benadryl.

Anyone with a medical condition should consider wearing a medic alert identification tag that identifies the problem and gives a phone number to call for more information. Contact **Medic Alert Foundation International** (P.O. Box 381013, Turlock, CA 95381; 800-344-3226).

Belize, filled as it is with quirky humanity, ancient crumbling cities and travel-poster islands, is a photographer's dream. At virtually every turn, you will find the makings of a great picture. But, be aware that the Adventure Coast can be tough on camera equipment, so unless you're competing in a photo contest, consider bringing something compact and inexpensive. Pocket-sized instamatic cameras hold up well, and are easy to tote around the jungle in a backpack. Disposable cameras are also practical because you don't have to worry about carrying rolls of film. I use an underwater camera that also takes decent above-water photos, and won't succumb to the Belize humidity.

The best way to protect your equipment is to keep it in a padded, zippered camera bag. Remember that if you tour on the mainland, you will be bouncing down rocky roads for hours on end. Belize's rains also wreak havoc on cameras, so keep a couple of ziplocked bags handy for sudden showers.

Definitely bring plenty of film; in Belize, film costs double or triple what it does in the U.S., and it's tough to find. Slide film is virtually unheard of. It's also wise to bring an extra camera battery and, if you're using a 35mm camera, a couple of clear lens filters. The jungle has a way of leaving its mark (scratches and dents) on camera lenses.

When it comes to toiletries, most towns in Belize carry everything you'll find in the United States, though usually at higher prices: toothpaste, deodorant, shampoo, soap, insect repellent, skin creams, shaving cream and bat-teries (buy the expensive ones; the cheapest kind often don't work). Im-ported items like tampons and suntan lotions are also widely available in larger towns, though they cost a lot more than in the United States.

Scuba divers should check with their lodge about available equipment. Few dive resorts carry enough for everyone, so plan to bring your own mask, snorkel, booties and fins, BC (buoyancy control device), regulator, weights and, of course, your certification card. Tanks are normally provided. Always pack your dive gear in a suitcase; a dive bag checked alone is a prime target for thieves—in the U.S., not Belize. Make sure your dive knife is in your suitcase, checked with the rest of your gear. I know of a foolish diver who, attempting to carry his knife on the plane, had to surrender it at a Miami departure gate.

Likewise, anglers staying at fishing lodges will want to bring along their rods and tackle. Check with your individual lodge about what it has on hand.

Take along some good paperbacks (hard covers don't hold up well in the jungle). However, in English-speaking Belize, where the literacy rate is over 90 percent, you'll have no trouble finding good books on all subjects. Many innkeepers stock superb libraries on Belizean and Maya history and culture and are happy to loan books while you're a guest. In archaeological areas, you will find English-language books about the ancient Maya civilization that are not available in the United States. In areas of Belize where American expatriates congregate, such as San Ignacio and Placencia, English-language novels are recycled endlessly. There are used-book or trade-in racks full of paperback potboilers left over from decades past at bookstores, hotels and restaurants where foreign visitors gather. No matter where you plan to travel, don't forget to bring your copy of *The New Key to Belize!*

ELECTRICITY

You'll likely stay in places without electricity, but those that do have it carry current the same as in the United States—110 volt, 60 cycles. If you need to convert appliances from other countries, bring your own adapters.

TRAVELING EXPENSES

Travelers accustomed to low prices in Guatemala and Mexico may be sur-prised to find their next-door neighbor more expensive. Belize is in fact on par with Caribbean destinations such as Jamaica, St. Thomas and Grand Cayman when it comes to lodging, restaurant and tour prices. And in 1996, Belize implemented a 15 percent Value Added Tax (VAT) on most travel expenses, including meals, car rentals, sightseeing tours and gifts. The hotel tax remains at 7 percent, though you should know that a three-star hotel that's US$10 a night in Guatemala will be US$45 a night across the border in Belize. The best jungle lodges and beach hotels charge over US$100 a night, and dinner at a "better" restaurant costs about US$30 a person.

If you're staying in remote areas, it will be necessary to have all your meals at your lodge. Expect to pay from US$30 to US$60 per person per day for these meals. While I have found the meals at some of these "all-inclusive" lodges to be exceptional and well worth the price, others have been marginal and overpriced. Throughout this book, lodges are critiqued on the quality and value of their meals.

Sightseeing tours are expensive. This is partly due to the poor condition of the roads, which can destroy tour vehicles in a matter of months. What else makes them so expensive, I have not been able to ascertain. Expect to pay from US$100 to US$250, for one to four people, for a day trip to a Maya ruin or nature reserve. Travel agencies in Belize City and Ambergris Caye sometimes arrange less expensive tours by organizing larger groups. In remote areas, however, your chances of joining a large group are slim. Single travelers will find tour prices exorbitant. Traveling alone, I have paid as much as US$200 for a six-hour tour to a ruin.

Groceries cost more (from 10 to 100 percent more) than those in the United States, particularly convenience foods and toiletries. Bus transportation is inexpensive, costing about US 25 cents to travel around Belize City and only US$4 to travel from Belize City west all the way to the Guatemala border.

Stick to local beer and rum. A bottle of Belize beer, a mild, tasty brew called Belikin, sells for US$1 to US$2 and is consumed by locals and tourists alike. Cocktails made with Belize's Caribbean White Rum are about US$2.50. Imported brands will run you two to three times that price.

INOCULATIONS

No inoculations are required to enter Belize. Cases of hepatitis, malaria, typhoid, cholera, dengue fever and other tropical diseases do occur but seldom afflict travelers. If you are planning to visit remote areas, your doctor may recommend yellow fever, tetanus, typhoid and gamma globulin (for hepatitis) shots and/or malaria pills.

ACCOMMODATIONS IN BELIZE

After you have stayed awhile in Belize, you will become accustomed to (and endeared to) the country's funky style of accommodations. A Belize City guesthouse, for instance, may offer drapes made of seashells and battered furniture painted every primary color. Decor in your seaside motel may include a lava lamp, a vinyl '50s-era chair and a boat oar parked on the wall, but hey, the room's got character! Lodge owners often furnish rooms with the same care and Belizean quirkiness they use in their own houses. Before long, you'll feel right at home.

Be aware, though, that funky doesn't mean cheap. The clean, comfortable, low-priced lodging that's abundant throughout neighboring Mexico and Guatemala doesn't exist in Belize. Lodging prices here are more in line with those in the Caribbean, and in popular resort areas of the United States.

Cabanas, made of stucco, wood or bamboo and crowned with palm thatching, are ubiquitous in Belize. They range from elegant bedrooms with glossy teakwood floors, mahogany furniture and canopy beds to basic round shelters with concrete floors and curtained closet doors. If you're staying in the jungle, make sure your room is properly protected from bugs by screens and other devices. During certain times of the year, insects migrate and can literally invade your room if it's not bug-proofed. I had this experience, and it is not one I wish to repeat.

Most towns and islands have at least one motel or lodge that offers electricity and, thus, air-conditioning. However, you will pay a premium for cold air, often twice as much as a room without air-conditioning—but it's worth it on suffocatingly hot days. Many lodges, particularly in the jungle, out islands and remote villages, receive their electricity from gasoline-powered generators. In some instances, electricity is rationed to a few hours after dusk. But their location makes the experience of staying there special enough to justify any mild inconveniences you might encounter. Indeed, I have found these jungle lodges to be some of the most memorable places in Belize.

During the November to April high season, and around major holidays like Christmas, Easter and National Independence Day, many hotels raise their rates and sell out weeks in advance. Reservations for these times of the year should be made at least two months ahead of time.

This book's lodging listings range from budget to very expensive, with an emphasis on unique or special midrange to upper midrange establishments. All price ranges are based on double occupancy, and *do not* include a 7 percent government tax. Lodging is rated as follows: *budget* facilities have rooms for less than $35 a night for two people; *moderate* hotels are priced between $35 and $70; *expensive* facilities offer rates from $70 to $100; and *very expensive* have accommodations at prices above $100.

Remember that, except for a few chain hotels in Belize City (such as the Radisson Fort George and Fiesta Inn Belize), most "expensive" and "very expensive" lodges will be neither fancy nor elegant. Rather, they will assure comfort and charm, picturesque surroundings and excellent meals, and plenty of assistance with local excursions. Unless otherwise noted, all lodges listed in this book offer electricity, hot water and private baths.

Note that many Belizean hotels charge an additional 5 percent if you pay for your room with a credit card. Some resorts also add a service charge of 10 to 15 percent to their rates.

NOTES FOR WOMEN TRAVELERS

Belize is quite liberated when it comes to women's issues. Women traveling here can expect at least the same freedom and respect they enjoy in the United States, if not more. Belize women are hard-working, independent individuals who are often family breadwinners. It is not uncommon to hear a Belize man complaining that his girlfriend is "too busy with her career" to settle down. After traveling around Belize for three months, the only sexual harassment I experienced was from American men!

NOTES FOR TRAVELING WITH CHILDREN

Should you bring the kids to Belize? That depends. If you plan to spend a lot of time in the cayes and other resort areas, then by all means, take them along. As you move into remote jungle areas of Belize, you may want to consider taking only older children. The jungle does hold limitless fascination for older children; they adore hiking through mysterious forests and exploring on horseback and in canoes. In archaeological areas, ancient temples and pyramids are great for climbing and poking into secret passageways, and the mysteries of a vanished civilization can tantalize young minds for weeks on end. Belizeans love children and are very family oriented. Numerous lodges across the country are owned by families, and children often join the guests at mealtime. Many travelers find it easy to enjoy both worlds—parenting and adventuring.

Remember to get a tourist card for each child. Children traveling with only one parent must have notarized permission from the other parent (or, if applicable, divorce papers, guardianship document or death certificate). Minors traveling alone must have a notarized letter of permission signed by both parents or guardians.

Prepare a junior first-aid kit with baby aspirin, thermometer, vitamins, diarrhea medicine, sun block, bug repellent, tissues and cold medicine. Parents traveling with infants will want to pack cloth diapers, plastic bags for dirty diapers, and a wraparound or papoose-style baby carrier. Strollers aren't practical on Belize's crumbling city roads and island sand streets.

Disposable diapers, baby food and medicines are available in larger towns. Outside Belize City and Ambergris Caye, few lodges have cribs or babysitting services. However, some lodge owners will help you find a local babysitter.

Belize restaurants are plenty casual for children, but the fare may not please picky eaters. You might want to bring some rolls, peanut butter and jelly, toaster pastries and other easy-to-pack munchies. In the meantime, encourage your child to try local foods. You'd be surprised how quickly they adapt to stewed chicken and beans and rice.

Go ahead and splurge on a rental car. Traveling with children, especially young ones, on public buses could be one stressor too many. If you tour by car with an infant, bring a portable car seat. For children of any age, be sure to pack toys, books and art supplies to drive away boredom during long trips.

Pace your trip so your child has time to adapt to changes. Don't plan exhausting whirlwind tours, and keep travel time to a minimum. Seek out beaches, parks, plazas and short excursions to amuse your child. The Belize Zoo is a wonderful place for children; thousands of local children visit each year. While you're there, pick up a copy of *Hoodwink the Owl*, a warm-hearted tale that introduces children to Belize's fascinating animals.

NOTES FOR SENIOR TRAVELERS

Belize has much to offer seniors, including adventures tailored to individual strength and endurance. In other words, not every trek to the ruins has to last 12 hours. Older travelers will find companionship everywhere, from the fishing and jungle lodges to tiny beach motels. They will also discover that Belize seniors are often in astoundingly good shape; I met several Maya bushmen who looked (and acted) much younger than their years.

There is, however, very little organized senior travel to Belize, mainly because modern tourism facilities, including transportation and roadways, are still developing. A good travel agent can recommend accommodations and sights to suit your needs.

Some of the most rewarding senior excursions to Belize are the work programs offered by **Elderhostel** (75 Federal Street, Boston, MA 02110; 617-426-8056). Travelers can join a Maya ruin dig, track dolphins off an atoll or help collect data on howler monkeys in the northern rainforests. These are no luxury trips: accommodations are usually very basic, and there is hard work to be done. But the opportunities to experience a country from a local point of view and to contribute to the environment are unmatched.

Be extra careful about health matters. Bring any medications you use, along with the prescriptions. Consider carrying a medical record with you—including your current medical status, medical history, your doctor's name, phone number and address. If possible, include a summary of your medical status and history. Check to see that your health insurance covers you while traveling in Belize.

NOTES FOR TRAVELERS WITH DISABILITIES

There are few sidewalks in Belize, and town roads tend to be narrow and bumpy. In the cayes, the streets are all sand. Most establishments and transportation systems do not provide special amenities, such as wheelchair access, for people with disabilities. You may want to get help from a good travel agent to track down facilities to suit your situation.

You may also wish to contact one of the following organizations: the **Society for the Advancement of Travel for the Handicapped** (SATH) (347 5th Avenue, Suite 610, New York, NY 10016; 212-447-7284); **Travel Information Service of Moss Rehabilitation Hospital** (Philadelphia, PA; 215-456-9600); **Mobility International USA** (P.O. Box 10767, Eugene, OR 97440; 541-343-1284); or **Flying Wheels Travel** (143 West Bridge Street, Owatonna, MN 55060; 800-535-6790). **Travelin' Talk** (P.O. Box 3534, Clarksville, TN 37043; 615-552-6670), a networking organization, provides useful information for travelers.

NOTES FOR STUDENT TRAVELERS

While there are few organized student tours to Belize, the country is well-suited to young people traveling on a budget.

Numerous lodges across Belize are popular with students from the United States, Europe and Latin America, and the public bus system is extensive and inexpensive. And, Belize's abundant outdoor experiences appeal to vigorous young travelers.

You'll find budget-priced rates and fellow students at the following lodges:

On Ambergris Caye, at **Lily's** (Barrier Reef Drive, San Pedro; 26-2059). On Caye Caulker, at **Vega Inn and Gardens** (located seafront, near the middle of town; 22-2142).

In Belize City, at the **Seaside Guest House** (3 Prince Street; 2-78339) and **Fort Street Guest House** (4 Fort Street; 2-30116).

In western Belize, at **Maya Mountain Lodge** (Cristo Rey Road, near San Ignacio; 92-2164) and **Venus Hotel** (29 Burns Avenue, San Ignacio; 92-2186). Maya Mountain Lodge even offers educational programs on natural history, archaeology and social science.

In Placencia, southern Belize, at the **Sea Spray Hotel** (on the beach in Placencia Village; 6-23148).

NOTES FOR TRAVELING WITH PETS

If you want to bring a pet into Belize, you must have an International Health Certificate for Dogs and Cats (Form 77-043) signed by a U.S. veterinarian verifying that the animal is in good health, as well as a separate certification that it has been immunized against distemper and rabies within the last six months. Belize also requires an import permit, available from the Veterinarian Office in Belize City (2-45230).

VISITOR INFORMATION

Because mainstream tourism is still relatively new to Belize, its only state-side tourist office can't provide extensive assistance, but it will send out a prepared list of Belizean hotels and tour operators. Contact the **Belize Tourist Board** (421 7th Avenue, Suite 701, New York, NY 10001; 212-563-6011, 800-624-0686, fax: 212-563-6033).

The best resource for travelers is in Belize City at the **Belize Tourist Board** (83 North Front Street; 2-77213, fax: 2-77490). For information on eco-tourism in Belize, contact the **Belize Audubon Society** (12 Fort Street, Belize City, Belize; 2-35004); the **Programme for Belize** (2 South Park Street, Belize City, Belize; 2-75616); or the **Belize Zoo and Tropical Education Center** (P.O. Box 1787, Belize City, Belize; phone/fax: 8-13004).

SAMPLE ITINERARIES

Belize may be small, but getting around takes a lot more time than you would imagine. Most of the country is still covered by forest, and paved roads are few. Towns and sights are spread out, sometimes separated by hours-long drives down rocky roads. Likewise offshore, many cayes are reached by boat trips that take two to four hours, depending on the height of the seas.

To get the most out of Belize, you should spend at least a week. Two weeks will give you a taste of every region, though you could return for two more weeks and still not experience all the best Belize has to offer.

First-time travelers to Belize who have only a few days usually spend them on Ambergris Caye, with maybe a day trip to a Maya ruin. It's not bad for a tight schedule, but then again, you won't get a real sense of the country. For those who have more time, I recommend the following itineraries:

ONE WEEK

Day 1   Fly to Belize City, rent a car and drive to San Ignacio in western Belize. Overnight in San Ignacio.

Day 2   Drive to Caracol for a morning tour, then explore Mountain Pine Ridge in the afternoon. Overnight in San Ignacio.

Day 3   Visit the Rainforest Medicine Trail and the ruins at Xunantunich in your rental car. Cool off in the late afternoon with a swim in the Macal River. Overnight in San Ignacio.

Day 4   Drive from San Ignacio to Belize City, stopping at Guanacaste National Park and the Belize Zoo along the way. Catch a late afternoon flight to San Pedro, Ambergris Caye. Overnight on Ambergris Caye.

Days 5 & 6   Relax, fish or dive at Ambergris Caye. One morning or afternoon, take a 15-minute launch over to Caye Caulker and explore the small, neighboring island. Overnight on Ambergris Caye.

Day 7   Fly from Ambergris Caye to Belize City, then fly home.

TWO WEEKS

Days 1–3   Spend your time in San Ignacio, as described in the one-week itinerary above.

Day 4   Drive from San Ignacio to Belize City, then fly to Flores, Guatemala. Overnight in Flores or at nearby Tikal.

Days 5 & 6   Spend the day exploring the magnificent ruins of Tikal. Overnight in Flores or Tikal.

Day 7   Fly from Flores to Belize City, then take the short flight to Placencia in southern Belize. Overnight in Placencia. (*Note:* If there are no connecting flights to Placencia, spend the night in Belize City, then take a flight the next morning.)

Day 8   Relax on the beach at Placencia, or take a trip to nearby cayes for snorkeling and lunch. Overnight in Placencia.

Day 9   Take a guided tour to the Cockscomb Basin Wildlife Sanctuary. Overnight in Placencia.

Day 10   Fly from Placencia to Belize City, then fly to San Pedro, Ambergris Caye. Overnight on Ambergris Caye.

Days 11–13   Relax, dive or fish around Ambergris Caye. Spend a day exploring neighboring Caye Caulker. Overnight on Ambergris Caye.

Day 14   Fly from Ambergris Caye to Belize City, then fly home.

If you prefer to spend all your time on the mainland, consider using days ten through thirteen to visit northern Belize. Take one day trip to Lamanai, and another to Altun Ha and the Community Baboon Sanctuary.

On the other hand, if you're a hard-core island person, think about spending one of your weeks at an out island. Lighthouse Reef, Turneffe Islands, St. George's Caye and South Water Caye offer splendid week-long, all inclusive packages.

SPECIAL WAYS TO VISIT BELIZE

To truly understand and appreciate Belize, it must be explored and then savored, like an exotic food one learns to enjoy. One way to experience the country's complex, multifaceted terrain and culture is to take a specialty tour. Specialty expeditions offer unusual insights into people, wildlife and places few travelers have seen, and encounters with a world virtually unchanged over centuries.

You can explore cool mountain pine forest on horseback, float along a river through caves of dazzling limestone or stroll the jungle during the black of night (accompanied by a bush guide, of course) at **Mountain Equestrian Trails** (Mile 8, Mountain Pine Ridge Road, Central Farm; 92-3310, fax: 92-3381). Located in western Belize in the Slate Creek Preserve, "M.E.T." (as it's called locally) offers overnight accommodations in simple cabanas, and meals and drinks at its popular cantina.

The educational field station at **Maya Mountain Lodge** (92-2164, fax: 92-2029, or call 800-344-6292 in the United States) located near San Ignacio is the starting point for **Archaeology and Natural History Tours** across western Belize. Two popular tours are the four-night **Ruta Maya Experience** and three-night **Mayan Adventure**. Also near San Ignacio, **Chaa Creek Cottages** (92-2037, fax: 92-2501) provides an array of nature and archaeological expeditions ranging from two to four days.

Hiking, flatwater canoeing, snorkeling and sleeping seaside in hammocks are all part of the ten-day treks offered by **Laughing Heart Adventures** (3003 Highway 96, P.O. Box 669, Willow Creek, CA 95573; 916-629-3516). Optional, multiday extensions allow you to visit a Belizean family, float through the River of Caves or go horseback riding in the jungle.

International Expeditions (One Environs Park, Helena, AL 35080; 205-428-1700, 800-633-4734), widely regarded as one of the best stateside organizers of specialty tours to Belize, offers several unique expeditions:

A nine-day **Rainforest, Reefs and Ruins**, with exceptional opportunities for seeing peccaries, tapirs, scarlet macaws and much more wildlife. Naturalist walks, horseback rides through the rainforest, river rafting, and a Garifuna cultural gathering are other highlights of the trip.

A nine-day **Pharmacy from the Rainforest** workshop, where travelers can help collect and prepare medicinal plants for National Cancer Institute research. There are many more unusual and rewarding experiences, including sessions with traditional Maya healers and village midwives. Traditional healers demonstrate how to identify the medicinal plants in the rainforest and in the ocean.

An 11-day **Naturalist's Quest** that takes in more than a half-dozen reserves, parks and sanctuaries, as well as the great Maya city of Tikal, Guatemala.

An 11-day **Maya Heartland** expedition that traces the Maya Route from northern and western Belize to the southern Yucatán, with a grand finale in Tikal. An optional three-day extension loops south to the Maya city of Copán, Honduras.

A five-day **Jaguars of Belize** tour, with three nights at the beachfront Jaguar Reef Lodge and one night camping inside Cockscomb Basin Wildlife Sanctuary, a jaguar preserve. Mountain biking, kayaking, swimming, sunning and excellent wildlife watching are included.

Perhaps the most exhilarating way to explore Belize's hidden cayes is to kayak them. Utah-based **Slickrock Adventures** (P.O. Box 1400, Moab, UT 84532; phone/fax: 801-259-6996) offers nine-night **kayak tours** to its private, eight-acre North East Caye at Glover's Reef. (Seven nights are spent on the island; the remaining two are in Belize City, where guests board a jet boat for a two-and-a-half-hour trip to Glover's Reef.) From North East Caye, kayakers can take day trips to nearby cayes and reefs for snorkeling, diving and sunning—or never leave the island. Everyone gets his or her own hammock. Cabanas provide basic overnight accommodations, and meals are cooked on propane stoves. There are daily activities, but don't think Club Med: things couldn't be more carefree on this castaway trip.

Island Expeditions Co. (368–916 West Broadway, Vancouver, British Columbia, Canada V5Z 1K7; 604-452-3212, 800-667-1630, fax: 604-452-3433) also offers a week-long kayak tour to Glover's Reef where travelers laze away the days on sand-fringed South West Cay. Schedule your trip between mid-December and the end of March and you can join a Garifuna gathering, usually held on Saturday or Sunday night, at Len's Cool Spot in the Sabal Community on mainland Dangriga. Garifuna culture is usually quite closed, and few travelers anywhere have the opportunity to experience the hard pulsing music and passionate dance of the punta.

High-school and college students as well as educators can sign up for independent programs at **Language and Travel Study** (30 East Yale Loop, Irvine, CA 92604; 714-552-8332, fax: 714-552-0740). Professor Steve Tash runs the programs through the University of California at Santa Barbara, the University of the Pacific and Seattle Central Community College. Students are eligible for college credit if they live with a Belizean family or attend a language school. Among the independent study courses offered: "Using the World as a Classroom" and "Spanish-Language Enhancement Through Experimental Activities."

A typical Belizean hut

FOUR

Once You Arrive:
Getting Around In Belize

LANGUAGE

While English is Belize's first language, don't expect everyone to speak your brand of English. Belizeans speak with a variety of accents, and may have just as much trouble understanding your English as you do theirs. In villages and areas near the Guatemala and Mexican borders, Spanish, Maya and other languages are spoken. If you know a little Spanish, or are good with body language, you'll have no problem communicating. Belizeans are gregarious people who enjoy making new friends.

MONEY MATTERS

CURRENCY

Belize currency, measured in Belize dollars (BZE$), is extremely stable. For the last few years, the exchange rate has stayed steady at BZE$2 to US$1. You'll have no trouble using U.S. dollars throughout Belize; in fact, many places now post their prices in U.S. currency to make them seem less expensive (which they rarely are). Foreigners, however, being respectful of where they are, should change their money and use Belize dollars. If you have any doubts about the issue, consider how you would like it if Belizeans insisted on using Belize dollars in the United States.

CHANGING MONEY

Be smart and protect your vacation by carrying traveler's checks. Even though you will get a slightly lower exchange rate, it's worth safeguarding your money. Well-known brands, especially American Express, are easiest to cash. You will need your passport to cash them. Canadian and European traveler's checks and currency can pose problems; some banks will not cash them.

Keep in mind that most villages have no banks, and it is usually impossible to cash traveler's checks there. On market days, there are often moneychangers around. At other times, only small-denomination local currency will work.

Most banks are open 8:00 a.m. to 1:00 p.m., Monday through Thursday. On Friday, hours are from 8:00 a.m. to 1:00 p.m. and 3:00 to 6:00 p.m. Banks often have specified hours for exchanging foreign money, which vary from bank to bank and day to day.

CREDIT CARDS

Credit cards are accepted at most lodges but only a few restaurants and shops, mainly those in Belize City. Many hotels add a surcharge if you pay by credit card. MasterCard, Visa and Discover are the most widely accepted cards; American Express cards are sometimes frowned upon because of their stiff fees to merchants.

If you need a financial transfusion while in Belize, most banks will provide a cash advance on your credit card. The transaction can take up to several hours, and there is usually a fee of three to five percent of the withdrawal amount. Money transfers can also be made via Western Union (*usually* taking one day) or via any big bank at home through one of its Belizean affiliates (which can take as long as three working days). Check before you leave home to see whether your bank offers this service.

TIPPING

Belizeans are not as gratuity-oriented as Americans, but they do appreciate a tip for good service. In general, follow the same customs on tipping as you would back home. Tip taxi drivers and chambermaids 5 to 10 percent; restaurant waiters and waitresses, 15 percent; and airport porters, US 50 cents per bag. Some hotels and restaurants include a service charge, so check your bill before tipping. Tour guides are some of the most knowledgeable, patient workers in Belize and deserve a generous tip when they do a good job.

LOCAL TRANSPORTATION

FROM THE AIRPORT

Taxis charge about US$15 for the nine-mile trip from Philip S.W. Goldson International Airport, in Ladyville, to Belize City. That's the maximum fare allowed by the government, so don't pay more. There is no bus service from the airport to Belize City.

TAXIS

The Belize government sets maximum fares for regular taxi routes around the country. Reputable drivers will have the fare schedule posted in their cars. The prices are high by U.S. standards, but considering the condition of Belize roads and the price of gas, they're actually quite reasonable. One driver who frequently travels to southern Belize, the land of rugged roads, replaces his car every year.

A few sample one-way fares from Belize City: north to Corozal, US$97; west to San Ignacio, US$85; south to Punta Gorda—a hellacious 202-mile ride on bumpy roads—nearly US$200. If you're going all the way to Punta Gorda, forget taxis; a 30-minute plane flight costs only US$50.

Most taxi drivers are good public relations for Belize: They're friendly, knowledgeable and in a hurry when you need them to be. Otherwise, they'll admonish you to slow way down, reminding that you are, after all, in Belize.

Indeed, some of the most memorable Belize experiences are in taxis. One American woman recalls how, in the middle of a trip, a driver asked for part of his fare in advance to buy his wife a chicken for dinner. After a brief stop at the market, the woman spent the rest of the trip in the back seat with a clucking, flapping chicken.

CARS FOR HIRE

Almost all taxi drivers double as tour guides, and will customize an itinerary and negotiate a fair fee. Many specialize in certain Maya ruins and wildlife reserves, and will act as bush guides. If you enjoy your tour, a tip of 10 to 15 percent is in order. Ask your hotel about qualified drivers, or check with the **Belize Tourist Board** (83 North Front Street, Belize City; 2-77213).

HITCHHIKING

Because bus service is widely available, there's really no need to hitchhike. Anyway, Belize is so small that if you do need a short ride, someone usually knows someone willing to give you a lift.

BUSES

There's only one class of bus in Belize, and it's closer to a school bus than a Greyhound bus. However, service is extensive and usually on time, and the fares are cheap. The express bus from Belize City to Corozal, near the Mexican border, is only US$3.75. To San Ignacio in the west, the fare is US$2. Be advised that if you're traveling during "rush" hour on a popular route, like the one between Belize City and Belmopan, get there early or you may not get a seat.

The **Z-Line** (Venus Bus Terminal, Magazine Road, Belize City; 2-73937) runs from Belize City to Belmopan, Dangriga and Punta Gorda, and points in between. **Novelos** (West Collet Canal, Belize City; 2-77372) services western Belize all the way to the Guatemala border, and offers connections into Guatemala. **Batty Brothers** (15 Mosul Street, Belize City; 2-72025), which offers similar routes through western Belize, will also take you to major points in northern Belize. Batty also has an express run from Belize

City to Chetumal, Mexico. **Venus** (7th Avenue, Corozal; 4-22132) offers service in northern Belize.

Current schedules and fares are available from the **Belize Tourist Board** (83 North Front Street, Belize City; 2-77213).

PLANES

Flying is by far the quickest, least tiring way to get around Belize, and is cheaper than hiring a taxi or renting a car. Most flights are aboard loud, twin-engine puddle hoppers (10 to 20 passengers) that feel like flying jalopies. The ride will either thrill or unnerve you, depending on your level of adventure, though you will no doubt find the scenery from above unsurpassed on the ground. Local flights leave from either the **Philip S. W. Goldson International Airport** in Ladyville, nine miles north of Belize City, or from the **Belize City Municipal Airport**, on the north end of town.

Tropic Air (2-45671 in Belize City; 26-2012 in San Pedro, Ambergris Caye; 800-422-3435 in the United States) operates an hourly shuttle from Belize City to San Pedro, Ambergris Caye, and also flies to Caye Caulker, Corozal in the north and points in the south. Tropic Air also has flights to Flores, Guatemala, the gateway to Tikal, that are more or less dependable. **Island Air** (26-2435 in San Pedro, Ambergris Caye; 2-31140 in Belize City) flies to the cayes. For flights to southern Belize, **Maya Airways** (2-31362 in Belize City; 800-552-3419 in the United States) is the best choice. Maya Airways also offers service from Belize City to Belmopan and San Ignacio, and from Punta Gorda to Puerto Barrios, Guatemala.

For service to Belize's out islands, such as Lighthouse Reef, and to remote inland areas of Belize and Guatemala, call **Javier's Flying Service** (2-45332). The charter company uses low-flying planes that offer enthralling views of the mountains and jungle, as well as the barrier reef running through iridescent blue waters.

BOATS

Shuttle boats cruise from Belize City to Ambergris Caye and Caye Caulker; there's usually a morning and an afternoon departure. Launches for Caye Caulker leave from the Texaco station near the Swing Bridge, on the north side of Haulover Creek. Boats bound for Ambergris leave at the south side of Haulover Creek, next to the Swing Bridge. You can also catch a boat for Ambergris at the dock across from the Bellevue Hotel (5 Southern Foreshore).

Some of the docks are attended by a number of sweet-talking skiff owners ("Hey nice lady, let me take you in my fast boat") anxious for your patronage. If there's not much business that day, you might negotiate a lower-than-normal fee. Otherwise, it's US$25 for the one-hour trip to Ambergris and US$25 for the 30-minute ride to Caye Caulker. Trips to St. George's Caye and other out islands can usually be arranged as well.

DRIVING IN BELIZE

Nothing makes you feel more Belizean than bounding down a rocky, washed-out jungle road in a rented four-wheel drive, Maya beads swinging from the rear view mirror and punta rock music pounding from a radio that's ready to pop out of the dash. The scenery is priceless—barefoot village kids racing through banana groves, iguanas darting across the road, Maya women toting fresh-cut corn for their tortillas—but the pace is painfully slow. Except for three paved "highways," inland Belize is a tangle of dirt and rock roads. After a few days, you will learn that every dirt road is not created equal, but fall into three general categories:

- Type 1: a wide, clay washboard surface that allows you to travel at a nice 35 mph clip.
- Type 2: narrow marl limestone road with scattered rocks the size of golf balls. Maximum speed: 25 mph.
- Type 3: a narrow, roller-coaster trail that looks like the scene of a bomb explosion. Rubble everywhere; rocks the size of baseballs. Maximum speed: 10 mph, with the windows clattering.

It is the Type 3 roads that often lead to the best lodges, Maya ruins and nature reserves, and so have to be reckoned with. After awhile, your body becomes used to the jarring, and you learn to accept how long it takes to go a short distance. And perhaps for the first time in your life, you become overjoyed at the sight of asphalt.

Belize's three paved "highways" (actually two-lane roads) are in fairly good shape. The **Northern Highway** runs from Belize City north to the Mexico border; the **Old Northern Highway** parallels the Northern Highway for about 40 miles; and the **Western Highway**, which starts near Belize City, heads west to the Guatemala border. On the Western Highway, distances are measured in "mile posts," little white cement markers planted beside the road.

The **Hummingbird Highway** is a formerly paved, severely potholed and rock-studded road that connects Belmopan in western Belize with Dangriga in the south. The **Coastal Highway** is a shortcut south, angling off from the Western Highway west of the Belize Zoo and hooking up with the Hummingbird just before Dangriga. From Dangriga, the **Southern Highway** extends 100 miles south to Punta Gorda—which locals call "painful driving."

I recommend flying to sights in southern Belize, but driving a four-wheel-drive vehicle everywhere else. If you visit during the rainy season, check local road conditions before setting off through the jungle. Many roads flood and are impassable from June through September.

Belize is so undeveloped that it's virtually impossible to get lost while driving. Most towns have only a handful of roads (many without names), and getting around is as easy as driving around the block. When asking directions, don't be surprised if you get a reply like, "Head toward the ocean and take a right at the third palm tree." Only Belize City requires any real navigation, and even there the streets are laid out in an easy-to-get-around fashion. Pick up a free city and country map from the **Belize Tourist Board** (83 North Front Street, Belize City; 2-77213). Car-rental companies also provide good maps.

CAR RENTALS

Renting a car gives you the freedom to explore at leisure (and avoid the hot, tiny public buses). Reputable companies recommend four-wheel-drive vehicle—a necessity for Belize's rocky roads. Be prepared to pay dearly; four-wheel drives run about US$80 per day, including unlimited miles and insurance. Beware of companies that offer lower rates for old, gas-guzzling American cars. After paying for gas (and possibly breaking down), you will have spent more than if you had rented a new four-wheel drive.

All the car rental companies are in Belize City. The one with the best reputation is **Budget Rent A Car** (771 Bella Vista Road, two-and-a-half miles north of Belize City; 2-32435, fax: 2-30237), which offers four-wheel drives in top condition. Budget owner Alan Auil will brief you on the area, and provide essential driving tips.

Elsewhere, try **Avis Car Rental** (at the international airport and the Radisson Fort George Hotel, Belize City; 2-52385, fax: 2-53062); **Safari Car Rental** (11-A Cork Street, Belize City; 2-35395, fax: 2-30268); or **National Interrent** (4½ Miles Western Highway, P.O. Box 1283, Belize City; 2-31587, fax: 2-31586).

In towns such as Corozal, San Ignacio and Punta Gorda, travel agencies can sometimes arrange a rental car for you. It may take several hours' advance notice or several days, depending on what local resident's car is available! In San Ignacio, try **Godsman Elis** (92-3264). In Punta Gorda, there's **AliStair King** (7-22126).

If you reserve a car through a company's toll-free U.S. office, be sure to reconfirm with the office in Belize City. The easiest, least expensive way is to send a fax. Anyone 25 years or older, with a passport, a driver's license and a major credit card, can rent a car in Belize. Take the optional extra insurance that lowers your deductible for damage to the vehicle. Rental cars in Belize lead hazardous existences, subjected as they are to the rocky, mountainous terrain and pothole-laced roads.

It is not currently possible to drive a Belizean rental car into Guatemala or Mexico or vice versa. It's best to take a bus or a taxi when crossing the border.

GAS

Belize gas is leaded. Sold by the gallon, it costs about twice as much as gas sold in the U.S. Most major towns have gas stations that are open during the day. If you plan a long excursion into the countryside, fill up beforehand.

Otherwise, if you stick to the paved Western and Northern highways, you're never far from a gas station.

BUSINESS HOURS

Professional and government offices are open from 8 a.m. to noon and 1 to 4 p.m., Monday through Friday. Bank hours are from 8 a.m. to 1 p.m., Monday through Thursday. On Fridays, banks also open from 3 to 6 p.m. Retail businesses open from 8 a.m. to 5 p.m. weekdays, except for Wednesday afternoons, when they are closed. Some stores are open Friday nights from 7 to 9 p.m., and all day on Saturday.

TIME ZONES

Belize is on Central Standard Time year-round. Daylight Savings Time is not observed here.

COMMUNICATIONS

TELEPHONES

Belize has a good phone system. Calling into Belize is almost as easy as calling long-distance in the United States (though there's usually a bit of static). The country code for Belize is 501, and local codes differ depending on where you're calling *from*. If you're calling from abroad, use the one-digit abbreviated local code (available from an international operator). If you're calling within Belize, use the full local code, which has a zero prefix. For instance, to call Belize City from the United States, you would dial 2. To call Belize City from elsewhere in Belize, you would dial 02. If this system sounds confusing, that's because it is!

Many establishments in Belize have no phones because of the expense and, in many communities, because it literally takes years on a waiting list to get one installed. For local or long-distance calls, your best bet is usually to ask your hotel manager for assistance in placing the call. You will pay any long-distance charges plus a small fee for the service.

AT&T and some other U.S.-based long-distance companies have special numbers you can dial in Belize that will connect you with an operator and let you charge international calls to your calling card, often at a lower cost than you would pay through the local phone company. Ask your long-distance carrier for a directory of international numbers.

To phone home without a calling card, go to any office of **BTL** (Belize Telecommunications Limited). You'll find offices in all major towns. Give your calling information to the person behind the desk, leave a deposit of US$15, and wait until the call goes through, which can take a few minutes or several hours depending on how busy international phone lines are. Then you can take the call in a private booth and talk as long as your US$15 lasts (calls to the U.S. are about US$1.60 per minute). At the end of the call, you will be reimbursed for any unused minutes.

For placing calls unassisted, here are some numbers to remember: long-distance operator: 91; international operator: 98; prefixes for dialing direct to the U.S., Canada and Europe: 95 (station to station) and 96 (person to person).

MAIL

A yellow-and-red-winged *Catonephele numilia*, a star-eyed hermit crab, a common lettuce slug—you never know what you'll find on Belize stamps. The beautiful butterflies and birds, beasts and blooms, sea life and even Maya ruins that adorn these little squares of paper are a celebration of the country's flora, fauna and history. Belize stamps are said to be some of most colorful and attractive in the world. Take a look and you'll surely agree. Stop by the **Belize City Post Office** (North Front Street, on the north side of the Swing Bridge; 2-72201) or at one of the many town offices across the country (some are run out of local homes). Besides decorating your postcards, stamps make unusual, inexpensive gifts. Postcard stamps to the United States are US 15 cents; stamps for letters are US 30 cents.

Unlike mail in other parts of Central America and in Mexico, Belize mail is highly reliable. From Belize to the U.S., mail takes one to two weeks; from the U.S. to Belize, about a week.

LAUNDRY

After watching the local women scrub laundry every day in the rivers, the idea of having your clothes dry-cleaned seems extravagant. However, there is the **Belize City Dry Cleaners & Coin Laundry** (3 Dolphin Street; 2-24213), which even offers delivery service that's more or less dependable. Outside the city, you can usually have your wash taken care of overnight at your lodge, though it's costly. I take a small bottle of laundry detergent, hand wash everything in the lodge sink, and hang it to dry in the trade winds.

PUBLICATIONS

U.S. magazines, newspapers and paperback books can be found in Belize City and at some lodges throughout the country. All major Belize publications are in English. The country's biggest newspaper is the weekly *Amandala*, which is tabloid-size and full of quirky tidbits as well as breaking news. There's also the *Reporter*, which covers issues from screwworm eradication to the number of Guatemalan "aliens" who sneaked across the border that week. Pick up a copy—it's local color at its best. More glossy but still offering gossipy details is the bimonthly *Belize Currents* magazine.

The *San Pedro Sun* of Ambergris Caye is a great little island weekly with a visitors guide, the local magistrate's court news and an advice column by the anonymous Doctor Love, "the island's and possibly the world's greatest authority on just about everything, though the doctor seldom addresses matters involving the law or religion. . . ." If you're on Ambergris, don't miss Doctor Love.

PICTURE TAKING

While on the cayes and in larger towns, you can take pictures freely in almost any public place. Outlying villages are a different story. Many villagers, particularly the older Maya and Garifunas, don't want their picture taken—a taboo that we, as visitors, should respect. If you want to photograph village people, ask first. You will no doubt be charmed by their colorful, elaborately handcrafted clothing and their exotic features with faces expressing everything from stoic nobility and ancient, mysterious wisdom to embarrassed amusement at the strange-looking tourist confronting them. With the coming of television to many villages, attitudes toward cameras are changing. Some people are more willing than in the past to pose for photographs. And if you converse with them for a while and let them get to know you, many people who would deeply resent having their likeness captured by a stranger are more than willing to offer it as a gift to a new friend. You may want to reciprocate with a small gift, either a monetary tip or a souvenir. Village children love pens, hair barrettes, sunglasses— most anything a tourist has to offer.

Have your film developed back home. Belize's developing labs are not only expensive but few and far between. If you just can't wait to see your snapshots, take your film to **Spooner's One-Hour Minilab** (89 North Front Street, Belize City; 2-31043), which offers fair prices and dependable service.

HEALTH PRECAUTIONS

HEALTH CARE

Medical clinics and doctor's offices are available in towns and villages across Belize, but the level of care does not measure up to U.S. standards. The country's hospitals are typically sad-looking, overcrowded places that are not equipped to administer advanced health care. A new Belize City Hospital, opened in 1996, has somewhat improved the situation. Belizeans who can afford it go to Miami or Houston for major surgery. For routine procedures and minor emergencies, **Belize Medical Associates Ltd.** (5791 St. Thomas Street, Belize City; 2-30303 or 2-30098, fax: 2-33837) is a private clinic recommended by some American expatriates. The facility employs seven physicians, including surgeons and specialists in internal medicine, pediatrics and obstetrics.

Outside Belize City, lodges can usually recommend the best local physicians. Contact your health insurance carrier before you leave to find out the extent of your coverage while abroad.

For true medical emergencies, a San Diego–based service by the name of **Critical Air Medicine** (call toll-free from Belize, 95-800-010-0268) provides air ambulance service to anywhere in Central America or Mexico—24 hours a day, every day of the year.

TURISTA

The illness some people may encounter is diarrhea, euphemized as *turista*. Caused by food and drink carrying unfamiliar strains of bacteria, a bout can range from a 24-hour case of mild cramps to an all-out attack with several days of fever, chills and vomiting, followed by a lousy feeling that lingers on for weeks.

However, *turista* is much less common in Belize than in Mexico. This author, who consistently gets ill in Mexico (despite drastic precautions), has had no problems in Belize. No doubt it is because Belize, despite its Third-World status, adheres closely to British standards of cleanliness and health. In Belize City, the British government has installed a modern purification system that seems to work just fine. In remote areas, motels and lodges usually provide bottled water in the rooms or will direct you to a grocery store that sells it. Always drink bottled liquids—mineral water, sodas, fruit drinks, soft drinks or beer—whenever possible.

Take it easy the first few days. If you sock your system with unfamiliar food and heavy liquor right away, your stomach may seek revenge. In other words, eating spicy stewed chicken followed by fried gibnut chased by Caribbean rum is asking for trouble.

Remember, those who stay healthy use the best defense: prevention. Eat with discretion. If you're in a jungle or island lodge frequented by tourists, the food is usually high quality and delicious. If you find yourself in a remote outpost, where the pickings are limited to a suspect Chinese hole-in-the-wall or a grocery store, opt for the grocer. Consume only thick-skinned fruits that you peel yourself, such as oranges and bananas, and vegetables that are cooked through. Nuts with shells, such as peanuts and coconuts, are pretty safe bets, too. Steer clear of raw seafood—*ceviche* is renowned for causing *turista*—as well as garden salads.

Be careful about street food, especially in small villages. Meat, seafood, peeled fruit used in drinks and candies on which flies have taken their naps are more risky. However, a lot of the food from stalls is delicious and very well prepared. I especially enjoy the street food in Belize City and in San Pedro, on Ambergris Caye. If the facilities look clean and the food is hot off the grill, it's probably okay. Be the judge and take your chances.

Many people believe in preventive medicine. Some take a slug of Pepto-Bismol before every meal; others, a shot of tequila, believing it will extinguish any threatening organisms. The antibiotic Doxycyclin is commonly prescribed as a preventive, although it causes sensitivity to the sun—a major inconvenience in the subtropics. Belize bush doctors prescribe jackass bitters, an awful-tasting potion brewed with jungle plants, as both a preventive and remedy. One traveler from Texas, who contracted severe diarrhea, said jackass bitters cured him in several hours—though he could barely endure the taste. I also met several people, including former residents of Mexico, who swear by garlic pills as the best prevention. Lime juice is also a traditional preventive for stomach problems.

Booby

If you take all the necessary precautions and still get hit with *turista*, try these remedies: Lomotil, the stopper-upper. Use sparingly. Not a cure, it's a morphine derivative that induces a kind of intestinal paralysis. Stop the dosage as soon as symptoms disappear. Paragoric, Kaopectate, Kaomycin, Imodium AD and Pepto-Bismol help keep the cramps down. For diarrhea with a fever, you can take Septra or Bactrium if you are not allergic to sulfa drugs. But remember that prolonged use of any antibiotic is not good for your immune system and can make you more susceptible to other tropical diseases.

Hot chamomile tea and peppermint tea soothe the stomach and often work wonders. Papaya restores the digestive tract. Light, easy-to-digest foods like toast and soup keep your strength up. Lots of nonalcoholic liquids—any kind—prevent dehydration. Carbonated water with juice of a lime is another popular stomach soother.

Rest and relaxation will help your body heal faster than if you run around sick and wear yourself down further. The symptoms should pass within 24 hours or so, and a case of *turista* seems to have an immunizing effect—any subsequent bouts you may have will be less severe, and eventually your body will adjust to the foreign water's bacteria.

In rare cases, diarrhea may be a symptom of a more serious illness like amoebic dysentery or cholera. See a doctor if the diarrhea persists beyond three days, if your stool is bloody or foamy, or if you have a high fever.

MOSQUITOES AND OTHER PESTS IN PARADISE

Ask anyone who's spent a night in the jungle and they will tell you: The most ferocious animal is not a jaguar but a mosquito. **Mosquitoes** fiercely protect their territory in this region of the world, known aptly as "The Mosquito Coast." The little buzzers are thickest in rainforests, swamp areas and along coastal bush. The best defenses are long sleeves and pants, and plenty of good insect repellent.

What works for you may not work for someone else. People who wish to avoid DEET, the active chemical in most commercial mosquito repellents, may want to investigate some other methods. Herb shops and health food stores in the U.S. sell good-smelling potions that are more or less protective lotions made from oils and herbal essences. Some people swear by daily doses of Vitamin B_6 or garlic, others by tobacco smoke. The new electronic mosquito repellent devices, which emit a sound pitched at the high edge of human hearing, got high marks from a visitor to Guatemala's dense Petén jungle. Many Belizeans, following an ancient Maya custom, burn abandoned termite nests to chase away mosquitoes. After trying dozens of different brands, pills and treatments, I found that only the strongest repellent (such as Deep Woods OFF!) keeps me bugless. For areas of moderate infestation, the pleasant-smelling Skintastic (also made by OFF!), sold either as a pump spray or lotion, does the trick.

Campers will find that mosquito netting is more important than a tent or a sleeping bag. Many jungle lodges drape mosquito nets over the beds, and provide mosquito coils that will burn all night.

Sandflies, also called flying teeth or no-see-ums, are mite-sized bugs with a giant bite. Like mosquitoes, sandflies steal the best part of the day, emerging in droves at dawn and dusk. Unlike mosquitoes, they will prey on the tiny grooves and crevices of the human body—ears, nose, eyelids. Besides a powerful repellent, wear a hat and a pair of sunglasses.

Less well-known but no less of a pest, **bottlass**, or "bottle-ass," flies are minuscule rainforest dwellers that inflict angry, itching blisters. As the flies fill with blood, their stomachs puff up and give the appearance of tiny flying bottles—hence the nickname.

Bottlass flies should not be confused with **botflies**, which don't bite in the traditional sense, but whose larvae burrow under the flesh after being deposited by a mosquito or bottlass fly. It causes only minor itching the first few days, but as the larva grows and feeds, its prickly body burns and pinches its victim. Botfly larvae breathe through a tiny hole in the victim's skin, so the way to kill them is to smother them by masking the hole (Belizeans use everything from Scotch tape and moistened tobacco leaves to petroleum jelly), then squeeze them out. If this sounds truly horrible, it isn't. Kids living and playing in the jungle get them all the time, and so do the animals.

And chances are, unless you spend many days in the jungle during rainy season, you will probably never experience a botfly.

Before you head out to Belize's beautiful seas, you should become acquainted with **sea thimbles**, **sea lice** and **stingrays**. The first is a tiny brown, thimble-shaped jellyfish that scoots along the surface of the water. If you swim along the surface, it will scoot with you and inflict little bites that later turn into big red welts. Sea lice, the larvae of sea thimbles, also lurk on the surface and bestow measles-looking bite marks that itch for a week. Unfortunately, sea lice are invisible.

You can usually avoid sea thimbles by not swimming where you see them. Occasionally, they are so small and pervasive, they look like underwater particles. Sea lice are impossible to avoid, but you can minimize the bites by rinsing your body in fresh water. Don't rinse until you've removed your swimsuit; fresh water trapped under your suit could cause the larvae to swell and sting you even worse.

Like sea lice, stingrays are tough to see. The flat slippery creatures camouflage themselves in the sand along shallow areas and can deliver a wicked puncture with their stingers. To avoid being stung, shuffle away. If you're stung, see a doctor at once.

For various bug bites, Benadryl ointment and pills take the itch out and reduce swelling. Caladryl (a blend of Benadryl and calamine lotion) also works well, as does lime juice. For sea thimble and sea lice bites, Belizeans splash on vinegar to reduce swelling and take the heat out. If you do get zapped with a rash of bites, avoid the sun for a few days. Direct sun causes even more swelling and inflammation, and slows healing.

DRUGS

Marijuana farms abound in Belize. If you have any doubts, check a local map; the bigger fields are often clearly marked. Out in the bush, when locals want some "Belize breeze," they visit the village pot farmer. They *do not* help themselves to a local field; doing so could result in physical harm. If you should happen upon a marijuana field, resist any urges to go exploring. Many growers protect their crop as though it were their lives.

Smoking marijuana out in the jungle will probably bring few consequences, but back in "civilization," partaking could land you in jail, where getting out can take a lot of time and money. In certain locales, such as Belize City, Caye Caulker and Orange Walk Town, you will receive offers from whispering, sometimes pushy, salesmen to purchase marijuana, cocaine, crack and other illegal substances, and you may even see locals using drugs publicly. But what the police may accept from locals, they rarely tolerate with tourists. All things considered, when traveling in Belize, it's better to stay out of the war on drugs.

SAFETY AND THEFT

Belize is sparsely populated and has little big-city crime. Plus, most Belizeans are extremely proud, family-oriented and peace-loving. Traveling here is like traveling through a jungle version of the American midwest—lots of country roads and friendly people. I spent several weeks crisscrossing Belize in a four-wheel drive by myself and had not one problem. Even in Belize City, where everyone seems to have an "I-got-robbed" story, I felt quite at ease.

But Belize City is famous for petty thieves, just as certain U.S. cities have a well-deserved reputation for crime. When choosing a hotel, make sure it's in a safe part of town, preferably one that's frequented by travelers. All lodges recommended in this book are located in safe neighborhoods. After the stroke of dusk, stay away from the Swing Bridge, the infamous hangout of petty thieves. Even if you are with a group, the Swing Bridge is not safe at night. During the day, however, feel free to cross as often as you like!

The safest place to be in Belize City at night is at your hotel; the second safest is the Fort George neighborhood. Areas of downtown where there is a lot of activity after dark are safer than outlying neighborhoods. Don't tempt fate by wandering around dark back streets late at night. Stay away from drug deals. In short, exercise the same caution you would use at home. Observe these common-sense precautions, and feel fortunate that you are not in New York City, where—unlike in Belize City—the petty criminals carry guns.

Be aware that whenever you are in public, any thief who happens to be around will be checking you out. Foreign tourists are natural targets for theft because they stand out in a crowd and seem wealthy in a country where the average income amounts to US$10 a day. Use common sense. Watch out for pickpockets, purse-snatchers and backpack-slashers, especially in public markets and other crowded places. Carry your trip funds, passport and other important documents in a money pouch or hidden pocket inside your clothing. Keep cash in your side pocket, never a back pocket. Carry day-packs under one arm rather than on your back. Don't leave wallets or cameras lying on the beach while you go for a swim or sitting on a café table while you go to the restroom. Always lock your hotel room and car. Park in a secured lot at night. Don't leave radios, gifts, cassettes or other temptations visible inside the car. Dress with humility; a thief will focus on the best-dressed, richest-looking tourist around, so make sure it's not you.

Once you leave Belize City, relax. Except for the town of Orange Walk, Belmopan and the island of Caye Caulker, which have their share of thieves and drug dealers, the rest of the country is rural and crime is rare. You should, of course, always exercise common sense. Never carry large amounts of cash or leave valuables unattended in public places. But don't be alarmed to find there aren't any locks on your lodge door—there are few thieves in the jungle!

EMBASSIES AND CONSULATES

Following is a list of foreign embassies and consulates in Belize:

Belgium Honorary Consul: Queen and North Front streets, Belize City; 2-45773

British High Commission: Embassy Square, Belmopan; 8-22146

Canadian Consulate: 83 North Front Street, Belize City; 2-31060

Commission of European Communities: Eyre and Hutson streets, Belize City; 2-32070

Embassy of Costa Rica: 49 Nanche Avenue, Belmopan; 8-23801

Honorary Consul of Denmark: 13 Southern Foreshore, Belize City; 2-72172

Embassy of El Salvador: 2 3rd Street, Belmopan; 8-23404

German Honorary Consul: 3 Miles Western Highway, Belize City; 2-77282

Embassy of Guatemala: 6-A St. Matthew Street, Belize City; 2-33150

Embassy of Honduras: 91 North Front Street, Belize City; 2-45889

Israel Honorary Consul: 4 Albert Street, Belize City; 2-73991

Italian Consular Representative: 18 Albert Street, Belize City; 2-78449

Jamaica Honorary Consul: 4 Eve Street, Belize City; 2-35672

Mexican Embassy: 20 North Park Street, Belize City; 2-30194

Netherlands Honorary Consul: 14 Central American Boulevard, Belize City; 2-75663

Panamanian Consulate: 5481 Princess Margaret Drive, Belize City; 2-34282

Swedish Honorary Consul General: 11 Princess Margaret Drive, Belize City; 2-30623

United States Embassy, Consular Section: 29 Gabourel Lane, Belize City; 2-77161

Embassy of Venezuela: 18/20 Unity Boulevard, Belmopan; 8-22384

NATIVE FOOD AND DRINK

FRUITS AND VEGETABLES

The Belizean landscape, so pristine and prolific, yields an extraordinary array of tropical fruits and vegetables. Many Belizean backyards are like "mini" produce markets, with selections ranging from papayas, mangoes and passion fruit to cacao beans, custard apples and habañero peppers. Banana plants and coconut palms abound, as do cohune palms, whose tiny white nuts taste like coconut and whose innermost cores, called hearts of palm, are considered a delicacy. You'll also find tamarinds, guavas, plantains and carambola, or star fruit, throughout Belize, and breadfruit on the cayes. Maize, or corn, is grown in *milpa* fields, and has been a diet staple of the Maya for thousands of years. In the tuber family, there are shaggy, white-fleshed malangas; the waxy, fibrous cassava, whose toxins are dispelled during cooking; and the knobby, rose-colored *boniatos*, the sweet potatoes of Central America.

For an introduction to Belize fruits and vegetables, visit the Belize City **Market** (Regent Street, at the southeast corner of the Swing Bridge), where bamboo bins display dozens of colorful varieties. Opened in early 1993, it's a gleaming, indoor place where Belize women are more than happy to tell you about each produce item.

Another excellent source of information are the Belize bush guides, who are infinitely versed in local fruits and vegetables. They'll tell you how the ancient Maya used the produce, and how you can prepare it today.

Even if you don't forage the countryside for fresh produce, you'll find yourself enjoying it at virtually every meal. Belize lodges take advantage of the earth's bounty to supply their tables, and many have organic gardens. For breakfast, wedges of papaya and mango might be tucked around the eggs, and slushy watermelon juice served alongside steaming tea or coffee. At lunchtime, when the sun is hottest and humidity highest, locals cool off with fresh squeezed lime juice, swirled with water and unrefined sugar. Dinner could bring malanga mashed with garlic or corn tortillas baked that very day. For the finale, it might be banana cake, mango fool (a custardy dessert, made with brown sugar, cream and sweetened condensed milk) or perhaps papaya slices flambéed with Belizean rum over ice cream.

Here are a few tips on identifying and using Belize's best produce:

Breadfruit: Breadfruit trees are massive, towering above houses and other trees, while the fruit, which is really a vegetable, is the size of a cannonball. Plucked when still green, it ripens quickly, developing soft, brown patches much like a ripening avocado. It is typically sliced in rounds and fried, though sometimes the flesh is scooped out and baked in a variety of ways, including into breadfruit bread.

Cashew: The cashew tree is a dull tree, with plain round green leaves covering a plain round canopy that disappears amongst the more beautiful Belize trees. Its only distinguishing characteristic is its fruit, the cashew apple, which appears in the spring. The apple is pale red and fleshy, and its sweet meat is turned into mild jellies and strong wines. At the apple's crown is the curly cashew nut, whose kernel is roasted and then coveted by people around the world. The best time to experience Belize cashews is in May, at the Crooked Tree Cashew Festival, held in the village of Crooked Tree in northern Belize. In case you're tempted to pick your own, be aware that the oily liquid inside the cashew shell is poisonous, and not only burns the skin but can kill you if ingested.

Cassava: A ruddy white tuber, and perhaps the humblest of Belize vegetables, it is a symbol of the Garifuna (African Carib) culture. In southern Belize villages, Garifuna women rise before the sun to dig hundreds of cassava roots from the hard clay ground. Then the roots are peeled, pressed through a grinder, and the juice wrung from it. The resulting mush is baked into a white waferlike bread. Other Belizeans use cassava widely, either mashing it like potatoes or slicing it into soups, stews and "boil ups," where it is boiled with whole fish, chicken or cow's feet.

Custard Apple: Like nature's own pudding cup, the custard apple has a creamy, rose-scented flesh designed to go straight from fruit to mouth with a spoon. About the size of an orange, with bumpy green skin that turns blackish-brown when ripe, the custard apple tastes best chilled. To eat, simply slice it in half and scoop out the black seeds.

Habañero Pepper: This is the hottest pepper on earth, registering 200,000 to 300,000 on the Scoville Chart, the Richter scale of chile peppers (jalapeños measure 5000), which sounds like enough to cause stomach meltdown. But the habañero can be eaten, indeed enjoyed, when tamed with shredded carrots and other vegetables and bottled as Marie Sharp's Hot Sauce. Marie Sharp's is consumed in mass quantities around Belize; the bottles sit on tables throughout the land. Many families have their own habañero bush. If you want to see fields of the lantern-shaped chilies, visit Melinda Farm in southern Belize, where Marie Sharp's is made (see Chapter Ten).

Hearts of Palm: It takes a great deal of strength and skill to hack into a palm tree and extract its heart. But once you have tasted the satiny core, encased in folds of delicate white flesh, you will understand why someone would go to all the trouble. After being wrenched from its tree, the heart is boiled until tender, then fanned across salads or served as a side dish, usually with a light sauce or a squeeze of lime juice.

Maize: Together with beans and rice, maize has been the foundation of the Maya diet for thousands of years. Maya villagers today still rely on corn as a primary staple; the men harvest it and the women soak it overnight in lime juice. The next day, the women grind the corn into a powdery meal, mix it with water, and knead it on a cornmeal stone called a *metate*. Then they shape it into wafer-thin disks called tortillas, and grill the disks over an open fire on a *comal*, or griddle stone. The tortillas are kept warm until the meal, at which time a typical Maya man may consume up to 20. If you are lucky enough to visit a rural Maya village, you can watch the women squatting over the fires, making their daily tortillas.

Mango: There are more than 100 varieties of mango, which can weigh anywhere from a few ounces to a few pounds, with flesh that can be fragrant, lush and golden or stringy and tasteless. The best way to tell a good mango from a bad one is to sniff it. It if doesn't smell sweet, it's probably no good. A choice mango smells and tastes like a cross between a peach, pineapple and banana. To eat a mango "on the half shell," slice the fruit right next to its flat pit to get two fleshy "cheeks." With the skin-side down, score each cheek into small chunks, then slice the chunks away from the skin.

A word of caution: Mangoes are in the poison ivy family; the juice and peel may swell and blister the skin of some people. But even those who are allergic to it can usually eat the ripe fruit without any side effects.

Papaya: American food writer Elizabeth Schneider likens the papaya tree to "an Indian fertility goddess." No doubt it is because the branchless trunk dangles its lobes of luscious fruit beneath a sprawling, lacy canopy. Yellowish-green to pinkish-purple, papayas have slippery peach-colored flesh and glassy black seeds that are edible. Simply cut it in half lengthwise and scoop out the meat.

Passion Fruit: One would hope this fruit was named for the sensations it arouses when eaten. Alas, it was named by a most dispassionate group, European missionaries, who upon landing in South America thought its flower looked like a crown of thorns and other Crucifixion symbols. The fruit, for its part, bears a sweet-tart, gelatinous pulp that is indeed sensory-heightening. To eat, slice the purplish-yellow globe in half and scoop out the pulp and edible seeds.

Soursop: There is nothing like the taste of soursop, so spicy and perfumed and tropically addictive. There is nothing quite like the looks of it either—pimply, plump and evergreen. Inside, the fruit's pale custardlike flesh is the color of pale pink abalone. The flesh is rarely cooked, but rather strained, and the soursop juice used in ice creams and rum drinks.

THE BEANS AND RICE SYNDROME

Except for Marie Sharp's Hot Sauce, nothing appears on more Belize tables than beans and rice. Since the time of the Maya, this fiber-starch duo has sustained generations of people on a short but endless cycle: They'd eat beans and rice to get energy to work in the fields planting, growing and harvesting beans and rice, which they'd eat for energy to work in the fields, starting the cycle all over again. Today, some villagers carry on the cycle, but most people who eat the dish do not grow it.

As humble as the dish sounds, beans and rice come in a variety of prepa-rations, from a fiery mélange of vegetables and ground meat or lobster stewed in coconut milk to a dry, bland combo cooked way too long. It's not hard to tell the difference. Good beans and rice look moist and colorful (the beans will be crimson red to bright purple and slightly cracked). Bad beans and rice look dry, and the beans will be cooked to little hard pieces. Most dishes are made with red kidney beans, though you will find concoctions prepared with black beans, turtle beans and even pink beans. Some of the tastiest beans and rice come from street vendors, who toss the brilliant mixture in drum-sized frying pans.

You may not become a beans and rice fan overnight, but you will quickly learn that the dish is remarkable human fuel. For climbing Maya ruins, hiking through the jungle or kayaking the seas, few foods keep you going like beans and rice.

Of course, beans aren't always paired with rice. One of the best dishes I had in Belize was the spicy refried bean dip served at Chan Chich Lodge. When the dip is brought out every evening at sunset, guests literally mob the bowl.

CHAN CHICH'S SPICY REFRIED BEAN DIP

½ pound dried red or black beans

1 medium green pepper, chopped

1 small onion, diced

2 pickled jalapeño peppers, chopped, plus 1 teaspoon of their juice

2 cloves garlic

¼ cup vegetable oil

salt and pepper to taste

tortilla chips, preferably blue corn chips

Rinse beans and place in a 2-quart pan. Cover beans with 2 inches of water, then cover with lid. Bring to a slow boil, reduce heat to medium-low, and simmer beans, partially covered, for 1½ hours. Add more water during cooking if necessary.

Remove beans from heat and cool. In a blender, combine beans and their water, green pepper, jalapeños and their juice, and garlic. Blend until smooth. In a large skillet, heat the oil over medium heat. Add the onion and sauté until pale brown. Stir in the blended bean mixture and cook over medium-low heat until thick, about one hour, stirring occasionally.

Cool slightly and spoon dip into serving dish. Serve with tortilla chips. Recipe makes about 2 cups of dip.

GIBNUT, BAMBOO CHICKEN AND COW'S FOOT SOUP

One reason people come to Belize is for adventure. That's why you might want to try gibnut, bamboo chicken and cow's foot soup. When cooked right, it's Belizean soul food at its best, food that's crisp-fried tender or simmered all day until the meat falls off the bone.

Gibnut, or paca, is a large nocturnal rodent whose tender white flesh is considered tastier than steak. Sometimes it's breaded and fried; more often it's stewed in a big, dilapidated pot over a gas stove or open fire. In the late

1980s, Queen Elizabeth elevated the dish to "royal gibnut" after she ordered it (and purportedly cleaned her plate) at a Belize City hole-in-the-wall called Macy's. But before the queen's discovery, it was plain old gibnut.

Bamboo chicken is the nickname for iguana, which, when fried or grilled, does look and taste a lot like chicken. Cow's foot soup is also just like it sounds: a broth made hearty by slow cooking with a cow's foot (or, if company's coming, two cow's feet). Carrots, onions, garlic, cassava and other vegetables are simmered with the foot, and sometimes a pig's tail, oxtail or chicken foot is thrown in. If you can get past the sight of feet in your soup, you will find the porridge is truly delicious.

Few hotel restaurants serve gibnut, bamboo chicken or cow's foot soup. Unless you're invited to a local home for dinner—an adventurer's dream— your best bet for soul food is a Belizean diner. These are typically tiny, meager establishments with fans teetering from the ceiling, a TV or transistor radio blaring, and a powerful-looking woman in the back hovering over numerous steaming pots.

The less adventurous will also find more familiar local cuisine. Fried chicken is ubiquitous, followed closely by "stew" chicken and "stew" fish, fried fish, fryjacks (sweet fried corn cakes) and johnnycakes (biscuits that are *not* fried). Street vendors sell spicy, flaky meat pies that are some of the best in the Caribbean. Tortillas and tamales are found in northern Belize, near the Mexican border, while lobster and conch prevail on the cayes. Order them only in season—July through October for lobster; October through June for conch. Chinese restaurants abound in certain small towns, with food of wildly varying quality. Some of the best Chinese food I ever had was in Belize, as was the worst. Ask around before you dine.

BEER AND RUM

Belize's national beer, Belikin, must have the best beer label in the world: a Maya temple. It's the Temple of the Sun God, found at Altun Ha. If you don't get to see the temple in person, you'll see its likeness all over Belize, since Belikin is wildly popular. The mild, medium-amber beer costs about US$1 a bottle in groceries and local restaurants, and double that in tourist areas.

There are several different rums made in Belize, but by far the best and most pervasive is Caribbean rum. It comes in light or dark, and both are surprisingly good, considering no one's ever heard of Caribbean rum. Buy some for your friends; a 750 ml bottle will only set you back about US$6.

Every Belizean has his or her own special recipe for rum punch. The one at Capricorn Resort on Ambergris Caye is a favorite of locals and travelers. It's a frosty swirl of just-picked tropical fruit and Belizean dark rum, with a dash of cherry juice, poured into a shapely hurricane glass and topped with sweet, heady crown of banana liqueur. If you can't find fresh fruit, substitute frozen fruit or canned juice—but it won't be the same.

CAPRICORN RESORT'S RUM PUNCH

1 cup chopped tropical fruit (such as papaya, mango, banana, pineapple, orange and lime)

dash of cherry juice

dash of strawberry daiquiri mix (optional)

1½ ounce dark Caribbean Rum (or other dark rum)

crème de banana liqueur

fresh fruit for garnish

Blend fruit in blender. Add cherry juice and strawberry daiquiri mix, to taste. Prepare a cocktail shocker with ice cubes. Pour fruit mixture over ice and add rum. Shake well. Pour into a tall hurricane glass and top with crème de banana liqueur. Garnish with wedges of fresh fruit, such as pineapple and orange.

Makes 1 tall rum punch.

RESTAURANTS

Belize is not known for its culinary achievements. In fact, its restaurants suffer a dismal reputation among travelers, a reputation that's not deserved. No matter where you travel in the country, you will have access to tasty, well-prepared food. The problem is, many eateries are inconsistent. The place that served a memorable meal one night may serve a forgettable one the next. Cooks hopscotch between restaurants, and high-quality ingredients are not always available. But if you ask around town, locals will point you to the best spot.

In populated areas, such as Belize City and Ambergris Caye, you can choose from fresh seafood, Italian, Chinese and the ubiquitous Belizean soul food. In remote areas, you will rely on your lodge for meals—not a bad option, considering Belize lodges offer some of the country's best fare. Jungle lodges often grow their food organically and employ Maya or Creole cooks who know their way around a kitchen. And don't be surprised to learn that your delicious, filling entrée was prepared with low salt and low fat and without meat. Many innkeepers believe healthy, no-meat diets are in keeping with the principles of ecotourism.

In this book, restaurants are separated into the following price categories: *budget* restaurants cost $5 or less for dinner entrées; *moderate*-priced restaurants range between $5 and $12 at dinner and offer pleasant surroundings and a more varied menu; and *expensive* establishments tab their entrées at $12 and over, featuring cuisine that's more sophisticated, plus decor and more personalized service. A few hotel restaurants add a 15 percent service charge, and all restaurants add the 15 percent government VAT.

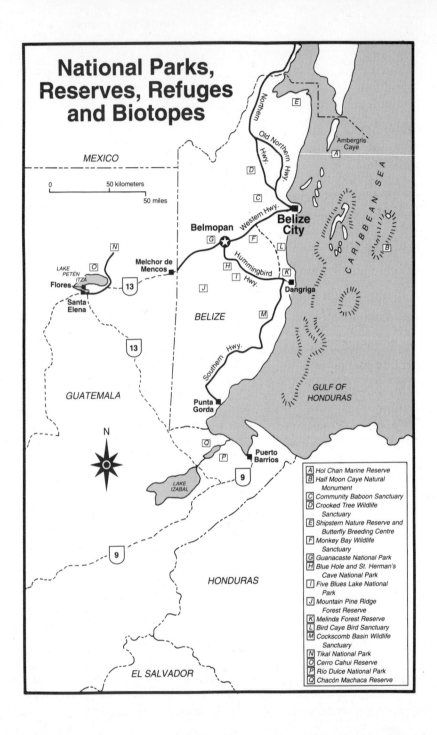

National Parks, Reserves, Refuges and Biotopes

MEXICO

0   50 kilometers
              50 miles

MEXICO

Northern Hwy.

Old Northern Hwy.

Ambergris
Caye

E

A

D

C

Western Hwy.

Belmopan

Belize
City

G

F

L

CARIBBEAN SEA

B

Hummingbird Hwy.

Melchor de
Mencos

N

O

LAKE
PETÉN
ITZÁ

Flores

13

H

I

K

Dangriga

Santa
Elena

13

J

BELIZE

M

Southern Hwy.

GUATEMALA

Punta
Gorda

GULF OF
HONDURAS

N

Q

P

Puerto
Barrios

9

LAKE
IZABAL

9

HONDURAS

EL SALVADOR

A Hol Chan Marine Reserve
B Half Moon Caye Natural
   Monument
C Community Baboon Sanctuary
D Crooked Tree Wildlife
   Sanctuary
E Shipstern Nature Reserve and
   Butterfly Breeding Centre
F Monkey Bay Wildlife
   Sanctuary
G Guanacaste National Park
H Blue Hole and St. Herman's
   Cave National Park
I Five Blues Lake National
   Park
J Mountain Pine Ridge
   Forest Reserve
K Melinda Forest Reserve
L Bird Caye Bird Sanctuary
M Cockscomb Basin Wildlife
   Sanctuary
N Tikal National Park
O Cerro Cahui Reserve
P Río Dulce National Park
Q Chacón Machaca Reserve

FIVE

The Outdoors

Belize *is* the outdoors. Here life revolves around the endless cycles of the rain-forest and the sea. The complexities of the outdoors, the mysterious web of birth, death and dependency, overshadow everything else. Those who seek out-door experiences and true adventures will find them everywhere—in the man-grove flats churning with fishing possibilities, in the primal forests riddled with hiking passages, and in the deliriously beautiful reefs offering incomparable scuba diving. You can explore 3000-year-old cities on horseback, canoe down rivers edged in jungle, bicycle to secret coves on hidden islands. You can even join a week-long climb up the treacherous, stony face of 3675-foot Victoria Peak—the ultimate Belize outdoor high.

NATIONAL PARKS AND RESERVES, WILDLIFE REFUGES AND ARCHAEOLOGICAL PRESERVES

More of Belize lies inside the boundaries of a reserve than outside of one. Some 80 percent of the country's original rainforests have been preserved (a sharp contrast to neighboring El Salvador, which has saved only 2 percent), and most are protected by the government. More than 25 parks, refuges and archaeologi-cal preserves exist today. Some are so wild and impenetrable, they are impos-sible to visit. But most can been seen, indeed extensively explored, by outsiders.

Access to reserves varies widely. By far the easiest to reach are Guanacaste National Park and Blue Hole and St. Herman's Cave National Park (not to be confused with the Blue Hole in the sea), located a short stroll off main roads. At the other extreme is the lost Maya city of Caracol, which requires an arduous, hours-long journey on rocky, oft-flooded jungle roads. Trips to Caracol require not only a special guide but a permit from the Belize Department of Archaeology.

The majority of reserves, however, fall somewhere in between. Prepare to spend at least an hour or two on rough roads (and don't lose your cool if the truck breaks down; Belize has a way of murdering vehicles!). And plan to do some serious walking and/or hiking—five miles in one reserve is not uncommon. Neither are 12-hour days.

No matter where you visit, go with a guide. Unless you've had guerrilla training, you won't know your way around the jungle. There is no substitute for having someone along who knows the land, and who can point out all the life hiding in the forest. Many Belize guides are Maya bushmen, earnest pioneers whose expertise range from baboon and jaguar calls to wild fern species and bizarre rituals performed by their ancient Maya ancestors. Some do not wear shoes, preferring to feel the jungle while they see and smell it. Their everyday conversations take on mystical proportions, with talk of Maya planet worship, universal energy and the healing secrets contained within the plants. When the day is done, they often retreat to the most comfortable home they know—the jungle.

For recommendations on bush guides, check with your lodge. For general information on reserves and wildlife refuges, contact the **Belize Audubon Society** (12 Fort Street, Belize City; 2-34985) or the **Programme for Belize** (2 South Park Street, Belize City; 2-75616). For information on archaeological preserves, call the **Department of Archaeology** (Belmopan; 8-22106).

CAMPING

There is little organized camping in Belize. You will find makeshift shelters scattered throughout the reserves, but you have to bring your own equipment, food and water. Sometimes that means toting it through the jungle, *after* driving down a long bumpy dirt road. If you do camp in the forest, make sure it's the dry season. Summer rains can not only wash away your camp (and hatch zillions of mosquitoes), they can flood surrounding roads and strand you for days. The best bet for camping is on the cayes, where palmy, open seashores make way for tents, and trade winds cool you down at night. Cayes camping, along with other places and ways to pitch your tent, are mentioned throughout this book.

FISHING

Belize has many secrets, not the least of which is this: There are fish in Belize. Fish so big and so plentiful that even the most amateur angler can catch his limit in a few hours. Fish so anxious to impale themselves on a hook that they will rush toward a skiff, or toward a pair of human legs wading in the flats.

Belize owes its fishing phenomenon to a remarkably diverse underwater world—it boasts one of the hemisphere's most healthy reef systems—and a lack of people. Whether you fish in one of the many inland rivers or on the mangrove flats, along the barrier reef or out in deep blue water, it is likely you will not see another angler *all day*. Of course, as more people "discover" these wonders, the solitude and diversity will diminish. In the meantime, if you love to fish, don't miss the chance to cast your line in Belize.

FLY-FISHING   If you're into angling's hottest trend, saltwater fly-fishing, you'll find it in Belize, where bonefish, tarpon and permit churn up the flats everywhere. Belize's most renowned flats are those around the Turneffe Islands, where the bottom is a mix of hard-packed sand and sea grass, and the water is virtually always wadeable. Turneffe's popularity means it is more crowded than other spots around Belize, though for those used to fishing in Florida or other "discovered" areas, it will no doubt seem secluded.

Also popular are the flats off Ambergris Caye, famed as one of the world's most lucrative tarpon spots. Year-round, you can count on at least a small tarpon (20 to 50 pounds), though 100-pounders also abound in these waters. Schools of scrappy ladyfish, jack crevalle, permit, bonefish and barracuda are plentiful here. The waters off Placencia are famous for permit, who thrive on the crystalline coral and mangrove "ocean flats" that emerge from deep water. The best time to try for them is at the end of an incoming tide, when tailing permit swarm the flats looking for food. Then even this most elusive of fish is inclined to strike your fly. Other superb places to cast your fly: the flats at St. George's Caye, Hickes Caye, Tobacco Reef, South Water Caye and Glover's Reef. If you're just learning to fly fish, most lodges offer instruction.

Peak fly-fishing seasons vary from place to place, but generally you'll find that tarpon are most plentiful from October through mid-December and in June and July; bonefishing is best from September through January; and permit fishing peaks from August through October and March through June. Be aware that March can be windy with scattered storm bursts, and July and August are usually rainy and buggy.

RIVER FISHING   If it's too windy to fly fish, or if you feel more comfortable with a spinning rod, Belize's rivers offer snook, snapper, jack and tarpon fishing in an incomparable jungle setting. One of the most scenic and prolific inland waterways is the Belize River, which climbs in an easterly direction across western Belize to empty into the Caribbean near Ladyville. Here along placid waters, walls of bamboo and troops of monkeys decorate the shore, and tarpon roll across the surface like a pack of piranhas thrashing at a hapless victim. Cast your lure into a pack of these tarpon, and you can't help but catch one, though don't be surprised when he rears up out of the water—several times.

South of Placencia, the deep Monkey River is similarly striking, framed with massive vines and sugar cane and teeming with tarpon and snook. Southern Belize's inland backwater lagoons, pockets of shallow, muddy water between the Caribbean Sea and the Maya Mountains, are ideal for permit fishing since they are sheltered from wind.

Remember that during the rainy season, from June through October, rivers often flood and drive the fish (and fishermen) out to sea. The best time to river fish is from February through May, when the water is low and clear and the fish most plentiful.

REEF FISHING   The ribbon of coral reef paralleling the Belize coast glints with healthy schools of big fish. Whether you're trolling or fishing the bottom, you're apt to catch big grouper, cobia, kingfish, wahoo, king mackerel, jack crevalles and prize snapper, including the ubiquitous yellowtail and the brawling cubera.

The barrier reef is so warm year-round, and the food so abundant, that reef fish do not migrate. Hence, expect good fishing here at any time.

Belize is not known for its blue water fishing. In fact, few charter boats are available for deeper waters. However, during the spring and fall, sailfish and marlin are occasionally caught along the seaward side of the reef.

FISHING LODGES   Belize has many first-rate fishing lodges offering week-long packages that include daily outings (usually ten-hour days) with an accomplished guide. Accommodations are usually rustic, but you can fish to your heart's content, assured that if you *don't* catch something, you are in the minute minority. Most locations feature every kind of fishing and include all meals. Tackle is not included, so bring your own. Fishing permits are not required in Belize. Details of the best fishing lodges are found throughout this book.

In the United States, **Angler Adventures** (P.O. Box 872, Old Lyme, CT 06371; 860-434-9624, 800-628-1447, fax 860-434-8605) arranges stays at Belize fishing lodges. The company offers a wealth of Belize fishing programs, and has a fine reputation in angling circles. With your reservation, you'll be informed about everything from weather conditions and the best tackle to what fish are running where.

If you'd rather schedule a day of fishing after you're in Belize, check with one of these Belize City companies: **Native Guide Systems** (P.O. Box 1045, Belize City; 2-75819); **Belize Land and Sea Tours** (58 King Street; 2-73897); **Mayan Land Tours Travel & Rental** (4 Cleghorn Street; 2-30515); **Zippy Zappy Boating Services** (36 St. Thomas Street; 2-32844); or **Blackline Marine Service and Dive Shop** (Northern Highway, two-and-a-half miles north of Belize City; 2-44155).

Fishing guides are abundant in Belize. In fact, some are former poachers who are now strict proponents of catch and release. On Ambergris Caye, check for a guide along the waterfront in San Pedro. On Caye Caulker, **Chocolate** (Belize City; 22-2151) and **Porfilio Guzman** (22-2152) offer customized fishing trips around the cayes. In Placencia, check with **Westby Guiding Service** (6-23138), **Whiprey Caye Guiding** (6-23130), **Blue Runner Guiding** (6-23153), **Kingfisher Sports** (6-23104), **Placencia Sportfishing** (6-22046) or **Ocean Motion Guide Service** (6-23162).

DIVING

Ancient Maya treasures may lie deep in the Belize jungle, but offshore, glorious treasures await in the mysterious underwater world of the sea. Here, on the world's second-longest barrier reef, dive spots come in endless varieties, from bright shallow waters marbled with dazzling reefs to deep, dark holes dripping with underwater stalactites. In most places, visibility averages 100 feet, though on a clear spring day 150 feet is not uncommon. The scenery often resembles a silent, blossoming dream or dazzling hallucination. To dive here is to enter another planet.

The coral reefs, though they look like inanimate rock, are actually living colonies of polyps that absorb food from the nutrient-rich Gulf Stream and have slowly grown into a coral jungle as complex as the Amazon. Finger coral, elkhorn, mountainous star, brain coral, purple leaf and orange tube, precious black coral with sepia age rings, plus green stinging coral and red fire sponges, which burn when touched, are a few of the species that bloom to towering heights on the sea floor. Hewn into breathtaking landscapes, this coral world is dappled with vivid sea fans, treelike gorgonia, prickly sea urchins, sea whips and lush anemones.

Throughout this subterranean garden are brilliant schools of fish and myriad other sea creatures: candy bass, shortnose batfish, spiny puffers all bloated and prickly, polka-dotted rays, stoplight parrotfish whose scales look tie-dyed, tiny blond razorfish diving into the mottled sand, coral crabs skittering sideways like moving shards of reef, turquoise angelfish, flamefish and sea cucumbers, colossal sea turtles and guitar-shaped guitarfish—an astonishing visual symphony rippling by, beautiful beyond belief.

But Belize's most famous place to dive is not on the barrier reef. The Blue Hole, a monstrous sinkhole in the sea, lies within an atoll—a ring of coral isles surrounding a lagoon. The hole does not glint with blinding color or fantastic fish. It is dim and eerie, a pit of inky water streaked with tiny tremors of light and looking like a scene from the Ice Age. Deep in its jowls, great shafts of rock imitate giant icicles and shelves of deep sand resemble snow banks. Prehistoric-looking sharks peer out from narrow ledges, and caves tunnel back into the walls. Caverns drip with stalactites formed by eons of percolating rain.

Back near the surface, the mouth of the hole is encased in exquisite coral, and the water is ten feet deep, swimming-pool-clear and wriggling with fish, sponges and sea fans.

Despite its fame, the Blue Hole doesn't attract crowds of divers, primarily because it is three hours by boat from the mainland. There is one nearby resort, **Lighthouse Reef Resort** (on Northern Caye; 800-423-3114 in the United States), accessible by plane from Belize City, which includes a trip to the hole in its extensive daily dive program. My favorite dive lodge in Belize, it offers a variety of dives around the gorgeous Lighthouse Reef atoll with views of walls and wrecks and basket sponges blossoming over a 15-foot span.

Several dive outfits offer excursions to the Blue Hole. From Ambergris Caye, **Fantasea Watersports** (at the Victoria House, San Pedro; phone/fax: 26-2576) offers day trips to the Blue Hole.

Like the Lighthouse Reef atoll, Belize's other two atolls—Glover's Reef and Turneffe Islands—are actually coral rock top hats of the Maya Mountains. The underwater ridges, valleys and ravines around the atolls make for sensational diving, and the varying terrain will please all levels of divers. And, because the atolls are circular in design, they always offer a leeward side where you can escape the wind and seas. Anyone who has dived in four- to six-foot swells—quite common on the barrier reef—knows the advantages of a leeward dive spot.

One of the most popular and challenging atoll dives is The Elbow, located in the Turneffe Islands, where the fish are big and the currents erratic. Turneffe is also famous for its miles of mangrove forests teeming with fish seeking shelter in the underwater roots. Manatees love the warm waters created by mangroves, and can sometimes be seen lumbering through the water.

Glover's Reef boasts different forests—ones comprised of luscious elkhorn coral that stretch up from depths of 100 feet. Dolphin, turtles and mantas are abundant in this remote southernmost atoll, and the waters are gin-clear and warm year-round. It's no surprise, then, that Glover's Reef is reputed to have some of the most extravagant underwater scenery in the Caribbean. Best of all, much of it lies inside the reef, where calm waters make for unparalleled diving.

Note: The fate of this resplendent scenery, and the rest of the Belize reef, lies with divers and others who visit it. Protecting the reef is as easy as not touching it. Even a slight brush from a fin is enough to damage a coral forever. No matter how tempted you may be, never take a piece of coral. That small souvenir will destroy in one second what it took nature thousands of years to build.

Always anchor your craft in the sand or grass flats, away from the reef. If you can't see where you're anchoring, send a diver down to check the sea bottom. Unfortunately, some Belize dive boats still anchor on the reef, lopping off huge pieces of coral and spreading disease. Perhaps if enough divers frown on the practice, dive operators will be more careful to preserve the future of their livelihood.

For your protection, avoid touching sea creatures. Inside crevices, where you should never poke a prying hand, live moray eels, whose saw-toothed fangs hold decayed food particles that can fatally poison an unsuspecting victim. Some anemones and sea urchins are poisonous, and their spines inflict painful, lasting wounds. An encounter with fire coral, a brownish, innocent-looking coral found everywhere, can leave you peppered with flaming welts that outlast your vacation.

Be a safe diver. Always dive with a buddy, preferably a Belizean buddy familiar with local waters and conditions. Stay well within the boundaries of the dive tables, and limit your dives at the beginning and end of your vacation. If you overdid the rum punches the night before, take the day off. A hangover can affect your judgment and even contribute to decompression sickness.

In case of decompression sickness, there is a recompression chamber (26-2851 or 26-2073) next to the airstrip in San Pedro, Ambergris Caye. However, some Belize dive operators prefer to send their guests to U.S. medical facilities. For a $25 annual fee, **Divers Alert Network** (Duke University Medical Center, Peter B. Bennett Center, #6 West Colony Place, Durham, NC 27705; emergencies: 919-684-8111, non-emergencies: 919-684-2948 or 800-446-2671) will provide air rescue from anywhere in the Americas, for dive accidents or other medical emergencies. The international, nonprofit organization also offers dive accident insurance.

DIVE LODGES   Whether you're a four-tank-a-day diver or one who enjoys the feel of a hammock as much as a BC, you will find your place in Belize. Half a dozen lodges specialize in diving, and another dozen offer some type of dive program. Most specialty lodges are located on secluded out islands and require minimum stays of four to seven nights. But they vary considerably when it comes to amenities (or lack of) and approach to diving. Some stress rigorous diving with little time for relaxation, while others strike a balance between diving and doing nothing. I stayed at one lodge that was so regimented, guests were either diving, eating or attending meetings about diving. This is dive dreamland for some people, but not for others. When making reservations at a lodge, ask about the facility's dive philosophy, the number of dives offered each day, and the experience of the divemasters. For critiques of individual dive lodges, see Chapter Six.

DIVE INSTRUCTION   If you've been thinking about getting certified to dive, why not do it in Belize? The pace is slow and the weather dependably warm, and there's not much to distract you from studying! More importantly, there are many experienced, first-rate dive instructors in Belize. Most dive lodges offer PADI or NAUI instruction, and most classes are so small (usually one to four people) you'll get special treatment. Allow at least four days for the course, which includes four open water dives divided between two days. Prices range from US$250 to US$400 a person, depending on the lodge and class size.

Many dive lodges also offer one-day resort courses for those who'd like a taste of diving, as well as advanced certification, refresher courses and specialty diving, such as rescue diving or night diving.

DIVE SHOPS   On Ambergris Caye, **Tortuga Dive Center** (Belize Yacht Club Marina, San Pedro; 26-2804) will take you to nearby reefs or farther out to the atolls. Also on Ambergris Caye is **Bottom Time Dive Shop** (at the San Pedro Holiday Hotel pier; 26-2348) and **Amigos del Mar** (seafront at Lily's hotel, San Pedro; 26-2706). On Caye Caulker, **Belize Diving Services** (22-2143) has scuba excursions. To rent snorkeling equipment on Caye Caulker, check toward the middle of town, across from the park, in a little building that says "Snorkel Rental-Pastries."

In Belize City, **Airs Dive Shop** (Mile Post 2, Northern Highway; 2-33187) offers many dive packages to the cayes. In Placencia, stop by **Rum Point Divers** (Rum Point Inn, two miles north of Placencia Village; 6-23239). The Belizean guides here specialize in scuba and snorkeling tours to remote areas such as Laughing Bird National Park. **Placencia Dive Shop** (Placencia Village; 6-23313) provides a variety of dive services, including certification courses.

If you'd like to record your dive for posterity, consider renting a camera. Underwater cameras, including video cameras, are available on Ambergris Caye from **Joe Miller Photography** (Seafront at Ramon's Village, San Pedro; 26-2577).

LIVE-ABOARD DIVE BOATS   The way to get in the most diving around Belize's fantastic reefs is to stay on a boat. Several live-aboard dive boats ply the waters around the cayes, dropping anchor at the Blue Hole, Half Moon Caye, the walls of Turneffe and other famous dive spots. Boats range from 16-passenger skiffs with dorm-style camping to 40-passenger yachts with staterooms. Trips typically last from one to seven nights.

The 50-foot **Offshore Express** (26-2013) takes you on two- and three-day trips to Half Moon Caye Natural Monument, where you can see red-footed booby birds, frigates and ospreys, and dive the Blue Hole. The fancier, 110-foot **Aggressor** (800-348-2628) has air-conditioned cabins that accommodate up to 18 people. By far the most luxurious is the 120-foot **Wave Dancer** (800-932-6237 or 305-669-9391 in Florida), whose air-conditioned staterooms are more than 90 square feet, twice the size of most live-aboard cabins. *Wave Dancer* offers a seven-night itinerary from Belize City, with a visit to the Turneffe Islands and Lighthouse Reef. The final night, guests stay at the plush Ramada Royal Reef in Belize City.

SWIMMING AND SNORKELING

Washed by stunning seas and crisscrossed with smooth-flowing rivers and jungle waterfalls, Belize offers many ways to get your body wet. Virtually anywhere inside the barrier reef, you'll find calm, shallow waters as clear as air, perfect for swimming and snorkeling. Unlike the Caribbean waters off the neighboring Yucatán, which are plagued by strong currents, the seas in Belize are sheltered by the barrier reef. Rip currents are rare, and the water is warm year-round—75 to 80 degrees in winter, and up to 85 degrees in summer.

But while the barrier reef provides protection, it prevents the formation of beaches. Like the Florida Keys, which have their own barrier reef, Belize's cayes are ringed with mangroves and pebbly dirt, not sugar-white sand. Except at the atolls and a few resorts with imported sand, swimming beaches are scarce. Better to swim and snorkel from a boat.

Take your mask, snorkel and fins to Belize. Rentals are expensive, and sometimes unavailable on remote islands.

Inland, freshwater rivers are framed in lush jungle, where you can watch monkeys play while you swim. Incidentally, when monkeys swim across a river, they thrash about like they're drowning. If you see one, don't offer your assistance or you will have one angry monkey on your hands!

Here are some of the top swimming spots in Belize:

❖ Hol Chan Marine Reserve, off Ambergris Caye, is the place to snorkel
❖ Valley of the Rays, a sandbar off Ambergris Caye, where you can swim among gentle sting rays and nurse sharks
❖ The shallow, protected lagoons within the Turneffe, Lighthouse Reef and Glover's Reef atolls

❖ The Sibun River beaches within Monkey Bay Wildlife Sanctuary
❖ The Belize River, especially at Guanacaste National Park
❖ Río On Pools in western Belize, where clear water tumbles down rock terraces
❖ Along the Curassow Trail at Cockscomb Basin Wildlife Sanctuary
❖ Blue Creek, outside Punta Gorda

BIRDWATCHING

Birders love Belize. They love rising at 5 a.m., sneaking into the darkened web of jungle, and listening for the *hoot-hoot* call of a blue-crowned motmot. To see one of these exquisite birds in the sun-dappled dawn is a great event, especially since they are somewhat rare. Daybreak brings out other species of extraordinary beauty, including oropendolas, red-legged honeycreepers, white hawks, great curassows and slaty-tailed trogons. Toucans and macaws are fairly common here, and so are unexciting to birders, although the layperson rarely seems to grow accustomed to seeing these ravishing creatures color the sky.

Birdwatching in Belize has only come into vogue in the past few years. As new trails are carved through dense jungle and bird sanctuaries made more accessible, birders are discovering the thrills of this little country. Several areas offer wonderful birding. At Chan Chich Lodge in northwestern Belize, exotic birds actually nest near your jungle hut. When was the last time you walked out your front door to see a toucan feeding her young? Or an ocellated turkey preening for a mate?

Other prime birdwatching spots are Half Moon Caye Natural Monument, Crooked Tree Wildlife Sanctuary, the jungles around Caracol and Cockscomb Basin Wildlife Sanctuary.

In the U.S., top organizers of birdwatching tours are scheduling more treks to view the beautiful birds of Belize. For dates and details of birding tours, contact the **Field Guides** (P.O. Box 160723, Austin, TX 78716; 512-327-4953, 800-728-4953), The **Massachusetts Audubon Society** (208 South Great Road, Lincoln, MA 01773; 800-289-9504) or **Victor Emanuel Nature Tours** (P.O. Box 33008, Austin, TX 78764; 512-328-5221, 800-328-8368).

Lineated woodpecker

Within Belize itself, the **Belize Audubon Society** (12 Fort Street, P.O. Box 1001, Belize City; 2-34988) is an excellent source of information and tips on birdwatching.

OTHER OUTDOOR SPORTS AND ACTIVITIES

KAYAKING

If you like the idea of navigating your own vessel, fishing for your own dinner, and sleeping under the stars on faraway islands, consider sea kayaking. Both **Island Expeditions Co.** (368–916 West Broadway, Vancouver, British Columbia, Canada V5Z 1K7; 604-452-3212, 800-667-1630, fax: 604-452-3433) and **Slickrock Adventures** (P.O. Box 1400, Moab, UT 84532; phone/fax: 801-259-6996, 800-390-5715) offer week-long trips to private islands within Glover's Reef atoll. Most of the cayes are uninhabited poster islands ringed with palms and sugar-fine sand, and the waters are brilliantly clear and filled with sea life.

Elsewhere around the cayes, you can rent kayaks by the hour or day. Check with your lodge. On Ambergris Caye, contact **Travel & Tour Belize** (Barrier Reef Drive, San Pedro; 26-2031).

CANOEING

Few experiences are so truly Belizean as canoeing down a silent, shimmering river draped in lavish jungle, fat iguanas sunning on tree limbs, monkeys skittering along the shore, parrots squawking in the air. Just 50 years ago, the rivers were the highways of Belize. Now that there are roads, the rivers are used by tourists as much as villagers, though they are hardly crowded.

The best place for canoeing is in the Cayo District, where the Macal and Mopan rivers offer splendorous scenery and splendid sightseeing stops. Several outfits offer canoe rentals or tours, including **Float Belize** (corner of Savannah, Wyatt and Riverside streets, San Ignacio; 92-3213), **Toni Canoes** (22 Burns Avenue, San Ignacio; 92-2267), **Windy Hill Cottage Tours** (Western Highway, just west of San Ignacio; 92-2017), **Chaa Creek Inland and Jungle Expeditions** (on the Macal River, about eight miles outside San Ignacio; 92-2037) and **duPlooy's** (nine miles outside San Ignacio; 92-3101).

Just east of San Ignacio, **Caesar's Place** (Mile Post 60, Western Highway; 92-2341) will also arrange various canoe outings. Near Belmopan, you can canoe along the scenic Belize River from **Warrie Head Ranch** (Western Highway, six miles west of Belmopan; 2-77185).

Birdwatchers will find the ultimate canoe trip at Crooked Tree Wildlife Sanctuary in northern Belize. Rentals are available at the visitors center or at nearby **Bird's Eye View Lodge** (2-32040) or **Paradise Inn** (2-12084).

BICYCLING

The most relaxing bicycling is on the hard-packed sand streets of Ambergris Caye and Caye Caulker. On Ambergris Caye, you can rent bikes at **Travel**

& Tour Belize (Barrier Reef Drive, San Pedro; 26-2031). On Caye Caulker, bike rentals are available at **Sea Horse Gift Shop** (in front of the police station; 22-2270). The ride from Corozal north to the Mexico border is nearly flat and quite scenic. Pick up a bike in Corozal from **Stephan Moerman** (37 1st Avenue, on the seafront; 4-22833).

HORSEBACK RIDING

What could be more enjoyable that a scenic ride through the countryside? Out in western Belize, **Mountain Equestrian Trails** (Mile Post 8, Mountain Pine Ridge Road; 92-3310, fax: 92-3361) is a popular, well-run facility offering rides across 60 miles of trails, including former logging trails. The ranch also features river cave float trips. In San Ignacio, **Easy Rider** (92-2253) offers half- and full-day rides through the Mountain Pine Ridge. The latter includes lunch along the Macal River.

HIKING

You could hike forever in the Belize jungles. Some of the best trails are in the archaeological zones, where ancient Maya cities harbor a labyrinth of trails through cool, exhilarating forest with views of temples, pyramids and the green countryside. My favorite place to hike is at Chan Chich, a lodge built on a Maya plaza and enveloped by 275,000 acres of interminable jungle. Nine trails, offering a variety of lengths, difficulty and scenery, cover eight miles in the forest. The lodge publishes an excellent book, *Exploring the Rainforest*, that details 130 marked sites along the trails, including tombs, creeks and "nest condominiums" often inhabited by toucans, woodpeckers and red-lored Amazon parrots. If you're feeling unusually adventurous, take one of the lodge's night jungle hikes. There's nothing like shining a flashlight into a pitch-black thicket, only to discover a pair of jaguar eyes glowering back.

Elsewhere, the Community Baboon Sanctuary and Cockscomb Basin Wildlife Sanctuary offer splendid hiking through dense broadleaf rainforest. Both facilities sell inexpensive trail maps (about US$1), and the wardens can point you to the best spots. For hiking through cool, mountainous slash pine forest, head for the Mountain Pine Ridge. The terrain harbors vast caves, thundering waterfalls, scenic lookouts, racing rivers studded with black boulders, and marvelous views of wild animals. Maps of various trails are available from most lodges in the pine ridge. One resort, the 18,000-acre Hidden Valley Inn, offers a trail system so vast it takes days to hike.

Around Belize, numerous companies offer hiking guides and/or excursions. They include: **Native Guide Systems** (P.O. Box 1045, Belize City; 2-75819); **Melmish Mayan Ecotours** (44 Barracks Road, Belize City; 2-45221); **Chaa Creek Inland Expeditions** (near San Ignacio; 92-2037); **Maruba Resort** (Old Northern Highway, about 40 miles north of Belize City; 3-22199); **Jungle River Tours** (20 Lovers Lane, Orange Walk Town; 3-22293); **Pelican Beach Resort** (north end of Dangriga; 5-22044); and **Placencia Tours** (Placencia Village; 6-23186).

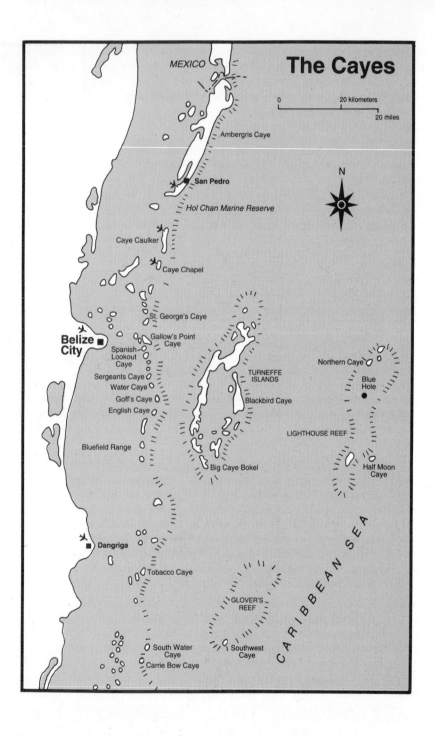

The Cayes

MEXICO

0 ___ 20 kilometers
___ 20 miles

N

Ambergris Caye

✈ ■ San Pedro

Hol Chan Marine Reserve

Caye Caulker

✈ Caye Chapel

St. George's Caye

Gallow's Point
Caye

Belize
City ✈

Spanish
Lookout
Caye

Sergeants Caye

Water Caye

Goff's Caye

English Caye

Bluefield Range

TURNEFFE
ISLANDS

Blackbird Caye

Big Caye Bokel

Northern Caye

Blue
Hole

LIGHTHOUSE REEF

Half Moon
Caye

✈ ■ Dangriga

Tobacco Caye

GLOVER'S
REEF

South Water
Caye

Carrie Bow Caye

Southwest
Caye

CARIBBEAN SEA

SIX

The Cayes

The Belize Cayes stretch eastward from the mainland, a sprinkling of coral rock and mangrove isles basking in the fabulous blues and greens of the Caribbean Sea. They range in size from tiny mangrove specks inhabited only by sea birds to substantial islands with thriving fishing villages. Their first inhabitants were the Maya, who established intricate island trading routes during the Classic Period, from 250 to 900 A.D. Seven hundred years later, British pirates used the isolated, scrubby isles to stash the treasure they had plundered from Spanish galleons. Today, little evidence exists of either the Spanish or the Maya, but the islands remain pristine and isolated.

The cayes (pronounced "keys") are why most visitors come to Belize, for here can be found some of the best diving and fishing in the world. Along this 200-mile-long barrier reef—the longest in the Western Hemisphere—is an underwater Eden of dazzling sea creatures, wildly colorful coral and see-through waters ribboned with sunlight. The marine life here, biologists say, is perhaps the most complex and diverse in all the Caribbean. Indeed, some claim Belize's reef sustains a greater variety of sea creatures per square foot than any other barrier reef in the world.

Beyond the barrier reef are secluded patch reefs with travel-poster islands, sandy flats superb for fly-fishing, and warm slurpy waters that beckon swimmers year-round. Then there are the atolls, pronounced a-TOLS, ringlike bands of coral isles surrounding lagoons. Belize's three atolls offer the ultimate in fishing and diving, for their circular shape ensures there is always a leeward side where you can escape wind and waves.

The pace of life is slow in the Cayes. There are no paved roads—only sand streets—and electricity is often provided by a generator, solar panels or even windmills. Getting to a caye usually means taking a small plane or boat, though hopefully the boat is not too small, as most voyages are from two to four hours. In fact, travel around the Cayes holds promise of adventure, considering the shaky dependability of boat motors and captains, the even less predictable weather, and the fact that Cayes' time is even slower than regular Belize time!

Though Belizeans don't particularly frown on nudity, there are no official nude beaches in Belize. However, there are dozens of deserted out islands with beaches perfect for sunbathing in the buff.

Surprisingly, beaches are scarce in the Belize Cayes, because, like the Florida Keys, they are formed of mangroves and coral rock. The choicest beaches are on the out islands, and so not within easy reach of the average visitor. On Ambergris Caye, the largest island, there is no official public beach, but good beaches can be found behind hotels on the north and south end of the island.

Lodging on the Cayes ranges from charming seaside motels and thatched bungalows on the beach to fishing cabins on a secluded island. Most of the upscale accommodations are on Ambergris Caye, Belize's largest caye, and those are not ultra-luxurious. In fact, most cayes' hostelries are what you'll soon come to know as funky-Belizean: full of charm and personality, but lacking in creature comforts. Only the expensive and very expensive few lodges offer air-conditioning, but sea breezes are adequate on all but the muggiest of summer days. To make sure you catch the breezes, ask for a room (preferably with lots of windows) on the windward side of the island. You'd be surprised what a difference a breeze will make—usually between a restful or a restless night.

Many cayes have only one or two lodges, offering that rare opportunity to stay at a castaway island. These out-island lodges are most popular with anglers and scuba divers who prefer nature over civilization. Some lodge owners take ecotourism quite seriously, even limiting the number of anglers allowed per week.

Lodge owners themselves can determine whether or not you love a place. When you're staying on a near-deserted island out in the middle of nowhere, the personalities running the show become quite crucial. (You should know that most lodge owners, like the guests, are Americans.) I have had experiences where lodge owners were so intrusive, it was difficult for guests to relax and have a good time. Lodging reviews in this chapter reflect my impressions of each place. Before you book an out-island lodge, however, it's helpful to talk to someone who's stayed there recently.

Depending on how "out" the island is, you may be required to stay at least a week. Any less would be impractical, since getting there requires a lengthy boat trip (four hours, in some cases) or chartering a small plane. All lodges will arrange your transportation. Most people find the journey not only an adventure but a marvelous window to the unspoiled Caribbean of Belize.

Like the lodges, Cayes' eateries possess those typical Belizean elements: eclectic decor, sand floors and fascinating characters hailing from all corners of the earth. Few restaurants keep "official" hours, but you'll always find something open to suit your needs. Besides the Belizean staple of rice and beans (which can be quite tasty), expect plenty of fresh seafood when dining on the islands. Here is a good place to try your first Belikin beer, Belize's ubiquitous national brew, which, by the way, happens to be very good beer.

On the out islands, you'll be dining at the lodge restaurant—the only one on the island—but most times you'll find the food quite good. A few resorts take advantage of their captive audience and charge ridiculously high prices for food. To avoid price gauging, buy a lodging package that includes meals. Most out island bars are run on the honor system—no problem if there are only 20 people on the whole island.

AMBERGRIS CAYE

Twenty-eight miles long and the country's biggest island, Ambergris Caye boasts the most and best resorts and the finest array of restaurants, shops and bars in all of Belize. Yet Ambergris is where people still go to get away, whether it be hippies escaping to a secluded campground or the rich and famous retreating to Journey's End, a posh resort literally at land's end. Ambergris also is still home to much wildlife, including many shore birds, nesting sea turtles and even ocelots, who find refuge in the swamps and mangrove forests unspoiled yet by people.

Situated northeast of Belize City, about a one-hour boat ride away, Ambergris is actually closer to Mexico than Belize. Only the skinny Boca Bacalar Chico Channel, dug by the ancient Maya, separates the north tip of the island from the Yucatán Peninsula. The caye gets its name from "ambergrease," the waxy secretions of sperm whales that was found on the beaches by 18th-century British explorers. Once a pricey substance used in making perfume, ambergrease can sometimes be seen today clouding sea waters in the area.

Most of Ambergris' activity is concentrated near the island's south end, in the seaside village of **San Pedro**. Named for Saint Peter, patron saint of fishermen, the fishing village was founded in 1848 and was a refuge for *Mestizos* (persons of mixed Spanish and Indian blood) fleeing Yucatán's War of the Castes. Eleven years later, Englishman James Hume Blake bought San Pedro and the rest of Ambergris Caye for just $625 during a bankruptcy auction by the British government. Soon coconut plantations abounded on Blake's island, and San Pedro residents made their living husking and shredding the nuts. By the mid-1900s, the coconut business had gone bust and most plantations abandoned, and San Pedroans returned to fishing for a living.

Today, a boat is just as likely to be hauling tourists as fish. Tourism is the biggest business on Ambergris. During high season, visitors to San Pedro outnumber its 2000 residents. No matter when you visit, the village will seem a busy little place, with golf carts and bicycles buzzing up and down the sand streets and punta rock music drifting from outdoor bars. Wobbly docks loaded with boats are strung along the seafront, and old clapboard buildings huddle against new concrete condominiums.

Unlike anywhere else in Belize, San Pedro has a definite feel of American influence, from the stark new buildings financed by American companies to the American-owned hotels, restaurants and bars. Indeed, the biggest-ever American development in Belize is under way on northern Ambergris Caye, once an isolated land of palms and scrub palmettos and mangrove shore and now the site of the immense, impending Royal Belize Village. It's a $250 million village, scheduled for creation over the next decade, with a 150-room resort, 350 condos, villas and apartments, a golf putting green and equestrian center, an airstrip and a water desalination plant. But none of these seem so alarming as the planned "gaming center"—Belize's first casino.

Yet, for now at least, Ambergris Caye is still a place where visitors aren't subjected to the rigors of mass tourism. Locals frequent the same restaurants and shops as tourists, and everyone is treated with the usual brand of Belizean hospitality. And though most residents are of Mexican descent, they are bilingual, and are just as happy to converse with you in English as Spanish.

Only about seven blocks long and three blocks wide, San Pedro is easy to navigate. It will take you all of about one hour to stroll every sand street, not including tiki bar stops! You'll soon learn that most everything happens on Barrier Reef Drive, also called Front Street, San Pedro's main drag and the street closest to the sea. Hotels and businesses are here, and so is the **San Pedro Town Hall** (26-2189), a humble seaside building with peeling paint and a hand-painted sign imploring readers to protect the Belize reefs. There's also **Travel & Tour Belize** (Coconut Drive; 26-2031), an excellent source for island information and excursions. Next to Central Park, you'll find the **Police Station** (26-2926).

Walking west from Barrier Reef Drive, you'll find Middle Street and Back Street. North are various unmarked and unnamed streets, and a couple of lanes called different local names just to keep things interesting. South is Coconut Drive, a sandy lane that boasts the latest developments, with new hotels and lodges lining the seafront. The scene starts around the 3000-foot **San Pedro Airstrip**, where visitors fly in and out every 20 minutes or so.

If you're lucky enough to be in San Pedro on a Saturday night, you'll see local families gather in the town square for their weekly get-together. It's a festive occasion, with folks cooking dinner on makeshift grills and kids playing basketball. Small children come all dressed up, then promptly get dirty playing in the sand streets.

About four miles southeast of town, the **Hol Chan Marine Reserve** is a five-square-mile underwater park accessible only by boat. Hol Chan is Maya for "little channel," and it was the Maya who first discovered the plethora of sea life in the narrow passage through the barrier reef here. Overfishing in the early 1980s nearly destroyed the area's fragile reef system and drove most of the life away. In 1987, the Belizean government made it a national reserve, and installed buoys for boats to tie to, thereby avoiding anchoring on the reef. Today, the reef is thriving again, and snorkelers can admire its brilliant brain and star coral, ethereal sea fans and resplendent sponges, bright blue damselfish and vibrantly colored parrotfish.

Most fascinating, though, are the green moray eels that inhabit the walls of the reserve's channel, which is only 15 to 30 feet deep. You will likely see divemasters feeding the eels (which they shouldn't), but don't try it yourself. Morays become aggressive when fed, and can nip off a finger in an instant. At a minimum, they can inflict a nasty poisonous sting.

Many dive boats also stop at **Mexico Rocks,** just outside the barrier reef and the reserve. Slightly shallower, with depths of 8 to 15 feet, the water is clear and etched with constellations of elkhorn and staghorn coral, and churning with exotic fish.

Coral Gardens, south of Hol Chan, is an incredibly healthy reef (for now, at least) with an average depth of 12 feet. Snapper and barracuda prowl the finger and brain coral and sea fans here. Nearby is **Valley of the Rays** (sometimes called Shark-Ray Alley or Sting Ray Alley), a sandbar where docile sting rays and nurse sharks gather.

The island's newest marine reserve, established in 1996, is **Bacalar Chico National Park**. Covering about fifteen square miles across northern Ambergris, it takes in sandy sea floors and canyons of coral; rock ledges and caves prowled by enormous grouper; lagoons and mudflats; and chunks of island where the scenery might be lush ridge forest or exposed limestone boulders, deep sinkholes or dry savanna. Bacalar Chico, however, is technically not a reserve, at least not yet, as no restrictions on fishing or diving had been set as of late 1997. Park officials hope to have regulations in place by 1999 and also have a visitors' center. In the meantime, travelers can charter fishing, snorkeling and diving trips to the park from San Pedro. For information, call 14-7308 on Ambergris Caye.

Snorkeling excursions to Mexico Rocks or Hol Chan can be arranged with one of the many boats at the San Pedro docks, or through most hotels.

LODGING   Budget and moderate accommodations can be found in the town of San Pedro, while expensive and very expensive resorts tend to be on the north and south ends of the island. Staying in town means you can walk to restaurants, stores and tiki bars, but town is also noisier, and there are no real beaches. Outside of town, you'll pay more for solitude and for having a generous beach out your back door. However, lodging on the north end is accessible only by boat or by a 4- to 5-mile, potentially mucky bike ride—something to consider if you plan to spend a lot of time in San Pedro. Hotels there do provide ferry service to and from town, though schedules are infrequent. Water taxis are another option, though remember that they operate on island time and can get quite expensive (about $US10 per person, roundtrip). If you stay on the south end of Ambergris, you'll need a bicycle or golf cart (available from most hotels) to get to town.

One of the southernmost hostelries is also one of the most engaging. Nestled on a sublime stretch of beach, the ✪ **Victoria House** (about two miles south of San Pedro; very expensive; 26-2067, or 800-247-5159 in the United States) boasts 29 rooms spread among a pretty Victorian plantation house, several row houses and Mexican-style *casitas*. Most desirable are the *casitas*, wrapped by spacious porches and warmly adorned with Mexican tile floors, hardwood furnishings, high-beamed ceilings and Belizean paintings. Rooms in the houses, though slightly smaller, are attractively appointed with white wicker. All rooms have small refrigerators. Complimentary bicycles, as well as van service to town throughout the day, are included in the rate.

Some of San Pedro's most comfortable and appealing accommodations are at ✪ **Caribbean Villas** (Coconut Drive, three-quarters mile south of San Pedro; ceiling fans; air-conditioning; expensive to very expensive; 26-2715, fax: 26-2885). The white-stucco buildings, resting right on the beach, offer standard rooms and spacious two-room suites with kitchens (including blenders, handy for frozen drinks). Hosts Will and Susan Lala have arranged the rooms with guests' comfort in mind—plenty of space and storage and constant views of the beach and sea. Two outdoor hot tubs are prime for stargazing. A 35-foot "People Perch" invites splendid opportunities for birding, and an artificial reef just off the dock has great snorkeling. The best part, though, is the golf cart tour of San Pedro by Wil Lala, who points out places to eat, drink, shop and just hang out.

Seafront **Coconuts Caribbean Hotel** (Coconut Drive, San Pedro; ceiling fans; air-conditioning; expensive; 26-3500, fax: 26-3501) is where you can unpack for a while. (One guest, in fact, booked a few days but stayed several weeks.) Owners Tim and Kathy Jeffers make guests feel right at home, offering breakfasts of fresh-baked breads, just-squeezed juice and hearty coffee. The 12 pleasant rooms have white tile floors and sleeper sofas piled with downy pillows. There is an extra charge if you use your air-conditioning.

If you enjoy cooking, consider **Corona del Mar** (Coconut Drive, San Pedro; ceiling fans; air-conditioning; very expensive; 26-2055, fax: 26-2461). The four suites have fully stocked kitchens and white wicker dining tables, as well as two double beds and a hide-a-bed. A few steps out the back door is a dock where boats will take you snorkeling, diving or fishing.

The stylish, spacious **Belizean Reef Suites** (Coconut Drive, San Pedro; ceiling fans; air-conditioning; expensive to very expensive; 26-2582) is great for families or anyone else who wants to spread out among one-, two- or three-bedroom digs. The three-story buildings of crisp white have arched porticoes and terraces and a white picket fence that wraps around the seafront grounds. Inside there's rattan and tropically patterned cushions, glass-topped tables and cool tile floors, and red ginger residing in vases. The beach out back is tiny, and perfect.

San Pedro's yuppie address is **Belize Yacht Club Hotel** (Coconut Drive, ceiling fans; air-conditioning; phone; TV; very expensive; 26-2777, fax: 26-2768), for where else can you sip espresso at the bar, pump iron in a weight room and then take a dip in a pool? Fashioned in Mediterranean style, this complex of white stucco and red Spanish tile harbors 44 suites with kitchenettes, Mexican tile floors and front porches—very nice, all in all. Most rooms have sea views.

Set just off the sea, the two-story A-frame **Changes in Latitudes** (Coconut Drive, San Pedro; ceiling fans; air-conditioning; moderate to expensive; 26-2986) has just six rooms, all small but quite stylish, and each with a private bath. Over breakfast (included in the rate) the congenial Canadian owners will help organize your day. Guests have use of the Belize Yacht Club pier next door.

Situated along a curving, palmy beach, **Ramon's Village** (just south of San Pedro; ceiling fans; air-conditioning in 29 rooms; phone; very expensive; 26-2071, fax: 26-2214, or 800-624-4215 in the United States) enjoys the liveliest atmosphere of any island hotel. The sands are alive with volleyball games, the freshwater pool is always filled with people, and the outdoor bar stays busy from morning till late night. Every Tuesday there is a beach barbecue, followed by a moonlight sail on Ramon's catamaran. Accommodations are in 60 *palapa*-style cabanas, squeezed together along the sand, with louvered windows, wood or tile floors and comfortable furnishings. The very expensive price buys atmosphere, not cushy rooms.

With its white-stucco arches, spindle rails and Mexican tile floors, the **Sun-Breeze Beach Resort** (seafront, south end of San Pedro; air-conditioning; phone; cable TV; very expensive; 26-2191, fax: 26-2346) recalls the architecture of San Pedro's native Yucatecans. The low-slung hotel enjoys a splendid location on a generous beach, right at the end of town. Everyone eventually shows up here and stays for a while, and that's why the place is always abuzz. Decor in most of the 39 guest rooms is brown and drab, though the air-conditioning, cable television and telephones more than make up for it. Best here are the five spacious rooms that feature modern decor as well as jacuzzi tubs.

Popular with divers, the seaside **Coral Beach Hotel** (Barrier Reef Drive, near the middle of San Pedro; ceiling fans; air-conditioning; moderate; 26-2001, fax 26-2864) is better known for its topnotch scuba program than its accommodations. Though unspectacular, the 19 rooms are clean and decorated with new wallpaper. Many offer views of the sea. There's no beach, but there is the uproarious Tackle Box Bar, which sits at the end of a pier. If you want to spend the night on the water, venture out on the live-aboard boat that makes an overnight trip to the Blue Hole.

Sea-weathered white clapboard, faded gingerbread and dormer windows make the **Barrier Reef Hotel** (Barrier Reef Drive, San Pedro; some air-conditioning; moderate; 26-2075, fax: 26-2719) look perfectly Belizean. This friendly seaside guesthouse, opened in 1907 and one of San Pedro's oldest, is also a good buy. The 11 rooms, with white plaster walls and Belizean tile floors, are basic but comfortable. Seven rooms have air-conditioning. There's also a swimming pool, a good restaurant and popular lounge.

Lily's (Barrier Reef Drive, San Pedro; ceiling fans; air-conditioning; budget; 26-2059) is a congenial, tumbledown sort of place, with a myriad of levels and cluttered rooftops. Wood-paneled walls and vinyl floors are standard decor in the ten bare but clean rooms. By far the best rooms are the three that face the sea. The owners, long-time residents of San Pedro, also offer delicious home cooking in a tiny restaurant.

If you prefer comfort to character, check into the newer, American-style **Mayan Princess Resort Hotel** (seafront, in the middle of San Pedro; air-conditioning; kitchen; very expensive; 26-2778, fax: 26-2784). Opened in late 1992, the coral-coated building boasts 23 stylish suites with white ceramic floors, whitewashed wicker furnishings, and French doors that open onto a private veranda. The well-stocked kitchens are especially helpful for families. Every room faces the sea.

Luscious landscaping on a generous expanse of sugary white beach makes the **Paradise Resort Hotel** (on the north end of San Pedro; ceiling fans; six rooms with air-conditioning; expensive to very expensive; 26-2083, fax: 26-2232) instantly appealing. To match the surroundings, 15 palm-thatched cabanas are outfitted with straw mat floors, bamboo closets and wood shutters. For those who crave less indigenous quarters, there are four contemporary villas and one condominium—all right on the sea.

If you're yearning for the luxuries of home, **Rock's Inn** (just north of San Pedro; air-conditioning; kitchen; expensive to very expensive; 26-2326, fax: 26-2358) offers some of the most modern, spacious rooms in all of Belize. Facing the sea, with a tiny beach, the white Mediterranean building houses 14 apartments with comfortable beds, sofas, dinettes, kitchens and big windows wrapped in pretty drapes.

Serious anglers will point you to ✪ **El Pescador** (located at the north end of Ambergris Caye; ceiling fans; very expensive; 26-2398, fax: 26-2977), whose nearby flats are world-renowned for tarpon and whose remote seaside setting feels worlds away from the daily grind. The two-story, wood-frame lodge is set among coconut palms on a lovely stretch of sand, and harbors 12 tidy but plain rooms typical of a homey fishing camp. There's also a two-bedroom suite. There is a four-night minimum stay, and packages include flats and/or reef fishing, daily guide, all meals, and the flight from Belize City.

Most visitors come to **Capricorn Resort** (north end of Ambergris Caye; one suite with air-conditioning, two cabanas with ceiling fans; expensive to very expensive; 26-2809, fax: 21-2091) for the superb food or the atmospheric bar, but there's no reason not to stay awhile, checking into one of two simple cabanas set right in the sand or the air-conditioned suite perched atop the main building and looking out to sea. Hardwood floors, beamed ceilings and primitive island art adorn the rooms, and hammocks are strung along the balconies.

Like some sanctuary for shipwrecked souls, **Captain Morgan's Retreat** (north end of Ambergris Caye; ceiling fans; very expensive; 26-2567, fax: 26-2616, or 800-447-2931 in the United States) is stashed on a deserted ribbon of beach, accessible only by boat. The 21 simple, thatched-roof *casitas* virtually disappear into the palm trees, and the bamboo restaurant and sand-floored bar look like they were built by Captain Morgan himself. Furnishings in the *casitas* are simple but tasteful, with louvered wood windows, plank floors, vaulted ceilings and roomy porches facing the sea. A favorite of honeymooners, and others who really want to escape.

Journey's End (north end of Ambergris Caye; air-conditioning; phone; TV; very expensive; 26-2173, or 800-460-5665 in the United States) is a sprawling, secluded retreat that seems to have it all: a palm-speckled beach, stylized swimming pool, lovely beach cabanas and modern hotel rooms with televisions (rare in Belize!), along with a friendly, accommodating staff. The restaurant's accomplished chef turns out daily gourmet creations. Besides all this, there's complimentary boat service to and from San Pedro (the resort is reached only by boat) several times daily.

If you want to be (almost) all alone, away from the buzz of San Pedro, check into the **Green Parrot** (ceiling fans; expensive; 21-2096, fax: 26-3293). Six simple, all-wood cabanas sit right on the sand at land's end, sequestered near the northernmost point of Ambergris Caye. A half-mile from the popular snorkel spot of Mexico Rocks, the bar is a popular stop for snorkelers on their way back to San Pedro. Green Parrot proprietors Bev and Stuart Coms, transplants from northern California, do all their own cooking—and aren't afraid to ask guests to pitch in—making the ambience friendly and family style.

RESTAURANTS   In a lovely South Seas–style building that looks across the beach, **Jade Garden** (a half-mile south of the airstrip, San Pedro; moderate to expensive; 26-2506) invites with its polished wood floors, soaring wood ceilings and pink and white linens. The Chinese fare does not shine as much as the decor, but it is a welcome change of pace. Chop suey, chow mein, sweet and sour and foo yong dishes are available, as well as American specials such as ribeye steak and seafood kebabs.

The margaritas at **La Margarita** (Coconut Drive, just south of the airstrip, San Pedro; moderate; 26-2222) are served in goldfish bowls large enough, the restaurant points out, "to easily accommodate five or six medium-sized fish." Sip your bowl slowly and order some enchiladas, fajitas or chile rellenos, enjoying the cactus garden or the veranda or the inside dining room that's low lit and decorated à la Southwest.

John Wayne mania in Belize? Strange, but true—just wander into **Duke's Place** (Coconut Drive, just south of the San Pedro Airstrip; moderate; 26-2666) and have a look at the Wayne memorabilia, including a saddle he actually used. More to the point, Duke's has the best breakfast in town: corn tortillas topped with refried beans, eggs, salsa, ham and grated cheese; and doughy, papery-thin fryjacks that have been deep fried and showered with confectioners' sugar. For dinner there's shrimp Creole, Parmesan fish and stewed chicken. Spinning fans, wood-paneled walls, CNN on the TV—Duke's is Belizean, through and through.

You don't have to take out at the **Tropical Takeout** (Coconut Drive, next to the San Pedro Airstrip; budget; 26-2288), where a generous round of tables invites one to relax and enjoy a traditional Mexican breakfast of eggs and tortillas, or a Belizean one with ham and bacon and johnnycakes. Lunchtime brings burgers, tacos and *tortas*.

Elvi's Kitchen (Pescador Drive, San Pedro; budget to moderate; 26-2176) has sand floors, long picnic tables, an enormous palapa roof and a tree growing up through the middle—the perfect venue for trading tall tales. Waiters in bow ties and starched white shirts serve burgers, fish sandwiches, fish platters, steaks and rice.

Hip New Yorker meets San Pedro and, instantly, there is **Lagoon** (Pescador Drive, near the middle of town; moderate to expensive; 26-2327). Swank as can be, the restaurant has ceilings washed in indigo, walls painted white and detailed with minimalist art, tabletops in zebra motif and chairbacks filigreed with black wrought iron. The international cuisine suggests new culinary heights for San Pedro (maybe even for Belize). Entrées to try: pork-and-apple fricassee, black-bean lasagna, chayote and lobsters lagoon (lobster sautéed in anise and cream and served in the shell over mashed potatoes). Arrive just before sunset and have a drink at the rooftop bar—one of San Pedro's best views. Steel drum bands accompany dinner on Wednesday and Sunday.

Of course, culinaria happens in some of the least expected places. Take **The Reef** (Pescador Drive, near the middle of town; budget; no phone), where from the simplest of white wood buildings comes fresh, hearty Belizean and Mexican fare. Baked whole snapper with beans and rice, rich and steamy cow's foot soup, tostadas and *garnaches* (fried tortillas stuffed with tomatoes and onions) are but a few of the offerings. Service can be slow, but who cares? This is the tropics.

Mary Ellen's Little Italy (Barrier Reef Drive, San Pedro; moderate; 26-2866) is an immensely romantic seaside venue with a touch of Southern charm. The latter comes from Mary Ellen, a former attorney from Tennessee. Classical music and sea breezes stream through the dining room, decorated with red-and-white checked tablecloths, flickering red candles and tropical flowers. The food is average to very good, from bubbling deep-dish pizza to chicken and pork dishes smothered in garlic and wine sauce.

If you arrive at San Pedro by boat, you'll immediately spot Fido's Courtyard, home to **Fido's Restaurant** (Barrier Reef Drive; moderate to expensive; 26-2056). Once a burger-and-chicken-wings joint, it's reincarnated as a civilized place where you can order such fashionable fare as hummus, black-bean dip or ceviche, grilled chicken salad or lobster salad. Dinner is more elaborate; try the filet mignon, chicken brochettes or mixed seafood platter.

Within Fido's Courtyard, you can also have a slice of Italian pie at the **Pizza Place** (26-2444) or a jolt of java at **Reality Cafe** (26-3586). The café is upstairs with a balcony to the sea and a good smelling kitchen funneling out plates of eggs and tortillas and refried beans from morning until night. For the health-inclined, there are terrific veggie sandwiches and tacos, fresh bread studded with bananas and frozen drinks plied with mango and papaya.

Celi's (at the Holiday Hotel, Barrier Reef Drive; moderate; 26-2014) is located on the waterfront in San Pedro's very first hotel. Long popular for breakfast, Celi's has some of the tastiest omelettes, waffles and Maya burritos (made with eggs, tomatoes and onions). For dinner, there's all manner of fresh seafood—stone crabs, shrimp, fish and lobster—that's equally as sumptuous.

Lily's (Barrier Reef Drive, San Pedro; budget; 26-2059) is widely known among locals for its hefty home-cooked portions. For breakfast, there's huevos rancheros and shrimp omelettes; for lunch or dinner, try the fried shrimp or fish simmered in Mexican barbecue sauce. The surroundings—battered rattan chairs, laminated wood clocks and turtle shells parked on the walls—are perfectly Belizean.

On a breezy seafront veranda, beneath the slope of a deep blue canvas, you can dine well at **Capricorn Resort** (northern end of Ambergris Caye; moderate to expensive; 26-2809) for lunch or dinner. Chef Clarence Burdes' menu has elements of French, Italian, Californian and Belizean cuisine, and there are daily chalkboard specials. Start with the Tuscan paté or the wedge of cream cheese smothered in sundried tomato pesto with Cajun baguette slices. Then order the seafood in a mushroom and sherry sauce piled high in a clamshell and baked; or the seafood or chicken crêpes. Finish with a creamy rum chocolate cake. There's intimate dining indoors or something more casual (with a limited menu) at the beach bar. Locals love this place, so call for a reservation (and a water taxi, if you're staying in San Pedro).

SHOPPING   **Eden Art** (Coconut Drive, next to the San Pedro Airstrip; 26-3149) is a marvelous little gallery with voluptuous urns and vases exotically painted, tiny and intricate woven baskets and tiny painted tables, radiant rugs and dazzling oils and acrylics. Most are works of American artist Katrina Samuels, who's also the gallery owner. Call ahead to make sure she's open.

For a terrific selection of Belizean art, stop by **Iguana Jack's** (Barrier Reef Drive, San Pedro; 26-2767). The cozy seaside gallery displays original paintings and color prints, painted clay vessels and exotic jewelry.

At Fido's courtyard, **Belizean Arts** (Barrier Reef Drive, San Pedro; 26-2638) carries original paintings of Maya and island scenes, as well as folk-art furniture. **Salty Dog** (26-2789), also here, has a good selection of artsy T-shirts.

Shop 1001 (Barrier Reef Drive, San Pedro; 26-2747) has lots of take-home items: Marie Sharp's jams and jellies, tropically flowered clothing and handsome silver jewelry, and canvasses depicting tropical scenery in oils.

Cohune-nut carvings, Maya medicinal potions, environmental-themed T-shirts—you'll find them all at **Rainforest Rescue** (Barrier Reef Drive, San Pedro; 26-3049). A portion of the profits go to the Belize Audubon Society.

NIGHTLIFE   San Pedro has the best nightlife in Belize, with possibilities ranging from intimate seaside bars to over-the-water pubs and sand-floored discos.

The **Purple Parrot** (seafront, south side of San Pedro; 26-2071) at Ramon's Village is a popular poolside location for evening drinks. Things heat up on Tuesday and Friday, when they barbecue on the beach.

Big Daddy's (seafront, toward the south end of San Pedro; no phone) is the last word on disco around these parts. Nothing fancy, the bamboo shanty on the beach rocks until the wee hours of the morning. Bands play on Saturday nights. Cover.

Tarzan's (Barrier Reef Drive, across from Central Park, San Pedro; 26-2947) is Big Daddy's rival disco, where the punta rock and dancehall reggae pulsate until 2 a.m. Cover.

The obvious choice for a pub is the ever-popular, sand-floored **Tackle Box Bar** (at the Coral Beach Hotel, seafront, San Pedro; 26-2001), perched over the water at the end of a pier.

For a before- or after-dinner drink, nestle up to the long padded bar at **The Pier Lounge** (seafront, near the center of San Pedro; 26-2002). The Monday night crab races and the Wednesday Chicken Drop (guess what the chicken drops) draw big crowds—for San Pedro, that is.

At sunset, make your way to the rooftop tables of the **Sunset Bar** (at the Hotel Casablanca, Pescador Drive, San Pedro; 26-2327). The drinks are good, the sea and island views even better.

Sandals Pub (on the main street, near the north end of San Pedro; 26-2281) is the local pool joint, with sand floors, recorded reggae and dusty sandals parked on the walls.

It is difficult to conceive of a more pleasant gathering spot than the bar at **Capricorn** (northern end of Ambergris Caye; 26-2809), big and open and wood-roofed, set among waving coconut palms and then the blue of the sea. The bartender will customize your frozen cocktail, serve it on a woven Guatemalan coaster and take you snack order (highly recommended: home-cooked tortilla chips with fresh conch ceviche). Go anytime, though I like late afternoon to early evening best. Call ahead to arrange for a water taxi from San Pedro.

GETTING THERE: If you're staying on Ambergris Caye, your lodge will arrange transportation from Belize City. If you're arriving on your own, Tropic Air and Island Air have regular flights to the San Pedro airstrip from Belize City. Or, shuttle boats make the one-hour cruise to Ambergris Caye from two Belize City locations: (1) across from the Bellevue Hotel, at 5 Southern Foreshore and (2) on the south side of Haulover Creek, next to the Swing Bridge. The one-way cost is about US$20 per person.

CAYE CAULKER

Just 20 scenic minutes by boat from Ambergris Caye, but decades away in spirit, is **Caye Caulker**. Despite its designation as the second-most populous caye in Belize, Caye Caulker hasn't changed much since the 1960s. Electricity did arrive in the mid-1980s, but there are still only a handful of old cars that cruise the sand streets. Life here feels like a slow-motion film, with dogs lazing everywhere, rickety picket fences running in all directions, and rows of battered clapboard homes tilting ever so slightly to the wind. Barefoot children tote tubs of bananas on their heads, and fishermen wrestle conch meat from their shells along crooked docks. The post office doubles as a store, and the pastry shop also rents snorkel equipment.

Spanning a five-square-mile area, Caye Caulker is mostly swamp and mangroves. The village itself is only four streets wide and ten streets long, all sand, of course. On the main drag, sometimes referred to as Front Street, there is a speed bump of knotted rope and a sign that cautions to "Go Slow," though no one is quite sure who they're meant for—maybe the island's four cars?

Perhaps it is the swamplands, or the island's thin ties with reality, that give Caulker its mysterious edge. Listen to the perpetual breezes that blow across the island and you will hear small-town whispers of strange people and places. There is a woman storyteller, locals will say, who spins yarns late at night, but only when storms are brewing. And somewhere is a lagoon filled with crocodiles, a disco that is haunted, and a mangrove forest where Maya cults worship. Who knows, they shrug, maybe it's the same place where the ancient Maya worshipped long ago.

Trumpetfish and Smooth trunkfish

Some 2000 years ago, the Maya were Caye Caulker's original islanders. Then followed the buccaneers, who never stayed very long but whose English accents gave the island its current nickname—Caye *Corker*. But most of Caulker's present-day residents are descendants of the *Mestizos*, who fled here after Yucatán's War of the Castes. In 1870, a *Mestizo* named Luciano Reyes bought the island for US$150 when he lost the bid for Ambergris Caye. Reyes' descendants still live on the island and are some of its most prominent residents.

Through the years, Caulker has always existed in the shadow of Ambergris, which is larger and more sophisticated than its tiny neighbor. Lately, Caulker itself is shadowed by a somewhat dubious reputation, no doubt due to the dreadlocked hustlers from Belize City, Honduras and other places who linger along the sand streets at night, pressing bypassers to buy a joint, some "blow," or some sex. Because of this, many travelers choose to take a day trip to Caulker, returning in the evening to their rooms on Ambergris.

Caye Caulker is still very much a fishing village; every afternoon along the seafront, crayon-colored sloops arrive laden with snapper, grouper and, in season, pearly conch and bright pink lobsters. Some sloops suggest they may be loaded with something else; notice the boats named "Suspect," "Miss Conduct" and "Bong" tied to the village docks. Right next to the docks is the tiny island cemetery, overgrown with weeds.

Caye Caulker's 800 residents are protective of their little paradise. When local officials announced plans to open an airstrip, residents rallied against it, saying it would bring too much tourism. In 1991, the airstrip did open, but so far the visitors are only trickling in. If you do arrive in one of the infrequent commuter planes, you'll be deposited in a place that looks like the mangrove boonies, with only one house in sight. Not to worry. Just pick up your bags and start walking north (toward that house), and you'll soon find yourself in town.

Lodging on Caye Caulker ranges from modest accommodations to bare-bones; the best hotel is the Tropical Paradise, though whose idea of paradise could well be a point of debate. Still, the island itself is filled with flowers and trees of raging color—flaming red flamboyants and purply bougainvillea, canary mandavilla and ruby hibiscus. Coconut palms are so plentiful their fruit litters every sandy street. Breadfruit trees grow so big they camouflage stilt houses, and their fleshy fruits dangle like green bowling balls. In the morning, village women pluck the fruit and turn it into breadfruit bread; you can smell it baking through their open windows.

Visitors can learn about the island, and Belize's fragile reef system, in a slide show offered most weeknights at **Sea-ing is Belizing** (near the soccer field, toward the north end of town; 22-2189; admission), a photo gallery and book exchange. The slides are taken by gallery owner James Beveridge, an underwater photographer and Belize conservationist. Other than the slide show, nighttime activities are pretty much limited to dining on catch-of-the-day, drinking rum at a tiki bar, or gazing at the stars.

For island information and tours to other cayes or the mainland, stop by **Dolphin Bay Travel** (Front Street, near the middle of town; 22-2214). Here is also the village message board with formal notices and odd bits of advertising ("Reflexology! Go to Little Blue House next door to Frenchies.").

During the day, snorkeling, scuba diving and fishing are top pursuits. Several boats offer excursions, but by far the most popular trips are with **Chocolate** (22-2151), the island's most famous boat captain. Chocolate lives in a thatched-roof house along the seashore with his partner, aptly named Annie Seashore. His manatee-watching trips, all-day excursions with a stop at Goff's Caye, are excellent and priced right: US$27.50 per person, including snorkel gear (but not lunch).

The Split was created in 1961 at the northernmost tip of town, compliments of Hurricane Hattie. It's now the place to hang with locals, who cool off in the air-clear aquamarine channel and warm up on little sun docks. The "public beach" is really a small patch of dirt with palm trees. There's a couple of marooned boats, and a popular tiki bar that looks like it may topple over any day now.

LODGING   If modest, back-to-nature accommodations are your style (and budget), you've come to the right place. Most lodging on Caye Caulker is a notch above camping, with clean, nondescript rooms that have ceiling fans and hot water that is more or less dependable. The water on Caye Caulker is not purified, so use only bottled water for drinking and brushing your teeth.

By far the best place to sleep on Caye Caulker is at ✪ **Chocolate's** (seafront, north end of town; ceiling fan and table fan; mini-refrigerator; moderate; 22-2151). There's only one room, a stylish and spacious second-floor perch staring at the sea, with a queen-size mahogany poster bed, vaulted mahogany ceilings, and pretty ceramic tile throughout. Chocolate's partner, Annie Seashore, runs the place, making sure there are freshly ground coffee beans in the coffeemaker every night. Call ahead for this room—it's a superb spot.

The second best place to sleep is, oddly enough, next door to the cemetery, at the **Tropical Paradise Hotel** (seafront on the south end of town; ceiling fans; some with air-conditioning; some with TV; budget to moderate; 22-2124, fax: 22-2225). Owned by the Reyes family, descendants of Luciano Reyes, the hotel offers rooms in a main concrete building or along two rows of tiny, tin-roofed, plywood cabanas parked next to the beach. The cabanas, by far the best choice, feature vinyl floors, wood-paneled walls and newly remodeled bathrooms. Thirteen cabanas have wall-unit air conditioners—offering the only air-conditioned lodging on the island.

Next door, the **Seabeezzz** (seafront on the south end of town; moderate; 22-2176) really is a breeeezzy place to stay. Constant trade winds cool three small clapboard buildings, where six tidy rooms provide clean, comfortable lodging. Best of all, the rooms open onto an immaculate courtyard brimming with tropical plants and exotic fruit trees. Open from November through April.

The road stops at Seabeezzz, so you'll have to walk along the beach to get to **Shirley's Guest House** (seafront, south end of town; fans; private and shared bath; moderate; 22-2145, fax: 22-2264). In a secluded, peaceful spot swept by sea breezes are ten rooms in a two-story building, as well as one duplex and one whitewashed cabin, all with Mennonite mahogany furnishings. The rooms and duplex share baths (including three outdoor facilities), while the cabin has a private bath.

The ✿ **Vega Inn and Gardens** (seafront near the middle of town; ceiling fans; budget to moderate; 22-2142) has a handful of tidy rooms and two suites for rent, as well as a lovely camping area right on the sea. The hot showers are the indoor-outdoor kind, but things seem private enough. The local family who owns the place treats the guests like family.

The prettiest pastel buildings on the waterfront can be found at the **Rainbow Hotel** (north end of town; ceiling fans; cable TV; budget; 22-2123, fax: 22-2172). Inside the 17 rooms are attractive green tile floors, battered dressers and mattresses that range from firm to lumpy. For television lovers, the cable televisions in 11 of the rooms are a real find.

RESTAURANTS   Caye Caulker's eateries are offbeat, super casual (don't mind the cats or dogs) and full of weird possibilities. A hippie will serve you tonight, but tomorrow night's waiter may be a moonlighting preacher or even a kid from down the street. Chairs and tables never match—that would be boring— and hours are apt to change with boating conditions.

Considering the norm, then, the restaurant at the **Tropical Paradise Hotel** (south end of town; budget; 22-2124) seems almost formal. Red and blue starched linens cover every table, and the service is dependably good. The breakfast, lunch and dinner fare isn't spectacular, but most meals are under $5. Fresh fish and shellfish, fried chicken, burgers and creole dishes are available.

Glenda's (budget; 22-2148) is a bit out of the way, tucked on a no-name side street near the middle of town, but anyone will be happy to point the way. Inside the blue wooden house with a tin roof, Glenda serves eggs with bacon, ham or beans for breakfast, and chicken tostadas, lobster tostadas, chicken burritos and rice and beans for lunch.

The place for lunch is **Syd's** (down a side lane, mid-island; budget; 22-2108), a battered little house with mesh screens and Christmas lights strung across the ceiling. Syd is not in sight, but his wife will gladly throw a cheeseburger or grilled cheese on the griddle, or whip up some burritos.

Paper lanterns, Mennonite mahogany tables and sea views lure diners to the **Sand Box** (facing the sea on the north end of town; budget; 22-2200). Once you're there, the talented chef and owner, a woman from southern Florida, treats you to fresh, inventive pasta and seafood dishes. Top choices are shrimp lasagna, conch fritters, and snapper stuffed with spinach, shrimp and mushrooms. Easily the island's best food.

Located on the bottom floor of the guest house of the same name, **Castaways** (north end of town; budget to moderate; 22-2294) is a cute little place that covers many culinary bases: chow meins, curries, pastas, steaks and seafood.

SHOPPING   Shopping is a loose term here; it's more like whatever you happen to find that's open *and* has merchandise that day. A few possibilities: **Galeria Hicaco** (south end of town), owned by a California marine biologist, who carries a fine array of Belizean arts and crafts; **Salty Dog** (middle of town; 22-2267), a good place to go for T-shirts and Guatemala imports, such as bags, hats, pants, purses and the like; **Toucan Gift Shop** (middle of town; 22-2219), which also peddles Guatemalan goods and T-shirts; or **Chocolate's** (near north end of town; 22-2151), where Chocolate's partner, Annie Seashore, sells good quality T-shirts, tropical wear and hammocks.

NIGHTLIFE   To really get into the Caye Caulker mood, walk upstairs into the **I & I Reggae Bar** (south end of town, a block from the Tropical Paradise; 22-2206) and have a drink. The outdoor terrace is as funky as can be, with haphazard tables, plants potted in plastic buckets, and reggae bands playing beneath the inky night sky. If you can't go late, go for sunset.

The Reef Bar (seafront, on the north end of town), a bamboo hut with sand floors, dart boards and pool tables, is popular though a little raunchy. Recorded blues and reggae entertains nightly crowds who gladly heed the bar's sign that says "No Shoes, No Shirts, No Problem."

GETTING THERE: Tropic Air and Island Air offer regular flights from Belize City to Caye Caulker. Shuttle boats make the trip to Caye Caulker from Belize City, leaving from the Texaco Station near the Swing Bridge, on the north side of Haulover Creek. The 30-minute trip is about US$12 to $15, one-way. From Ambergris Caye, shuttle boats leave from the San Pedro docks and charge approximately US$7.50 one-way to Caye Caulker.

ST. GEORGE'S CAYE

The idyllic caye called St. George's is nearly two miles long and 800 feet wide at its broadest point, and is shaped like a wriggly crescent. From Belize City, it's just 20 minutes by boat across the clear sand flats, making it Belize's most accessible isle of escape. Little wonder that St. George's is a weekend haunt for wealthy Belizeans, whose charming stilt homes of painted clapboard are propped along the beach.

Given the island's eye-blink size, it is difficult to imagine that for two centuries it was hotly fought over by the Spanish and British. In fact, the Spanish called the island Cayo Casino even after the British made it the capital of the Belizean colony in 1650. By then, the island's residents were mainly English logwood and mahogany traders who grew numerous crops on the caye, despite the ban on crop growing, which kept the colonies dependent on the Crown. The Spanish regularly raided the crops. As one islander tells it: "Every couple of years the

Spanish Navy would sail in, burn all the crops, hoist up the Spanish flag, and sail away. By the time the crops were good and growing again, the Spanish were back. It was a frustrating cycle."

The tug-of-war continued until 1798, when the Spanish lost the Battle of St. George's Caye. Belizeans commemorate the battle with a national holiday and much revelry. Some, however, claim it was not a battle at all, but simply some Spanish galleons retreating after being confronted by a ragtag band of Belizeans in boats. Official history, however, records the presence of a British schooner and the volleying of many cannon balls before the victory.

Appropriately, a single cannon on the beach remembers the battle today. Near the cannon are several graves, some occupied by early settlers and others by the recently deceased. A footpath wends past the graves to St. George's other inhabitants: two lodges, a few lobster fishers whose rickety traps are stacked higher than the palm trees, an aquarium builder (you can peek your head in, but there's not much to see), and the British Joint Forces "Adventurous Training Centre." The training, judging from the troops' activities, involves playing volleyball in the sand and drinking Belikin beer by the sea.

LODGING **St. George's Lodge** (some rooms with ceiling fans; very expensive; for reservations, call 2-12121 in Belize City, or 800-678-6871 in the United States) is ideal for hard-core divers who prefer a rigorous schedule. Each day's agenda, organized and directed by owner Fred Good of Texas, calls for diving interspersed with dive instruction and discussion, with time for three meals but little time for relaxation. Which is too bad, considering the lodge enjoys a picturesque location on the sea. Guests can choose from six rustic cabanas perched on stilts over the water or ten bedrooms in a main house that are narrow and breezeless, quite monkish in design. Meals, dives and boat transfers from Belize City are included in the rates—among the highest lodging rates in all of Belize—and, in my opinion, not worth it.

At the opposite end of St. George's Caye is ✪ **Cottage Colony** (air-conditioning; expensive to very expensive; for reservations, call 2-77051 in Belize City, fax: 2-73253), where six prim cottages are painted in sherbet colors, trimmed in gingerbread and framed by a white picket fence. Their interiors are airy and modern, with hardwood floors and white wicker furniture, and their porches face a shady courtyard next to the beach. About half have air conditioners—lifesavers on hot days! The official gathering place is the second-floor bar and restaurant overlooking the sea. Main activities: diving, fishing and beach bumming. Rates include meals and boat transportation to the island.

GETTING THERE: Guests of Cottage Colony and St. George's Lodge will have prearranged boat transfers from Belize City to St. George's Caye. Independent sightseers can usually hire a boat from the docks at the Texaco Station near the Swing Bridge, or from Blackline Marina, two miles north of Belize City on the Northern Highway.

THE ATOLLS

Farther out to sea lie three atolls, coral isles that form rings around lagoons. These dazzling island necklaces actually sit atop the Maya Mountains; over the eons, the coral blossomed on the mountains until it rose above the sea. The sea, in turn, pulverized their rocky shores into cushiony white sand that makes the atolls look like some exotic Pacific isles. Most of the world's atolls do in fact lie in the Pacific. Only four exist in the Western Hemisphere, and three of these are in Belize. The fourth atoll, Chinchorro, is in Mexico just across the Belize border.

From the air, the Belize atolls appear as stunning oddities, with the calm emerald waters of the lagoons seemingly corralled by the blustery blue waters of the sea. On land, the scenery is just as compelling. The faraway isles that make up Turneffe Islands, Lighthouse Reef and Glover's Reef atolls are the quintessence of tropical paradise: pearly beaches studded with swaying coconut palms and washed with warm, shallow waters. Bird life is prolific and bountiful, and giant sea turtles build their nests in virtual privacy. Northern promontories attract swarms of grouper and snapper, who spawn each year with little interruption from a hook and line.

Just offshore, the sea bottom plummets, then becomes wildly etched with spiked ridges and rolling canyons and lattice-like caverns. The ridges have brought down many a ship, laid them to rest in what is now a virtual nautical graveyard of the 18th and 19th centuries. These sunken ancients, together with the many sheer walls webbed with sea life, make the surrounding waters an extraordinary place to dive.

Only a few years ago, Belize's atolls were considered the outer limits of Caribbean diving. But as word spread, they have become the "in" place to dive;

Frigate bird

their virtues are whispered on the diving grapevine and exalted in glossy dive magazines. The place most divers hear about first is **Turneffe Islands**, the largest and westernmost of Belize's atolls, located about two-and-a-half hours from Belize City by boat. Here, one can dive the Black Beauty, where ebony coral blankets a reef, and The Elbow, where curtains of huge fish waft up and down a 150-foot wall of coral. There is an excellent dive lodge on Turneffe, as well as a fishing camp and an ecotourism retreat.

Besides its size and fantastic diving, what really sets Turneffe apart is its mangrove forests. Brilliant orchids drape from the mangrove limbs, and schools of fish seek protection in their roots. Mangrove lagoons provide safe haven for many manatees and dolphins, which are the main reason **Blackbird Caye Village** opened in 1991. The research center and ecotourist resort is the venture of Belizean Ray Lightburn and American Al Dugan, who have hired scientists to study marine life in the area. The 4000-acre island and its surrounding waters are still extremely pristine, and sea life is profuse. The village focal point is a dolphin research center, where scientists are studying the communication and other behaviors of the gregarious mammals. Lightburn and Dugan hope the village will make the Turneffe atoll a national park.

There are few mangroves on the **Lighthouse Reef** atoll, but there are ravishing beaches, whose promenades of luxuriant, crisp white sand are sprinkled with palms and washed by pleated seas dyed green and blue and, at sunset, blazing violet.

Within the atoll are numerous natural wonders, most notably the **Blue Hole**, explored in the 1970s by Jacques Cousteau. Actually an ocean sinkhole, it measures a spectacular 1000 feet across and plunges 480 feet down from the atoll's ten-foot-deep lagoon. Riddled with stalactites and stalagmites and pitch-black caves, the Blue Hole is difficult to reach (on a calm day, it's three hours by boat from Belize City), but that only adds to its mystique. Several dive operators offer one-day trips, but dedicated scuba divers should consider staying at **Lighthouse Reef Resort** (800-423-3114 in the United States), which includes a trip to the Blue Hole in its one-week package.

The resort also offers excursions to **Half Moon Caye Natural Monument** (for information, contact the Belize Audubon Society; 2-34988 in Belize City) at the southeast corner of Lighthouse Reef. The 45-acre sanctuary, Belize's first national park, boasts sensational beaches and about 4000 red-footed booby birds, who nest on the southern end of the caye and are very rare. Among the other fascinating creatures living here are mangrove warblers and frigate birds, wish-willie lizards, and loggerhead and hawksbill turtles, who lay their eggs on the eastern beaches. A raised platform provides bird's-eye views of all the animal action. Arrive at dusk and you may catch one of nature's intense shows: aerial bird fights between the frigates and boobies.

Because of its extreme remoteness, Belize's southernmost atoll is also its least visited. **Glover's Reef** is two-and-a-half to five hours (depending on the size and type of boat) from Belize City—not a pleasant trip on rough seas. But on calm days, it is a fantastic voyage, with mesmerizing vistas of sapphire waters that meet blue skies and the tiniest, most serene little islands.

The atoll is named for English buccaneer John Glover, who set up camp here during the 1700s, not knowing he was living on the hemisphere's most shapely atoll. Glover's coral outcroppings form a nearly unbroken oval whose vertical sides fall away to inky depths. If drained of their seas, they would look like a Pacific volcano.

Inside the coral lies an 80-square-mile lagoon of the most intensely beautiful water, riddled with hundreds of patch reefs and sea creatures of flamboyant colors and shapes. Outside its borders are the wrecks of five 18th-century English merchant ships, which met their doom on jagged coral. Glover's has but six cayes, all fringed with fabulous white sand and palm trees, and all located on the southeastern corner of the atoll.

LODGING   The most popular atoll resort is ❂ **Turneffe Island Lodge** (Caye Bokel, Turneffe Islands atoll; ceiling fans; very expensive; for reservations, call 2-12011 in Belize City, or 800-874-0118 in the United States), situated on a private 12-acre caye. A cluster of charming frame bungalows, swallowed in palm trees, line the sandy shore and offer comfortable rooms with private baths and views of the sea. Guests spend most of their time in the sea, either diving the fabulous reef or fishing the flats. The waters around Turneffe are renowned for bonefish. To help keep them that way, the lodge limits the number of anglers to eight per week. The minimum stay is three nights; included are all meals and boat transportation from Belize City—about a two-and-a-half-hour trip.

Kayaking, snorkeling, occupying a hammock—these are the primary pursuits of those fortunate enough to check into **Blackbird Caye Resort** (Turneffe Islands atoll; ceiling fans; very expensive; for reservations, call 888-271-3484 in the United States; fax: 713-658-0739). Set on a 4000-acre, jungle-covered island and surrounded by water that's deeply turquoise, the resort offers woodsy accommodations in 11 thatched beach cabanas. Nature trails curl through the tropical brush, dolphins frequent the surrounding mangrove lagoons and three piers offer hook-and-line possibilities. Minimum stay is one week. Meals and transfers from Belize City included in the rate.

For thousands of years, the site of **Turneffe Flats** (on Northern Bogue, on the northeast side of the Turneffe Islands atoll; ceiling fans; very expensive; for reservations call 800-815-1304 in the United States) has been a fishing camp, first for the Maya and now for visiting anglers who come armed with fly rods. Flats fishing is naturally the big draw, but guides are also available for reef and deep-sea fishing. The lodge can also arrange dive trips. Guests stay in one of sixteen comfortable wood-frame bungalows with porches on the beach. A 24-hour generator turns the ceiling fans in each room and provides the hot water for showers. There's a bar and family-style dining room, where Belizean entrées are the highlight. Minimum fishing or diving package is one week, which includes one night in Belize City at the Fiesta Inn, all meals and guides.

Lighthouse Reef Resort (Northern Caye, Lighthouse Reef atoll; air-conditioning; very expensive; for reservations, call 800-423-3114 in the United States) resembles a tropical illusion: a castaway island, ringed in coconut palms and powdery white sand, with lovely cabanas strung along the beach. Offshore, the underwater panorama is no less spectacular, which explains why so many scuba divers stay here. Dives are offered several times a day and at night, including trips to the famous Blue Hole. Guests may also use the resort's sea kayaks. Accommodations are in casual, roomy concrete cabanas or in gleaming suites. Every room has modern decor and a porch with lawn furniture. The restaurant serves unusually good food, and there's a real feeling of camaraderie among guests. Weekly packages only; all meals and air transportation from Belize City included.

Two-and-a-half hours by boat from the mainland, ✪ **Manta Resort** (Glover's Reef atoll; ceiling fans; some air-conditioning; very expensive; for reservations, call 2-31895 in Belize City, or 800-326-1724 in the United States) is a seclusionist's paradise. It's nestled on its own 12-acre fantasy island, with nothing but fluffy white sand, palm trees and sapphire waters that plunge to inky black depths. The attention-getter is a vast thatched cantina, stuck way out in the sea at the end of a pier. Here, guests meet for eating, drinking and partaking of the gorgeous sea views. The accommodations are nothing fancy: 12 thatched-roof cabanas made of mahogany and featuring tiny porches with hammocks over the sand. For those who want more creature comforts, there's a modern two-bedroom family house with air-conditioning, kitchen, and even television and VCR (unheard of in the out islands!). Rates include all meals and boat transfers from Belize City.

GETTING THERE: Boat or air (in the case of Lighthouse Reef) transportation to the atolls is arranged through your resort.

OTHER CAYES

Hundreds of other beautiful cayes are scattered off the Belize coast, including many that are uninhabited but can be visited by boat. Such is the case with **Spanish Lookout Caye**, **Sergeants Caye**, **Water Caye** and **Goff's Caye**. About 45 minutes by boat from Belize City, the teeny sandy cayes are popular day destinations for Belizeans who love to picnic and snorkel here. Also popular is nearby **English Caye**, which marks the entrance to the shipping channel and has a lighthouse, a lighthouse keeper and a few private houses.

South of Belize City, you can experience the life of a lobster fisher on the string of mangrove isles called the **Bluefield Range**. Belizean Ricardo Castillo runs a commercial lobster camp on one of the islands, and also runs **Ricardo's Beach Huts** (moderate; for reservations, call 2-31609 in Belize City). He invites guests who stay in his four super-rustic stilt huts (no showers—the sea is your bathtub) to accompany him as he fishes for lobster. Or, guests can do their own fishing and snorkeling in the surrounding crystalline waters. Meals (including much lobster, of course!), a day trip to surrounding cayes, and boat transfers from Belize City are included in the rate. For the true adventurer who doesn't mind really roughing it, this is a memorable experience—even for Belize, where *everything's* an adventure.

Looking like a wedge of sand and palm trees set adrift, **South Water Caye** is encircled by the clearest, shallowest water, and beyond that, the resplendent coral reef, beckoning for exploration. Unlike most of the "other cayes," South Water has a little more going on, thanks to the **Blue Marlin Lodge** (ceiling fans; air-conditioning; very expensive; for reservations, call 800-798-1558 in the United States), which has lately become popular with anglers and divers. Here, numerous buildings are sprinkled atop the sand, including several clapboard ones with casual, beachy rooms, and several concrete cabanas that offer air-conditioning but smell musty—a hazard of island existence. The most coveted room is a spacious wooden bungalow that juts right out over the water and catches constant sea breezes. There's a glorious sand beach here and congenial thatched-roof restaurant and bar with a floating dock. Minimum stay four nights. Rates include all meals and transportation from Belize City.

Next door, you'll notice a sandy jewel called **Carrie Bow Caye**, spanning all of one acre, and acting as a field station for the Smithsonian Institute during the spring and summer. Smithsonian researchers, searching for a good field station site, accidentally landed on the island in 1972 during a bad storm. They fell instantly in love, and struck a deal with the Bowman family of Dangriga, who own the island, to use it for half the year. If you swim or motor over to Carrie Bow, the scientists will be happy to show you around. Research changes every season, of course, but past study has included the mating habits of worms and jellyfish.

GETTING THERE: Day trips to these outer cayes can be arranged through **S & L Travel** (91 North Front Street, Belize City; 2-77593, fax: 2-77594).

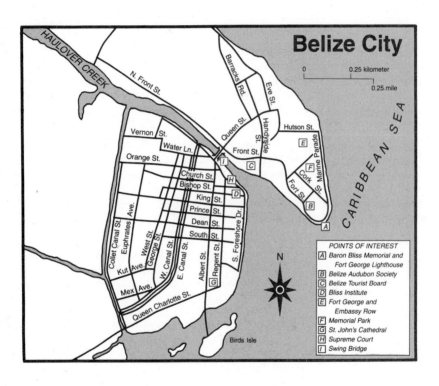

Belize City

0.25 kilometer

0.25 mile

HAULOVER CREEK

N. Front St.

Barracks Rd.

Eve St.

Queen St.

Handyside St.

Hutson St.

Vernon St.

Water Ln.

Front St.

Orange St.

Church St.

Bishop St.

King St.

Prince St.

Dean St.

South St.

Collet Canal St.

Euphrates Ave.

West St.

George St.

W. Canal St.

E. Canal St.

Albert St.

Regent St.

S. Foreshore Dr.

Kut Ave.

Mex. Ave.

Queen Charlotte St.

Cork St.

Fort St.

Marine Parade

CARIBBEAN SEA

Birds Isle

N

A

B

C

D

E

F

G

H

I

POINTS OF INTEREST

A Baron Bliss Memorial and
     Fort George Lighthouse
B Belize Audubon Society
C Belize Tourist Board
D Bliss Institute
E Fort George and
     Embassy Row
F Memorial Park
G St. John's Cathedral
H Supreme Court
I Swing Bridge

SEVEN

Belize City

Although the Cayes are the most popular destination in Belize, Belize City is the place most travelers see first, after arriving at the international airport. Unfortunately, it is not the best introduction. Sweltering hot all the time, it is crowded with crumbling streets, tin-roofed shanties and British colonial buildings that have seen better days. Murky Haulover Creek slices through the center of the city, bubbling with sailboats and makeshift skiffs and fed by open sewage canals that line the streets. The 52,670 people who live and work here create a continuous grind of activity—quite unlike the rest of the country, where life is slow and the land virtually empty.

In the early 1700s, the city was conceived by a band of British Baymen, logwood cutters who were former pirates but who still clung to their buccaneer ways. From their stilt-shack settlement at the swampy mouth of the Belize River, they would occasionally cut logwood and load it onto ships headed for England. Most of the time, however, "their chief Delight" was "in drinking," rum punch being their favorite, according to Captain Nathaniel Uring in 1720, who adds he "had a very unpleasant time living among these people." Little wonder that 18th-century mapmakers obelized, or marked the settlement with a symbol warning of a corrupt place, which, over time, was supposedly corrupted into the word "Belize."

More than a hundred years later, when Maya explorer John Lloyd Stephens sailed into the port city, conditions had changed considerably. Gleaming white colonial houses paraded up and down the waterfront and nearby streets, culminating in the elegant Government House, designed by famous 19th-century architect Christopher Wren. There was also an ornate Gothic church with a soaring spire and groves of coconut palms that, from the sea, reminded Stephens of the palm trees of Egypt and "gave the appearance of actual beauty."

Despite its new-found sophistication, vestiges of the unsavory Baymen remained deep in the city's foundation. As late as 1917, workers who dug down 60 feet found "mahogany chips mixed with rum bottles, with surprising regularity," according to one account in *The Baymen's Legacy, A Portrait of Belize City.*

It is a city that should not have been built, for its land is swampy and low-lying, confronted by water on three sides and forever vulnerable to rains and tides and hurricanes. The no-name hurricane of 1931 extinguished ten percent of the capital city's 15,000 residents, most of whom tragically believed the barrier reef would prove a natural force field. Thirty years later, Hurricane Hattie virtually picked up Belize City and flung it out to sea in a day of hell described by many as "an earthquake in a storm." It was Hattie that finally drove the country to move its capital inland, to a place called Belmopan.

Today, Belmopan is the official capital, but Belize City is the life pulse of Belize, the country's only genuine city. Despite its teetering existence, "it continues to swell and expand against all odds and without any plan," or so said the *Amandala*, Belize's biggest newspaper, in a 1986 editorial that became an infamous essay on Belize City. The editorial denounced the city as having a culture that "copies America too slavishly, and which has no stomach for sacrifice. But it is the culture that gives Belize City identity and makes it flashy and attractive, like a Saturday night hooker."

It is also that culture, that spicy slice of post-Colonial life by the sea, which eventually tends to win visitors over. Of course, Belize (as locals call the city) does have its high points, not the least of which is its people. Like all Belizeans, city residents are gregarious, laid-back and ever helpful to newcomers. Some are too helpful, though, as they hustle visitors to lend pocket change, buy drugs or join them in finding "some action." But visitors who stick to the better neighborhoods, and avoid venturing out alone at night, will find Belize City safer than big cities back home. At night, the infamous scene of petty crime is the Swing Bridge; avoid walking it from dusk to dawn, no matter how many people you're with.

The very best neighborhood is the **Fort George neighborhood**, named for the fort built here in 1803 but since destroyed. At the time, the area was a swampy island, but today it is draped across the tip of a peninsula on the northern side of Haulover Creek. The neighborhood's beauty lies in its big old whitewashed homes trimmed in filigree and framed by white picket fences and well-groomed lawns, and in the lavish traveler's palms and poinciana trees that decorate the yards and street corners. Here, along the waterfront Fort Street and Marine Parade, is **embassy row**, where several countries are represented by picturesque architecture (and, hopefully, competent staffs). One of the most appealing buildings in all of Belize, the **United States Embassy** (29 Gabourel Lane; 2-77161) is a distinguished, whitewashed building that was actually constructed in New England and brought to Belize in the 1800s.

At the tip of the peninsula stands the stately **Radisson Fort George Hotel**. Built in 1953 as a hotel, it once boasted the only swimming pool in Belize.

(Times have changed, and now there are more than two dozen.) A block from the hotel is the **Baron Bliss Memorial** (Marine Parade), an unspectacular slab of stone commemorating a spectacular act of generosity. In 1926, Englishman Henry Edward Ernest Victor Bliss, known as Baron Bliss, sailed into the harbor at Belize City. Sick with food poisoning he'd contracted in Trinidad, he was unable to leave his boat. For the next few months Bliss lived onboard, fishing and trying to recover from his illness. He never recovered, but he did befriend many Belizeans, who brought him food and took care of him. When he died, he left his $2 million fortune to the people of Belize.

The baron's generosity made him a national hero and paid for numerous public buildings, including health clinics, schools and the Bliss Institute museum. And though he never walked on Belize in life, he is buried here in a tomb, where land meets the sea. The **Fort George Lighthouse** stands sentinel nearby.

North on Marine Parade and facing the sea, **Memorial Park** is a rambling grassy area with queues of concrete benches, a tin-roofed gazebo, amphitheater and obelisk honoring the 40 Belizean men who died in World War I. Around the bend is the headquarters for information on Belize. The **Belize Audubon Society** (12 Fort Street; 2-35004, fax: 2-34985) will help plan excursions to the country's parks and preserves. Maps and books on Belize, as well as volumes on birding, wildlife and ecotourism are for sale. Over on Front Street, the **Belize Tourist Board** (83 North Front Street; 2-77213) has helpful employees, as well as maps and guides.

Continue west a few paces and you'll notice the white clapboard **Paslow Building** (Front and Queen streets), looking tired but dignified, and housing numerous government offices, including the **Belize Post Office** (2-72201). On the west side of the building, hiding out in a teeny room, is the **Belize Philatelic Bureau**, showcasing the country's marvelous stamps. You can purchase souvenir sheets of various editions; my favorites: the dazzling Coral Reef series and the poignant, infinitely detailed Maya Monuments.

From here, you can spot the **Swing Bridge** and its constant hum of activity. The city's geographic frame of reference, the bridge crosses Haulover Creek and swings open at about 6:00 a.m. and 5:30 p.m. daily, causing instant gridlock. Built in Liverpool, England, and brought to Belize in 1923, it is thought to be the only manually operated swing bridge still being used in the world. If you watch the four skinny men straining with their long poles to open the bridge every morning and night, you will know why it is the only one.

South of the bridge lies the heart of the city, centered around Albert and Regent streets and the Southern Foreshore. Here, buildings crowd shoulder-to-shoulder and street vendors hawk baskets of bread and tropical ices. Bicyclists, pedestrians with parasols, rickety old school buses and kamikaze taxis compete for the same narrow stretch of pavement. At high noon, the roadside park benches get so hot they burn right through your jeans.

At the southeastern foot of the Swing Bridge, you'll be met by the sparkling, modern, yellow-with-black-trim **Belize Commercial Center**. Opened in 1993, it feels like a mini-convention center, with a first floor crowded with Creole and Latin American foods and second and third floors lined with vendor-style shops, businesses and eateries. The first-floor **market** features wobbly tables and baskets overflowing with produce, from glassy red scotch bonnet peppers and shaggy boniato (a tuber) to silky red beans and juicy passion fruit. You'll also find catches of the day—anything from grouper and snapper to live iguana and sea turtles. The latter are endangered, so don't support the industry. If you have questions about produce, the friendly Belizean women (anxious to make a sale) will happily answer them. *Remember:* Buy only what you can peel yourself, and wash everything in purified water.

Away from the bridge, and where everyone seems to be heading, is **Brodies Department Store** (255 Albert Street; 2-77070). It's Belize's official department store, but don't expect Macy's; it's more like a crowded K-Mart with iffy air-conditioning.

Near here, Belize's own **Central Park** (bounded by Albert, Regent and Church streets) is bustling, small and strange, a sort of outdoor way station for street vendors, street people and salesmen of questionable character. Banks and other businesses line the park, and so does the white clapboard **Supreme Court** (Regent Street across from Central Park). The third Supreme Court to be built on the site (fires destroyed the first two), it's an attractive two-story building with neoclassic columns, a four-sided clock tower (pay no attention to the time—it's usually wrong) and a filigreed iron balcony, the prettiest in town.

A couple of blocks over along the sea, you'll find the **Bliss Institute** (1 Bliss Promenade; 2-72110, fax: 2-70726), a weathered white concrete edifice and center of Belize culture. Inside, there are a few permanent exhibits, including limestone altars uncovered from the ancient Maya city of Caracol. Traveling exhibits, sponsored by the resident Belize Arts Council, feature bamboo crafts and paintings by Belizean and international artists.

Near Regent Street's southern end, visiting dignitaries are often entertained at the graceful **Government House**, built around 1812 and designed by famed architect Christopher Wren. Across the street, you'll instantly recognize **St. John's Cathedral** (Regent and Albert streets) by its manicured lawns and dignified red-brick facade. The oldest Anglican church in Central America, it was built by slaves from 1812 to 1826, who were conveniently emancipated by the church in a formal ceremony in 1838. Despite many fires and hurricanes, St. John's still boasts its original sapodilla roof, mahogany beams and 1826 organ.

For a slice of Belize City life, wander the side streets between Regent Street and Southern Foreshore. Under the canopies of shady poinciana trees, brilliant parrots squawk from cages and women scrub their wash in big tubs.

Children tote heavy strings of fish, fresh from the wooden sloops bobbing in the nearby harbor.

West of the city center are neighborhoods not worth visiting but whose street names are worth mentioning: Armadillo, Iguana, Antelope, Gibnut and Pelican.

Yellow-headed parrot

On the north end of Belize City, you can look over to **Moho Caye**, a half-mile offshore from the airstrip. Earlier this century, the mite-size island yielded more historical mementos than all of Belize City. Pottery shards, pottery rings used as fishing sinkers, spear heads and two burial grounds testify to its days as a Maya fishing outpost. Even more remarkable were the thousands of manatee bones washed on the northern shore. Today, manatees still seek the warmth of nearby waters, and the tiny island is owned by **Maya Landings** (2-33075, fax: 2-30263), a marina and dive/sail boat operation offering week-long trips to the Blue Hole and to the Río Dulce in Guatemala.

You can also board a sailboat to Sergeant's Caye or Goff's Caye for a day of snorkeling and fishing. **Discovery Expeditions** (126 Freetown Road; 2-30748, fax: 2-30750) offers full-day trips, which include a box lunch, snorkel and fishing gear, and use of a dinghy and motor. Discovery has several locations around Belize City, including one at the Fiesta Inn Belize.

LODGING   For the most part, accommodations in Belize City are extremely basic, with four walls and a bed, plus a ceiling fan if you're lucky. Considering the often suffocating heat and the nagging problem of street hustlers, I highly recommend you take a room in or near the Fort George neighborhood, where several pleasant hotels offer air-conditioned rooms, or at the Ramada Royal Reef in the King's Park neighborhood.

The city's most distinguished establishment is the **Radisson Fort George Hotel** (Marine Parade; air-conditioning; cable TV; very expensive; 2-77400, fax: 2-73820), whose 100 rooms are among the plushest in Belize—and worth the price. Favored by business travelers, its lush, walled grounds with brick lanai and pool seem worlds away from the bustling street life. Rooms in the main building offer commanding views of the sea, and have that Belize rarity, cable TV. Near the gardens, rooms take on a tropical flavor. A fine restaurant and lounge round out the amenities.

Across the street, also owned by Radisson, is the pretty **Villa Belize** (13 Cork Street; air-conditioning; expensive to very expensive; 2-77400, fax:

2-73820). Everything in the lobby is vivid and tropical, from the green wicker settees to the shiny ceramic floors. Of the 41 rooms, 30 offer splendid sea views. There is a little swimming pool, but it overlooks neighboring apartment balconies strung with laundry. Of the many pluses: a helpful staff, topnotch restaurant and terrific location in the Fort George neighborhood.

Located in the Fort George neighborhood and definitely one of the town's best bargains, the 1930s colonial ✪ **Colton House** (9 Cork Street; private and shared baths; ceiling fans; two rooms with air-conditioning; moderate; 2-44666) invites with its front porch with double swings, polished pine floors, lacy draperies and shelves lined with good books. Congenial innkeepers Alan and Ondina Colton make sure guests are comfortable in the four spacious rooms. Each room has pine floors, plush carpets and a private entrance; two have private baths. There's also a separate garden room, complete with private bath, air-conditioning, refrigerator, microwave and TV. Rates include complimentary coffee.

If the Colton House is booked, try the **Fort Street Guest House** (4 Fort Street; shared bath; ceiling fans; budget; 2-30116, fax: 2-78808). It's not as classy, but the six bedrooms are quite cozy with their tongue-in-groove ceilings and floors, woven Guatemalan rugs and assortment of battered furniture. Unfortunately, the beds take up most of the room. It gets hot in the summer.

The pink **Château Caribbean** (6 Marine Parade; air-conditioning; cable TV; expensive; 2-30800, fax: 2-30900) is showing some wear, but it still imparts an island charm. Overlooking the sea, with a large pool encased in palmy grounds, the colonial mansion has 19 pleasant rooms with private balconies.

Close to the Swing Bridge, **North Front Street Guest House** (124 North Front Street; cold water; fans; budget; 2-77595) has eight featureless rooms that, nonetheless, are immaculate. The shower's cold, the bath's down the hall, but the price is right. Take heed of the disco across the street—it can get loud, especially on weekends.

In the upscale (for Belize City) neighborhood of King's Park, you'll find the **Fiesta Inn Belize** (Newtown Barracks; air-conditioning; cable TV; very expensive; 2-32670, fax: 2-32660). The best choice for young couples and families, the attractive teal building is set along the Caribbean Sea and boasts a fantasy pool (the best in Belize) with swim-up bar. There are 118 rooms, each with a sea view and decor that's contemporary but tropical: textured concrete walls, cane headboards and striking tones of plum, teal and auburn. Amenities include a hair salon, marina, several good restaurants and bars, and a gallery showcasing a different Belizean artist every month.

If you have to stay downtown, a good choice is the **Bellevue Hotel** (5 Southern Foreshore; air-conditioning; moderate; 2-77051, fax: 2-73253), whose two-story brick facade with arched windows curve along the seafront. It's a comfortable, timeworn place with a little garden, a wedge-shaped swimming pool and a bar called the Maya Tavern. All 37 rooms are carpeted and decorated with seashell-patterned bedspreads and rattan tables and chairs in unexciting shades of brown and olive. A few have a view to the sea, but, unfortunately, it's through chain link tacked over all the windows.

Reminiscent of a youth hostel, the Quaker-owned **Seaside Guest House** (3 Prince Street; shared bath; cold water; fans; budget; 2-78339) has dormitory accommodations plus five rooms with single beds. Sea breezes help cool things down, but it's still hot and noisy. Check out the extensive orchid collection. Hot breakfasts are US$3. Clean but funky.

Even if you don't stay at the **Mopan Hotel** (55 Regent Street; ceiling fans; some air-conditioning; moderate; 2-73356, fax: 2-75383), you should stop by and meet Jean and Tom Shaw. For decades, the two environmentalists have attracted a coterie of archaeologists, zoologists and other conservation devotees, who converge at the hotel bar for nights of impassioned discussion, and who don't seem to mind that the hotel is entirely run-down. The 12 bedrooms, scattered between an old frame house and a concrete block addition, are spartanly furnished but have clean sheets and private baths, and jalousie windows that let in the city noises. Several rooms have wall-unit air conditioners.

RESTAURANTS   Despite its reputation as a rice-and-beans country, Belize has much to offer in the way of skillfully prepared seafood dishes and gratifying home cooking. In Belize City, fine dining exists in hotel restaurants, while soulful fare can be found in seedy diners tucked here and there.

When the heat in the city becomes too much, cool down at **Scoops** (17 Eve Street; 2-44699; budget), an old-fashioned ice cream parlor. The ice cream is creamy and the milkshakes will satisfy any sweet tooth.

It may not be paradise, but the **Paradise Restaurant** (120 Eve Street; 2-31130; moderate to expensive) does sit right on the sea, enjoying water views and pretty decor. Colorful Belizean artwork is parked on the walls, and bright green cloths cover the tables. Seafood is the star. Order lobster, king crab, or shrimp sautéed with garlic, parmesan and jalapeños.

The fresh, inventive cuisine at **St. George's** (at the Radisson Fort George Hotel, Marine Parade; moderate; 2-77400) is not only delicious, it's reasonable. Situated along the sea, with pink starched linens and vases brimming with tropical flowers, the handsome dining room turns out dishes such as grouper filet with shrimp and white wine sauce, shrimp amaretto, bouillabaisse, lobster thermidor (in season) and stuffed baked stone crab. For breakfast, there are thick slabs of french toast and saucy eggs ranchero; for lunch, try the cobb salad, bacon cheeseburger or American-style pizza.

Glimmering oil lamps, brilliant tropical flowers and white eyelet tablecloths make **Fort Street Guest House and Restaurant** (4 Fort Street; moderate to expensive; 2-30116) an intimate place to dine. Set in a big whitewashed colonial house, the piped-in blues and Bogey and Bacall decor give a feeling of bygone days. The chalkboard menu is read tableside, listing about ten items the cook has prepared for the evening. Cajun shrimp, kingfish with sour cream and pineapple, and Caribbean chicken with vegetable stir-fry are a few choices.

The Grill (164 Newtown Barracks; moderate to expensive; 2-45020) has a reputation as an on-again, off-again establishment, but when I tried it, I found it exceptionally good. Fresh seafood, beef and chicken, grilled or bathed in light sauces, are served in a seafront room framed by candlelight and white linens. Tables are well-spaced for privacy, and the service is above par.

Goofy's Restaurant (6 Douglas Jones Street; 2-32480; budget) is family style, ultracasual, with a cluster of tables and TV shows radiating from the corner set. Among the Jamaican and Belizean specialties here are jerk chicken and pork, steamed beef, curry chicken and fried fish.

The dining room at the downtown **Bellevue Hotel** (5 Southern Foreshore; moderate; 2-77051) would be the last place you'd expect complex dishes. But here they are, served in a small but entirely cozy room of rattan chairs and carved wood sculptures by friendly, but slow-moving waitresses. For starters, try the smoked Belizean blue marlin, then move on to entrées such as grouper with cucumber cream sauce, chicken breasts filled with herbed cream cheese and served on a bed of pineapple and brandy sauce, or rock fish olé (stuffed with capers, olives and onions and topped with spicy tomato sauce).

Around the corner, on the first floor of a lovely whitewashed building decorated with arches and gingerbread, **GG's Café & Patio** (2-B King Street; budget; 2-74378) serves down-home Belizean fare like stewed pork, beef or chicken, pork steaks and burgers slathered with hot sauce. Nothin' fancy, the inside is a mishmash of nautical and south-of-the-border decor, with plastic tablecloths, wood chairs and wood-paneled ceilings. Or, dine out on the shaded patio.

Dit's (50 King Street; budget; 2-73330) is as Belizean as they come: friendly and uproarious, with plastic tables and local artwork, and Campbell's soup cans sold at the cash register. Choose from meat pies, "fry" chicken, *garnaches* (fried tortillas stuffed with tomatoes and onions), and rice and beans with stew chicken, beef or fish.

The funkiest diner in town, **Macy's** (18 Bishop Street; budget; 2-73419) became famous in the late 1980s when England's Queen Elizabeth dined here on gibnut (a large rodent). The rodent has been elevated to "royal gibnut" on the menu. Right beside it is oxtail soup, and more traditional offerings like stew rice and beans and grouper. Sweet local fruit juices, from pulpy papaya to slushy watermelon, come in tall cool glasses. It's all served in a little room with folding iron chairs, clanking screen doors and a TV playing American soap operas.

SHOPPING   For a wide selection of Belizean arts, go to the **National Handicraft Sales Center** (Fort Street; 2-33636), where the work of over 100 artisans is displayed, including carvings of zericote, mahogany, redwood, jabillo, rosewood, garandillo and Santa Maria woods. The store also features ceramics, stone carvings, pottery, baskets and jewelry.

Few people would think to go shopping at the **Belize Philatelic Bureau** (in the Paslow Building, corner of Front and Regent streets), but the country's exquisitely designed stamps really do make great gifts. Souvenir stamp sheets include dozens of historical and environmental themes.

You'll find vintage greeting cards at **The Book Center** (4 Church Street; 2-77457), as well as Belizean literature, two-day-old copies of the *Miami Herald*, and references on local cuisine, history and art.

The pleasant, colorful **Go Tees** (23 Regent Street; 2-74082) purveys tropical clothing, wood jewelry, postcards by Belizean artists and books on Belize.

The **Belize Bookshop** (corner of Regent Street and Rectory Lane; 2-72054) stocks everything from coloring books and tattered, third-generation paperbacks to excellent books on Belize.

If you'd rather slum it for bargain prices, walk along King Street between Albert and Canal streets. The narrow stores here are jammed with electronics, sneakers, cosmetics, lingerie and T-shirts.

NIGHTLIFE   Most local bars are seedy joints and not places for tourists. Stick to the hotel bars, such as the Radisson Fort George's **Paddle Lounge** (Marine Parade; 2-77400), where a big-screen TV shows the latest American sports.

The most pleasant place for a drink in Belize City is **Calypso** (Newtown Barracks; 2-32670) at the Fiesta Inn Belize hotel. High-ceilinged and open to the sea, it's cooled by breezes. There's live calypso on Thursday and Friday, reggae on Saturday, and Latin sounds on Sunday. Indoors at the Fiesta Inn, the **Blue Hole Lounge** (2-32670) is not nearly as happening, but you can settle into a cane-back chair and watch the big screen or gaze at the swimming pool. A stereo plays punta rock and American tunes.

The Belize Arts Council sponsors concerts and national and international theater and dance performances at the **Bliss Institute** (1 Bliss Promenade; 2-72110).

GETTING THERE: International flights land at Philip S. W. Goldson International Airport in Ladyville, nine miles from Belize City. The easiest way to get into Belize City is by taxi, which costs US$15 (the maximum fare allowed by the government, so don't pay more). During the day buses regularly run between the airport and the city and while it's not as speedy as taking a taxi, it only costs US$2.

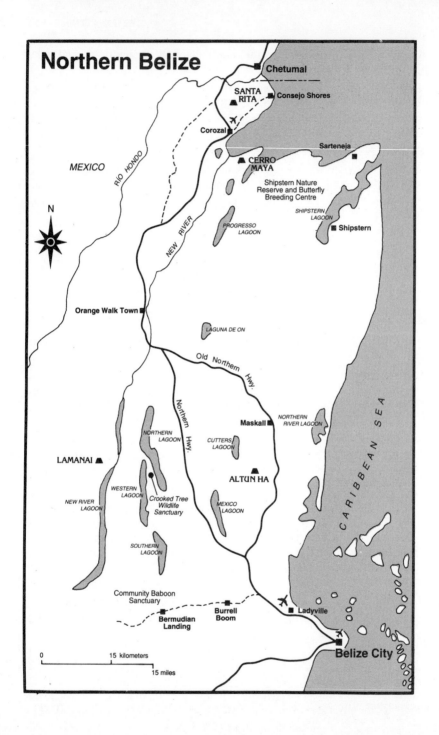

Northern Belize

MEXICO

N

RÍO HONDO

NEW RIVER

Chetumal

SANTA
RITA

Consejo Shores

Corozal

Sarteneja

CERRO
MAYA

Shipstern Nature
Reserve and Butterfly
Breeding Centre

PROGRESSO
LAGOON

SHIPSTERN
LAGOON

Shipstern

Orange Walk Town

LAGUNA DE ON

Old Northern Hwy.

Northern Hwy.

NORTHERN
LAGOON

Maskall

NORTHERN
RIVER LAGOON

CUTTERS
LAGOON

LAMANAI

NEW RIVER
LAGOON

WESTERN
LAGOON

Crooked Tree
Wildlife
Sanctuary

MEXICO
LAGOON

ALTUN HA

CARIBBEAN SEA

SOUTHERN
LAGOON

Community Baboon
Sanctuary

Bermudian
Landing

Burrell
Boom

Ladyville

Belize City

0   15 kilometers

15 miles

EIGHT

Northern Belize

Just three decades ago, northern Belize was a forbidding land choked by dense jungle and mired in swamps, and the only road was a potholed trail that rarely got you from here to there without some calamity. Today, the Northern Highway is fairly smooth and lined with small villages, fields of shaggy sugar cane, and ponds populated by wood storks and egrets. Of course, the jungle retains its hold—thanks to conservation efforts by Belizeans—and "highway" traffic is just as likely to be a sprinting Jesus Christ lizard as a car.

From Belize City, the Northern Highway wends 100 miles to the Yucatán border, past several modern-day villages and two magnificent and mysterious ancient cities that are testaments to Maya greatness, Altun Ha and Lamanai, as well as endless remnants of stone houses and walls. Traveling this northern corridor, you are constantly reminded of the ancient Maya civilization, whether it's the house mounds at one's jungle lodge or the 1000-year-old well near a swimming hole.

LADYVILLE TO CROOKED TREE

The first town north of Belize City is neither ancient nor mysterious. Rather, **Ladyville** is best known as the site of Belize's **Philip S. W. Goldson International Airport**. It's pint-sized, as international airports go, but locals love to hang out on the receiving deck and watch the 747s come booming in. Just south of the airport on the Northern Highway, and one of the first sites visitors see in Belize, stands a steel monument depicting five Belizeans, each representing one of the country's five major ethnic groups—Creole, Garifuna, *Mestizo*, Mopan Maya and Kekchi Maya. North of the airport is "downtown" Ladyville: a gas station, tumble-down schoolhouse, several no-name bars and usually dozens of children playing along the street.

LODGING   If you need a room near the international airport, the place to stay is the **Belize Biltmore Plaza** (Mile 3, Northern Highway; air-conditioning; expensive; 2-32302, fax: 2-32301). Opened in 1991, the low-slung, coral-washed buildings encase a lush courtyard of traveler's palms and oleanders, a swimming pool and pond. The lobby is done in British colonial style, with white-paned glass, white wicker and attendants in pith helmets. Each of the 90 rooms opens onto the courtyard and gives the feeling of a spacious motel with contemporary comforts such as bathtubs (unusual in Belize), cable television and telephones. Popular with business travelers, who enjoy the hotel's clubby bar and semiformal restaurant.

Just around the corner from the airport but worlds away in ambience, the **Belize River Lodge** (Northern Highway, Ladyville; very expensive; 25-2002, fax: 25-2298) offers total escapism. Here, tucked along a flourishing river-bank, with stands of coconut palms and banana plants and carpets of green lawn running down to the river, are several clapboard cottages whose ma-hogany walls harbor decades of fish tales. The lodge is indeed reputed among anglers, who return each year to stalk the giant tarpon that seethe, piranha-like, in the river. For those who prefer flats or reef fishing, Belizean owners Marguerite Miles and Mike Heusner have an ample fleet of skiffs and top-notch guides to take you just about anywhere. They also offer six- and seven-night fishing "cruises" aboard their larger cruisers. Those who stay at the lodge will find cozy, all-wood cottages with eclectic touches such as driftwood lamps, brown patchwork quilts and comfortingly worn books lining the shelves. Minimum stay is six nights, and includes family-style meals and guide for five days, with only two anglers per guide—the best way to fish.

RESTAURANTS   Rich maroon carpets, sheer lacy drapes and mahogany ta-bles and chairs give the **Victorian Room** (at the Belize Biltmore Plaza, Mile 3, Northern Highway; expensive; 2-32302) a slightly formal air. For many travelers, it's a welcome change from the wear-your-flip-flops funkiness of most Belize eateries. Plus, the extensive menu satisfies both the domestic and international palate. For soups, there's onion gratinée, goulash or fish-erman's soup; for salads, a tossed caesar or Belizean potato. Entrées include everything from spaghetti bolognaise and filet mignon to grouper with ar-tichokes and stew chicken with beans and rice.

NIGHTLIFE   Your best bet is an after-dinner drink at the American-style **Squire's Lounge** (at the Belize Biltmore Plaza, Mile 3, Northern Highway; 2-32302). It's dark and cozy, with entertainment ranging from local bal-ladeers and Caribbean artists to karaoke parties.

GETTING THERE: If you've just arrived at the international airport, it's easy to rent a car inside the terminal. If you're coming from Belize City, you can take a Batty Brothers or Venus bus, which have frequent daily service. Taxis can also be chartered but are expensive, about US$15 one-way from Belize City.

CROOKED TREE AREA

From Ladyville, the patchwork asphalt called the Northern Highway launches into wide-open savannah and low-lying mangrove forests, with occasional pit stops like the cinderblock Chillville Lodge, announcing "cool A/C and

TV," but looking unlike like any place one would stop lest she were positively down on her luck, or had imbibed an unconscionable amount of Belizean rum.

After several miles comes the turnoff for the village of **Burrell Boom**, which will take you nine miles down a dusty, rocky trail into forests of pine-oak and cohune and swamp, until you arrive in **Bermudian Landing**. The Landing and surrounding villages were originally settled by Maya, who left their calling cards in the form of house mounds, which still pepper the wooded landscape, and in the Maya people—many direct descendants—who live and farm here. It was formerly called Butchers Landing because local cattle were brought here to be slaughtered before heading downriver to Belize City markets. Several decades ago, it was renamed for the band of Bermudian buccaneers who settled on this high bank in the 1600s.

It was the logging industry that shaped the area, starting in 1650 and continuing for some three hundred years. Villages testify to those logging days with their whimsical names of "boom," "landing," "bank," "walk" and "pen." Loggers first settling an area called it a landing or bank (for riverbank); once established, they would stretch a boom, or heavy iron chain, across the river to trap floating logs. They might also plant fields of crops where you could "walk," or raise cattle in pens. Today, you'll find villages such as Flowers Bank (formerly Flowers Walk), Lime Walk, May Pen and Isabella Bank. There's also Scotland Half-Moon, named for its Scottish settlers, and Ben Bow Creek, the namesake of one pirate Admiral Ben Bow, who supposedly spent several rum-crazed nights in these wilds.

Bermudian Landing may seem just as wild to visitors today. Few people own cars and fewer have telephones, but most any teenager can tell you the jungle cure for stomachache, and even small children know the difference between a good snake and a bad one. Absorbing exhibits on snakes, and on endangered black howler monkeys, await in the museum at the **Community Baboon Sanctuary** (admission). Black howlers, which are also known as baboons, are found only in Belize, southern Mexico, the Yucatán and northern Guatemala, and are rarely spotted in great numbers.

Little was known about the howlers in 1980 when Dr. Robert Horwich, a Wisconsin primatologist, watched a documentary titled *Amate—The Fig Tree*. It was made by well-known filmmaker Richard Foster, who lives in Belize and who had captured footage of an endearing troop of howlers living in a fig tree near Bermudian Landing. Horwich immediately flew to Belize and began research on the howlers. What he found was not only a healthy population of the monkeys, but a group of villagers willing to protect them.

In 1985, at a small gathering in a tiny clapboard house, the villagers of Bermudian Landing and surrounding areas formally opened their Community Baboon Sanctuary. The event not only secured the future of the howlers, it began what was perhaps the world's first grassroots sanctuary, where resi-

*Howler
monkeys*

dents—not the government or some conservation organization—rallied to save the wildlife in their own jungle backyards.

Eleven villagers first signed a pledge to change their farming methods in a three-square-mile area. Their mission was to protect vegetation along the Belize River banks, various corridors of trees, and other areas where the howlers thrive. For the villagers—most of whom were surviving at poverty level—it meant using even less land to grow their crops; hence, less food for their families.

Over the years, the hardships have pulled the villagers together, and today 125 farmers and ranchers are members of the sanctuary, which, in turn, has blossomed to 20 square miles. Former howler and jaguar hunters now serve as sanctuary guides, and local families earn small fees by hosting visitors in their homes. Studies by sanctuary manager Camille Young show that about 90 percent of the villagers have kept their promise to protect the vegetation. Perhaps the most convincing evidence of success, however, is that while there were 500 howlers here in 1985, today there are more than 1400.

Which means that visitors to the Community Baboon Sanctuary will most certainly see a howler, even a whole family of howlers, who are instantly appealing with their cherublike faces, beseeching eyes and tiny hands and feet. Their narrow throats magnify their thunderous roars—often mistaken for jaguar screams—so they can be heard more than a mile away.

To find the howlers you will, of course, need a guide, and a museum attendant will be happy to fetch you one from "downtown" Bermudian Landing. Local guides are infinitely versed on the native flora, pointing out the spiny bamboo, red ginger, bromeliads and guanacaste trees that line the three-and-a-half miles of trails and the Belize River, which flows through the sanctuary.

Spiny bamboo, one learns, protects the riverbanks from erosion, and red ginger is called forest "Visine" because its juice takes the red out of irritated eyes. The petals of the bromeliads can store up to two gallons of water and provide a home for 12 species of insects, while the trunk of the guanacaste tree was used by the Maya to make dugout canoes. The acidlike sap of the poisonwood tree is so poisonous it burns its own trunk. The stately kapok tree—the rainforest's tallest—towers more than 200 feet, but alas, all its limbs cling to its crown. Here, also, are many mapola trees, whose canopies are loved by howler monkeys. On most days, you'll spot families of monkeys scurrying through the treetops. The babies are not much bigger than your hand.

The monkeys are just some of the thousands of jungle residents you're apt to see. Foot-wide butterflies dance in and out of forest shadows and red-eyed tree frogs emit flashes of color. Iguanas sun on splintered logs poking out across the river, and leafcutter ants parade across the jungle floor, hoisting freshly cut leaves in their own antish, Herculean style. My guide and I even encountered a boa constrictor, all seven feet of him, stretched across the footpath.

If you'd rather explore the sanctuary on horseback or by canoe, guided excursions are available. Fishing guides are also available for those who'd like to try for tarpon, snapper or catfish in the Belize River—though it's strictly catch and release. To find out about tours, call the Belize Audubon Society at 2-35004.

Back on the Northern Highway, about 19 paved miles north and 4 miles west down a white marl road, lies a bird sanctuary. The centerpiece of the 3000-acre **Crooked Tree Wildlife Sanctuary** (admission) is the vast Northern Lagoon, whose shallow waters are perennially darkened by flocks of fantastic birds. Birdwatchers and birders (there is a difference, the former being a more casual observer) also flock to this place, setting up their telescopes and cameras along the shores, scouting out such unusual creatures as purple gallinules and ruddy crakes, social flycatchers and lesser yellow-legs, olive-throated parakeets and white-collared seedeaters. Most species have funny local names; the spot-breasted wren, for instance, has been creolized to "katy-yu-baby-di-cry," no doubt because a man claimed its song mimics the voice of a certain woman.

The unusual creature most people come to see is the jabiru stork. The Western Hemisphere's largest flying bird, it is formidable and fascinating, boasting a 12-foot wing span. Arrive during the dry season (October through February is the very best time), when the storks and thousands of other birds, including peregrine falcons and boat-billed herons, create a flurry of activity.

It is usually easy to get close-up views of the birds from the paths that wend along the Northern Lagoon, as well as from the Western Lagoon, located on the opposite side of Crooked Tree Village. Along the paths are many anhingas, who dive underwater to snag fish, then emerge to dry their water-gorged wings on a tree branch. Locals rent boats and offer guided boat trips, but they're expensive (up to US$80), and the scenery is much the same. When the rainy season starts, the sanctuary floods and many birds leave.

Before you visit, call the **Belize Audubon Society** (2-35004 in Belize City) to check current conditions.

Once at the sanctuary, stop by the **visitors center** and pick up a map and list of birds. The warden there can also provide other information or arrange for a local guide, and can tell you about **Crooked Tree Village**, home to 700 people and seemingly just as many pigs, chickens and skinny dogs. Half a dozen dirt roads wind through the village, past Jones Bar, Alice Store, the town telephone, and the town generator that gets turned off at midnight (it used to shut down earlier, but local barflies complained).

If you have some time, take one of the horse-and-buggy rides (ask at the visitors center) offered by several local farmers. Ask them to point out all the mango and cashew trees the village is known for. Every May, at the Crooked Tree Cashew Festival, locals go all out with nonstop parties, including Caribbean folktelling and outdoor theater. Attending visitors are invited on nature walks, river trips and tours of the nearby Maya ruins.

ALTUN HA   Just south of Crooked Tree Village and the sanctuary is a fork where the Northern Highway meets the **Old Northern Highway**. Formerly *the* highway in northern Belize, this sliver of lonesome, well-worn pavement bumps and turns for 40 miles past cohune palms, thick bush and a scattering of clapboard houses. It is so narrow, a taxi driver points out, that when he meets a car, "we play chicken."

The road is the reason **Altun Ha** (Old Northern Highway, 31 miles north of Belize City; admission) was discovered. In 1957, quarriers looking for stone to build the road selected some 2000-year-old specimens at this Maya site. As they dug, they uncovered more than just rock mounds. There were 13 structures surrounding two plazas, including one 60-foot temple now called **Temple of the Sun God**. Several years later, as archaeologists did their own digging at the temple, they made a thrilling find: the head of Kinich Ahau, the sun god, carved around 600 A.D. from a single piece of jade. The largest carved jade artifact ever discovered on the Maya Route, it weighs nearly ten pounds and is masterfully sculpted. (Unfortunately, you won't be able to look upon its hideous countenance—forked tongue, crossed eyes and cauliflower ears—as Kinich Ahau now resides in a Belize bank vault.)

What made the jade head even more spectacular was that it was located next to the remains of a priest. The holy man had been laid atop a wooden platform, adorned with jaguar and puma skins and necklaces of oyster and jade, and buried in a small pyramid. Rarely did the Maya bury their dead in temples, so what was the significance? The excavation team, led by Canadian archaeologist David Pendergast, never reached a conclusion. What they did find, however, were six more priests entombed in the temple—an exhilarating discovery in the first full-scale excavation in Belize. Several of the crypts had been defiled by fire, soil or broken roof slabs. The desecrators were not modern-day looters but early Maya—an indication, Pendergast wrote, that the society may have collapsed at the hands of revolting peasants.

A Classical city that reaches out for one-and-a-half miles, Altun Ha was a link in the Caribbean trade route that ran north through the Yucatán. It was a town and minor ceremonial center, lacking any stelae, yet Pendergast found remnants of jade and copal tree resin obviously used in rituals—a practice rare among the Maya. Many of the fragments were found on the round altar atop the Sun God temple, known as **building B-4** in **Plaza B**, including exquisitely carved pendants that had been shattered and cast into a blazing fire. Pendergast believes that this altar held some unique significance, noting that "the bits of jade, resin and charcoal were scattered over the floor around the altar, and left as some sort of fossilized ceremony, to be discovered some 1300 years later."

Like many Maya structures, the Temple of the Sun God was constantly being improved on; Pendergast noted eight separate construction periods. And while it was obviously the premier building, Altun Ha boasts five additional temples, surrounding **Plaza A**. Four are dedicated to the forces of nature—the sun, rain, wind and moon—while the fifth, the **Temple of the Green Tomb**, held human remains and hundreds of pieces of jade jewelry, some quite elaborate.

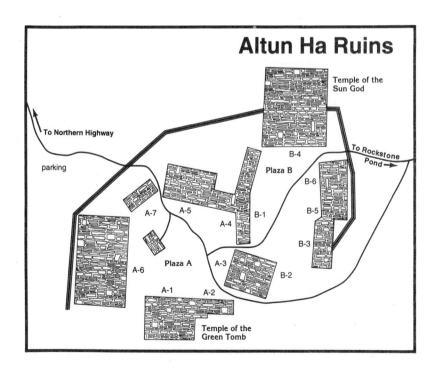

Altun Ha Ruins

Temple of the Sun God

To Northern Highway

parking

B-4

Plaza B

To Rockstone Pond →

B-6

A-7   A-5

B-1   B-5

A-4

B-3

A-6   Plaza A   A-3

B-2

A-1   A-2

Temple of the Green Tomb

Away from the plazas, a quarter-mile trail through the jungle leads to a misty, lime-colored reservoir. Called **Rockstone Pond**, the clay-lined, spring-fed basin was enlarged by the Maya, as evidenced by the sharp stone blocks—probably digging tools—found around the shoreline. At the south end, they built a dam of stone and clay to keep the water from seeping into surrounding swamps. The reservoir is surrounded by house mounds, the remains of waterfront residences.

Standing at the lip of the pond, watching the parrots skip through the trees, listening to the *hoot-hoot* call of blue-crowned motmots, spying the tail of a fleeing opossum, it is impossible not to wonder if the occupants of those houses saw and heard these same creatures, felt the same steamy haze before an afternoon rain, inhaled the skunky smell of the forest floor. After all, more than 1000 years have passed, but the jungle has remained virtually unchanged.

And therein lies Altun Ha's added appeal. Though it is one of Belize's most popular Maya sites—it is close to Belize City and easy to find—Altun Ha still belongs to the rainforest. Except for the occasional mid-morning and mid-afternoon tour buses, there are no crowds—only mosquitoes, whose swarms will blacken your skin and attack your body in the most troublesome places. Coat yourself in repellent, then sightsee at leisure, exploring the ceremonial structures and house mounds sprinkled around the lush jungle clearing.

LODGING AND RESTAURANTS   Birders know **Chaux Hiix Lodge** (ceiling fans; very expensive; for reservations, call 800-765-2611 in the United States) as one of the choicest spots for catching a glimpse of Belize's unusual winged creatures. Of course, it doesn't hurt that the lodge is wonderfully remote, located downriver from the Crooked Tree Wildlife Sanctuary and upriver from the Community Baboon Sanctuary. Just getting to Chaux Hiix usually involves animal encounters, as guests travel 45 minutes by boat down jungle-lined Spanish Creek from the outpost of Lemonal. Four rooms in two duplex cabanas aren't fancy, but they are comfortable enough, offering hot showers and screened jalousie windows. Three new cottages offer a little more privacy, with hot showers and air-conditioning. The lodge rests on the widest point of Sapodilla Lagoon and is enveloped by more than 4000 acres of jungle and low pine ridge. More importantly, it borders the ancient Maya town of Chaux Hiix, where archaeologists from the University of Indiana are still uncovering fascinating clues to its existence, including structures dating all the way from 1500 B.C. to 1500 A.D. There is so much yet uncovered that workers attempting to dig outhouse trenches kept finding layers of relics. Tours of the ruins, as well as guided nature tours, fishing excursions and canoeing trips, meals and snacks and transportation from Belize City are included in the rate. Because getting there is so time consuming, a three-night stay is required.

In the village of Crooked Tree, three rustic lodges open their doors to visitors. All are extremely basic, so expect to rough it:

Red-eyed tree frogs

On the rim of Northern Lagoon, facing a dirt beach and a wobbly pier, **Crooked Tree Resort** (moderate to expensive; 2-77745, fax: 2-74007) features ten round bamboo cabanas peaked with thatch roofs and shaded by bullet trees. Furnishings are simple but clean, with well-swept mahogany floors, pine walls and private baths with hot water. There's a small restaurant serving home cooking, and the village bar is spitting distance—not a good situation if there's a party going on. Two birdwatchers I met stayed awake several nights, listening to the boom-boom-boom of a band that played until dawn. Translation: Before you book a room, ask if there are any special events scheduled at the bar.

The five cabanas at **Paradise Inn** (fans; moderate; 2-12084) look remarkably like the ones at Crooked Tree Resort, located just south along Northern Lagoon. All face the water and catch a perpetual breeze. Belizean specialties, including local fish plied with cashews from village trees, are served in the budget-priced restaurant here.

On the opposite side of the village, set along a picturesque shore of a lagoon, **Bird's Eye View Lodge** (ceiling fans; moderate; for reservations, call 2-32040 in Belize City, fax: 2-24869) is a drab yellow cinderblock building whose two rooms are surprisingly attractive and comfortable. Belizean tile covers the floors and hot water emanates from the private bath. The dining room is the fanciest in Crooked Tree.

Local villagers built the ten massive cabanas of **Pretty See Jungle Ranch** (Mile Post 39, Old Northern Highway, Maskall Village; ceiling fans; very expensive; phone/fax: 31-2005), as well as a great lodge whose thatched roof is in the style of Tahitian longhouses. The ranch opened in 1996 on 1360 acres of wild savannah with five miles of rivers and a crocodile pond (go at sunset, when the crocs cruise the surface like silent missiles). The cabanas are spread apart and have soaring thatch ceilings and skylights. The interior features beautifully carved wood and furnishings, mahogany floors and big poster beds with sculpted jaguar feet. You can shower or bathe by moonlight on private verandas (all cabanas have indoor showers, too), listening to the sounds of crickets and frogs and birds all around, or to the Mozart CD that's been slipped into your stereo. Take your meals on the big porch of the lodge, enjoying fat French toast in the mornings and lasagna, chicken piccata, or shrimp with pesto cream sauce in the evenings. Other pursuits: horseback riding or a ride in a horse-drawn carriage, river canoeing, guided jungle hikes, and boat trips to Ambergris Caye. Bring lots of repellent: it's extra buggy in this part of Belize, especially in rainy season.

GETTING THERE: It's easy to drive to Crooked Tree Wildlife Sanctuary and Altun Ha. Both have on-site guides who will show you around.

ORANGE WALK TOWN AND LAMANAI

The modern-day hub of northern Belize lies 37 miles north of Altun Ha along the Old Northern Highway. You'll know you're getting close to **Orange Walk Town** when you see the old trucks stuffed with cut sugar cane, and notice a sweet molasses smell in the air. Sugar cane is the number-one business in this working town, one of Belize's biggest. Home to 11,000 people, Orange Walk was originally a logging outpost that became a refuge for *Mestizos* fleeing the Caste War in nearby Yucatán. Mexican influence is evident everywhere, from the tortilla bakeries and Wild West–style storefronts to the weathered mission churches.

Over the past few decades, Orange Walk has attracted a rich ethnic mix that includes Chinese, Hindu Indians, Maya and Mennonites. The latter, dressed in tattered straw hats and baggy overalls cinched with twine, ride into town in horse-drawn buggies to trade crops for sugar or supplies. There isn't much in downtown to attract a traveler, considering it's mainly tired cinderblock buildings, ice factories and a string of churches. In fact, the number-one reason most people come to Orange Walk is Lamanai.

The Maya would no doubt be pleased with the present-day way to arrive at **Lamanai**: a two-hour, backwater boat trip. After all, Lamanai means "submerged crocodile," a name befitting a city sprawled on the jowls of a gorged lagoon. The trip starts near Orange Walk, on the New River, which winds southward past an old rum factory, slash-and-burn farms, and Mennonite villages.

Along the way, women wash their clothes in the clear warmth of the water, and long-nose bats sleep in hollow tree trunks above the river. Long-legged jacana birds, flaunting fluorescent green wings and neon yellow beaks, trot across colossal lily pads, and fields of emerald sea grass wave beneath the water's surface. Shy boat-billed herons hide along the riverbanks, and snail kites whisk through the sky.

It would be enough just to witness the surreality of the river, but what awaits afterward is even more riveting. Here, where the river yawns into a wide lagoon, several thatched buildings gather at the water's edge. At their flanks is a once-grand city that still presides over this part of the jungle—an ancient Manhattan, some 720 buildings spread across 950 acres, obscured in a mantle of massive trees and greedy vines. Leaf and rubble paths curl between Lamanai's buildings, many of which tower above the jungle canopy and form a mystical maze. The rattling purrs of unseen cicada insects flood the forest, and the panicked squawk of a brown jay—the jungle siren—warns of impeding danger.

The waterfront thatched buildings (including a mini-museum, gift shop, and restrooms) are left over from the days of Canadian archaeologist David Pendergast, who excavated the area during the 1970s and 1980s. While Pendergast's teams resurrected buildings, they also sought clues to the lifestyles of Lamanai's former inhabitants. They took samples of lagoon sediment, for instance, which revealed good levels of pollen and suggested the Maya were growing corn as early as 1500 B.C. And they combed the primeval rot of Lamanai's garbage dumps, only to find that these ancient Manhattanites fancied deer and turtle.

Pendergast also brought some modern-day gentility to the jungle setting, for when *Equinox* writer Ronald Wright dined with him in the late 1980s, he recalls that their meal "was followed by cookies and tea, and it would have been hard to imagine oneself in the heart of Belize were it not for the tarantula that (one of the archaeology students) discovered in the teapot."

Today, Maya caretakers live in the thatched village, and excavations and restorations continue on several of the ancient buildings. Wandering around the hulking stone structures, it is difficult to believe that this great ceremonial center was begun around 1500 B.C. Even more astounding, it was still inhabited in the 19th century, making it one of the longest occupied Maya sites.

In 1860, the British Honduras Company Ltd. showed up on Lamanai's shores with dreams of building a sugar factory. It did indeed construct a mill and import laborers from Jamaica, Barbados and China, but the workers were not trained in making sugar and the mill was too primitive for the task. In 1875, sugar making became history at Lamanai, though the brief attempt is remembered today in the ruins of the old mill, including a flywheel and boiler, located south of the city center.

Two hundred years earlier, the Spanish had come to Lamanai and, eager to force their religion on the Maya, built a Christian church. The Maya were not so eager to convert and destroyed most of the building. Missionaries soon arrived and put up a second, more stylish church, but the Maya were not impressed. This, too, they tried to demolish, though more of it survived. Remnants of both missions can be seen today north of Lamanai's center.

Far greater than those houses of worship are the Maya ceremonial structures. The one known as **Lag**, or **structure N10-43**, rises to 112 feet and was the tallest in the Maya civilization when it was created in 100 B.C. Today, it is the largest Preclassic building on the Maya Route. A sturdy flight of stairs runs up the front, depositing visitors on a platform that looks across the pastoral Maya lowlands and slow, snaking New River. It is on this platform that the Maya likely performed complex religious ceremonies. Among the more bizarre, men pierced their penises with stingray spines and women dragged strings of thorns across their tongues. Prisoners of war were typically beheaded, though noble ones received special treatment: their hearts were torn out while still alive.

Lag faces a good-sized **ball court**, where Maya athletes played *pok-ta-pok*, a basketball-style sport using a small rubber ball. In the center of the court Pendergast found a massive stone disc; under the disc, he made one of his most thrilling discoveries: a pool of liquid mercury, the first ever uncovered at a Maya site. The mercury was among several pottery vessels containing jade and shell objects that were no doubt part of a special offering.

The offerings made at **structure N10-7**, south of the ball court, seem to have included children. Here, behind a remarkably detailed stone stelae of a Maya ruler, Pendergast found the bones of six children. Why the people of Lamanai would sacrifice their own children remains a mystery, since human sacrifice was not customary among the Maya. Across the plaza stands the **Jaguar Temple (structure N10-9)**, built in the 6th century and embellished with stairs in the 8th and 13th centuries. Among the finds here: a giant red and black bowl, a jade mask and a pair of Early Classic jade earrings.

North of here, the 60-foot-tall Mask-Decorated Temple, or **structure N9-56**, rises hauntingly along the New River Lagoon. It is wildly adorned with stone masks, though the eye is instantly drawn to one particular visage—the 12-foot-tall face of a man, his nose fat and flattened, his eyes heavily lidded and slitted like a jaguar's, his features markedly Oriental. The temple's architecture reveals four separate construction phases, beginning in 200 B.C. and ending, incredibly, some 1500 years later.

There are numerous other masks and stelae, and buildings containing flint and pottery, at Lamanai. In fact, it takes at least four hours to explore the two-square-mile city center—with a guide, of course. But don't count on finding any at Lamanai; it's best to hire a guide a day before you plan to visit.

LODGING   Set up high along the banks of the New River Lagoon, with views of the water and the lofty temples of Lamanai, is **Lamanai Outpost** (ceiling fans; expensive; for reservations, call 2-33578). The 18 wood and palm-thatch cabanas are attractive, entirely restful, and located but a stone's throw from the Lamanai archaeological reserve. Explore the ruins at leisure or take a canoe or windsurfer for a jungly lagoon ride. There's a dining room (meals cost extra, but are reasonably priced) and bar, and plenty of daily excursions for the asking. Round-trip transportation from Belize City is included in the rate. Spend the night here—you won't regret it.

Few travelers have the need (or desire) to stay in Orange Walk Town, but if you find yourself stuck for the night, try **Hotel Barons** (40 Belize-Corozal Road; some rooms with ceiling fans, some with air-conditioning; some rooms with phone and cable TV; budget to moderate; 3-22518). The downtown hostelry looks a little weary, but has basic rooms that are fairly clean and come with battered furniture, assorted tile designs and plenty of street noise. For a little more, you get cable television, a telephone and air-conditioning that not only keeps you cool but drowns out that pesky street noise.

RESTAURANTS   Of the many Chinese restaurants in Orange Walk, **Lee's** (11 San Antonio Road; budget to moderate; 3-22174) stands out. The interior is cool, clean and modern, if not utilitarian, and the portions generous and tasty. Besides the traditional sweet and sours, chop sueys and chow meins, there's baked fish and grilled pork chops.

GETTING THERE: Orange Walk is easily accessible by car or by taking a Batty Brothers or Venus bus from Belize City. Lamanai, however, is best reached with a guide.

Boats leave from various points around Orange Walk Town for the four-hour round-trip ride to the ruins. One of the more popular launch spots is **Jim's Cool Pool**, at the Northern Highway toll bridge south of Orange Walk. Brothers Joel and Anthony Armstrong, who live with their families and flea-bitten dogs in an old yellow school bus along the river, will usually take you to Lamanai in their motorboat. Excellent Lamanai tours are offered by **Herminio Novelo's Jungle River Tours** (Lovers Lane, Orange Walk Town; 3-20348 or 3-22293), with extensive narrative on birds and other wildlife, medicinal plants and archaeology. Or try **Discovery Expeditions** (2-31063, fax: 2-30750 in Belize City), which offers excursions aboard the *Lamanai Lady* riverboat.

During the dry season (November through February), it is possible to drive to Lamanai from Orange Walk down a rocky, rutted path that looks a lot like a road. It's 36 miles one way, but the jarring trip takes about two hours. Before you strike out on your own, check road conditions and get directions from a local hotel or travel agency. **Caribbean Holiday and Travel Service** (51 Main Street, Orange Walk Town; 3-22803) is a good place to try.

COROZAL

If you've been awed by the brilliant butterflies weaving around the Belize forests, don't miss the **Shipstern Nature Reserve and Butterfly Breeding Centre** (about an hour's drive north from Orange Walk). Here, on a sunny day, butterflies are so thick they appear a constant whirlwind of color (they hide in the foliage on cloudy days). More than 200 species reside within a mesh enclosure that resembles a mini-forest. Visitors can wander through, learning about the butterflies' breeding cycles and extensive research being done here. Of course, many more creatures reside within this 22,000-acre reserve, which is unique in Belize because it takes in both hardwood and mangrove and swamp, or bajo, forests. Wading birds find the miles of salt lagoons and mangrove marshes safe places to raise their young, and white-tailed deer, brocket deer and tapir take shelter in the vast hardwood forests. Botanical trails offer peeks at these animals; guides are available at the reserve's visitors center. Tours to the reserve are offered by **Tony's Inn** (south end of Corozal; 4-22055).

North of the reserve, the last real town before the Mexico border is **Corozal**. Curving along a pale blue, blustery sea, with a shore saturated in coconut palms, Corozal is scenic and peaceful. The expensive homes sprinkled along the water hint that this is a town with money, albeit mostly foreign money. Wealthy Belizeans do own vacation homes here, but it's the Americans and Europeans who fuel much of the real estate market. Local pride shines through in the picturesque **central park** (1st Street North, one block from the sea) with its pretty fountains and canopies of poinciana trees. Around town, you'll also notice the hand-written signs, tacked to electric poles, that read: "Don't Be Mean. Keep Corozal Clean."

On the outskirts of Corozal, two minor Maya sites offer interesting side trips. It's best to take a boat to **Cerro Maya**, located south of Corozal, near where the New River empties into Corozal Bay. Boats leave from downtown Corozal; or, check at **Tony's Inn** (south end of town; 4-22055). Cerro Maya, meaning "Maya Hill," is spread across more than 50 acres of forest, though the city center—resting on a gentle hill—is easily explored in an hour. Several plazas are surrounded by pyramids, including one that's 72 feet tall. Like these buildings, the ball courts and artifacts here date from 400 B.C. to 100 A.D.

Archaeologists believe **Santa Rita** (off the Northern Highway, just north of Corozal) was the Maya city of Chetumal, located about 35 miles south of today's Chetumal, Mexico. Situated on Corozal Bay, near the New River and Río Hondo, Santa Rita likely controlled the trade arteries that funneled cacao, honey and vanilla from Belize to the northern Yucatán. The city was discovered around the turn of the century by Thomas Gann, amateur archaeologist and Corozal's town doctor. Gann uncovered fantastic Mixtec-style frescoes, jade jewelry and pottery, though the frescoes have since been destroyed. Today's site will not impress visitors as it did Gann. Only one structure survives: a Classic building, riddled with doorways and connecting rooms, including a main room where burnt offerings were made.

For the eight miles from Corozal to the Mexico border, the Northern Highway yields rural vistas of wide-open pastures, scrub forest, and fields swelled with corn, bananas and sugar cane. There are a few eye-blink towns, including the pueblo-like Santa Clara and Santa Elena Concepción, that look more like Mexico than Belize. Mexico officially starts at the bridge spanning the Río Hondo. The **border crossing** is quick and simple on the Belize side, long and often complicated on the Mexican side, especially if a public bus has just disgorged its riders. American citizens, who need a passport, will be issued a Mexican tourist card. The card will be reclaimed by the border officials upon reentering Belize. Most people crossing into Mexico are taking a day trip to **Chetumal**, mainly to shop the crowded, inexpensive markets. Buses are the cheapest way to go, costing about US$1.25 each way. Taxis are extremely expensive; the one-way trip is about $20.

LODGING   Twelve miles south of Corozal and four miles off the Northern Highway, **Santa Cruz Lodge** (in the village of Santa Cruz, just beyond the village of Libertad and the sugar cane factory; ceiling fans; air-conditioning; phone; satellite TV; some rooms with kitchenettes; expensive; 4-22441, fax: 4-22442) resides amid sugar cane fields and groves of mangoes, grapefruit and soursop. Four primly painted houses each have four to five rooms, all with modern comforts—air-conditioning, telephones, satellite TVs, reverse osmosis water systems, minibars—unheard of in these parts. Three rooms have kitchenettes. Tennis courts, swimming pool, a swingset and playing field make this an ideal place for families. There's indoor and outdoor dining, and a gazebo bar.

By far the best choice for Corozal lodging is **Tony's Inn** (south end of town; ceiling fans; some rooms with air-conditioning; some rooms with satellite TV; moderate to expensive; 4-22055, fax: 4-22829), which feels like an upscale motor court. The crisp white two-story buildings enjoy a breezy seaside locale, complete with outdoor palapa bar and precious patch of white beach. The rooms are big and modern, with tile floors.

If you're short on cash, check out the **Hotel Maya** (south end of Corozal; budget; 4-22082), across from the sea. The 20 rooms are very clean, but the dressers are beat-up and the draperies look like sheets. The owners are a friendly local family.

RESTAURANTS   The fare is not spectacular, but **Tony's Inn** (south end of town; moderate to expensive; 4-22055) easily wins as Corozal's top restaurant. Choose from a variety of seafood dishes, baked, broiled or fried, as well as pork chops, fried chicken, and rice and beans. Linens cover the tables, and jalousie windows funnel in sea breezes. Breakfast and lunch are also available.

With only four tables, the **Hotel Maya** (south end of town; moderate; 4-22082) feels like someone's private dining room. In a way it is, since it belongs to a family who prepares homestyle meals for a loyal local following. The menu changes depending on what's fresh each day, but entrées might include fried chicken or T-bone steaks. Breakfast features omelettes and eggs with refried beans.

NIGHTLIFE   It's scarce around Corozal. There are a couple of in-town bars, but things can get rough. I like sitting on the beach at **Tony's Inn** (south end of town), listening to the waves slap at the shore, watching the silent leaps of lightning across the nighttime sky.

GETTING THERE: Batty Brothers and Venus buses service this area regularly from Belize City, although Corozal and most other points are easy to reach with a car.

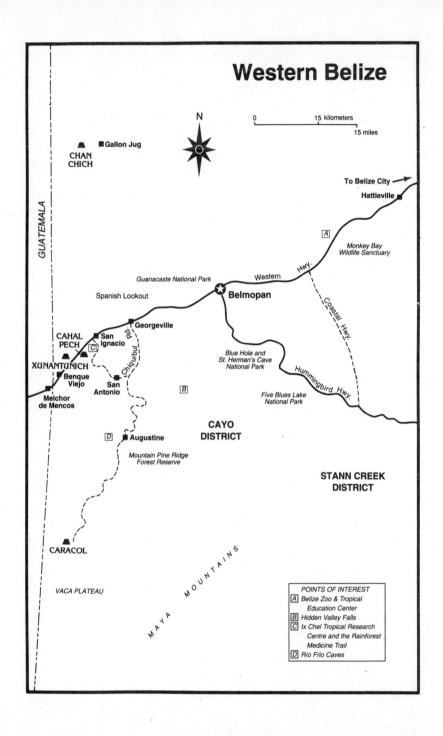

Western Belize

N

0   15 kilometers
                    15 miles

CHAN CHICH
■ Gallon Jug

To Belize City →
Hattieville ■

Ⓐ
Monkey Bay
Wildlife Sanctuary

GUATEMALA

Guanacaste National Park   Western Hwy.

Spanish Lookout   ★ Belmopan

Georgeville

CAHAL PECH
San Ignacio
Ⓒ
XUNANTUNICH
Benque Viejo
San Antonio
Melchor de Mencos

Chiquibul Rd.

Coastal Hwy.

Blue Hole and
St. Herman's Cave
National Park

Hummingbird Hwy.

Ⓑ

Five Blues Lake
National Park

CAYO
DISTRICT

Ⓓ ■ Augustine

Mountain Pine Ridge
Forest Reserve

STANN CREEK
DISTRICT

▲ CARACOL

VACA PLATEAU

MAYA MOUNTAINS

POINTS OF INTEREST
Ⓐ Belize Zoo & Tropical
    Education Center
Ⓑ Hidden Valley Falls
Ⓒ Ix Chel Tropical Research
    Centre and the Rainforest
    Medicine Trail
Ⓓ Río Frio Caves

NINE

Western Belize

While the Belize cayes offer visitors a window to the world at sea, barely an hour away, western Belize opens onto a world of luscious jungle, forest-clad mountains and mighty temples shrouded in mystery. The gateway to this world is the Western Highway, which runs 82 paved miles from Belize City to the Guatemala border. Heading west from the city, the landscape is at once lonely and rugged, with scrub palmetto, mangrove swamps, and a few clapboard homes on stilts. Then mountains are slowly etched on the horizon, jagged summits with intense green forest cascading down their slopes.

This western route is measured in mile posts; you'll begin noticing the concrete posts with white signs and black numbers as you leave Belize City. You'll also notice the weedy cemetery, whose sunbaked, bone-white, above-ground tombs bid goodbye as you head west.

Western Belize is a land of country cottages, ranches and jungle lodges that seem etched into the earth. Many lie more than an hour from the paved road, down winding, rocky trails that look down the sides of hills. Most have not progressed to electricity (kerosene lamps light up the night), but accommodations are usually quite comfortable. Best of all, the nature encounters and cultural experiences are unmatched.

BELIZE ZOO AND MONKEY BAY

The first village is not for 16 miles, and it wasn't even meant to be a village. After Hurricane Hattie nearly blew away Belize City in 1961, survivors fled inland and set up a temporary camp that was, naturally, called **Hattieville**. Belize City was eventually rebuilt, and the capital of Belmopan opened to the west, but many people preferred to stay in their new clapboard homes dotting the scrub palmetto. Today, the homes don't look so new, but the 1179 residents of Hattieville enjoy their status as suburbanites.

Around Mile Post 29, you'll see a small sign for the **Belize Zoo & Tropical Education Center** (admission; phone/fax: 81-3004). A wonderful introduction to Belize's wildlife, the zoo is home to Rambo the toucan, Balboa the boa constrictor, Pete the jaguar, Sarge the crocodile, Boomer the jabiru stork and many other rare and colorful creatures. It seems inaccurate to call it a zoo, since the more than 100 species of animals do not occupy cages. Instead, they dwell in patches of forest veiled in wire mesh. Their spaces are so big and private that, if an animal is so inclined, he or she can hide from visitors, reiterating that this is *their* world.

Gravel paths wend through thick stands of slash pine trees dripping with moss and bromeliads, past a preening curassow, a fanged crocodile snoozing in the mud, a statue-still jaguar hunching beneath a palm frond, locking his eyes onto yours. His are not the beaten-down eyes of a zoo animal, but of a retired king come to rest in a comfortable home. Signs sprinkled among the enclosures plead for the animals' autonomy: "I'm a great black hawk, but guys who take shots at me are Great Big Turkeys," says the sign where a black hawk lives. And at the spider monkey home: "Listen! We make bad pets! We would much rather spend time with other monkeys than with human primates!"

The clever signs are the work of Sharon Matola, an American biologist who founded the zoo in 1983 after several animals were abandoned by a wildlife filmmaker. Since then, the zoo has gone from a funky little place with a few pens to one of Belize's shining ecotourism stars. In 1991, when a bigger and better Belize Zoo opened next to the old one, *National Geographic* filmed the animals moving into their new homes for a television special on animal caretakers. Included in the documentary were accomplished zoo curator, Belizean Tony Garel, and a staff of more than 20 villagers, some of whom were former wildlife poachers.

Many animals are born at the zoo, but those who aren't come from other zoos or from people who donate wild pets. Poachers are told to take their quarry elsewhere. Iguanas are among the animals being born at the zoo lately. The Green Iguana Breeding Project, started in 1995, hopefully will help replenish Belize's iguana population, fast diminishing because of overhunting (iguana, nicknamed "bamboo chicken," is a popular Belizean dish). Educating residents about iguanas, and teaching them to raise the reptiles much as they would raise chickens, is also part of the project.

In fact, public education is one of Matola's main goals. Back in the early zoo days, Matola constantly pestered schools to offer field trips. She would hop on her Kawasaki 650, with a boa constrictor and slide show in tow, and visit classrooms in rural areas. Today, the Tropical Education Center regularly hosts student groups who study native animals and the human threats to their survival. Belizean schoolchildren visit the zoo nearly every day, and though the youth of Belize may not know about Mickey Mouse, they are well acquainted with April, the tapir, which is Belize's national animal.

While Matola is known around Belize as an animal rights radical, she has also been elevated to folk hero, a Belizean version of Dian Fossey (portrayed in *Gorillas in the Mist).* The former Florida lion tamer, Mexican circus show-girl and Central American fungi specialist has received publicity from *Sports Illustrated, National Geographic* and numerous other magazines.

Today, Matola lives about a mile from the zoo in a thatched bungalow where, in the predawn hours of the jungle, she writes children's books. One of her titles, *I Live In An American Forest,* features an accompanying sound-track of animal voices. During her early mornings, the former showgirl also pumps iron in a screened, thatched-roof gymnasium she built single-handedly. Working out keeps her in shape for the expeditions she leads across Belizean mountains and through the jungles. In summer of 1992, she led the first all-woman expedition to the top of Victoria Peak, Belize's highest at 3675 feet. A few months earlier, she was the only woman on a grueling ten-day hike across the Maya Mountains divide. The expedition included British military troops who acquired jungle training and researchers who learned about Maya history at numerous ruins along the way.

Some of Matola's hiking terrain lies just two miles west at the 1070-acre **Monkey Bay Wildlife Sanctuary** (Mile Post 31, Western Highway; 8-23180, fax: 8-23361). Here, in a privately owned reserve that welcomes visitors, slash pine, scrub palmetto and supine savanna stretch for miles against a hazy backdrop of jagged foothills. There are no monkeys (the park is named for its founders, Monkey Bay Wildlife Sanctuary Tokyo), but there are many species of birds to be found, as well as peccaries. An arboretum with labeled plants and trees introduces visitors to the vegetation. A picturesque beach on the Sibun (pronounced Si-BOON) River is ideal for daytrippers who don't mind hiking 40 minutes from the sanctuary entrance. There are more than two miles of solitary trails waiting for hikers; ask for directions at the wood stilt house near the entrance. The house is a loosely run place that is the sanctuary headquarters and home to various wayfarers getting to know Be-lize. It has an extensive library on native flora, and is also home to American Matt Miller, who runs Monkey Bay, organizing visits from numerous United States student groups each year.

Within the next mile, looking like nothing much but being two of Belize's most famous stopovers, are **Cheers** (Mile Post 31¼, Western Highway; 14-

Collared peccary

9311) and **J.B.'s** (Mile Post 32, Western Highway; 14-8098). Naturally, each watering hole has its own story. J.B.'s has been the stomping grounds of many a British soldier, Belizean politician and imported movie star (Harrison Ford hung out here during the filming of *Mosquito Coast*), having begun its illustrious career in the late 1970s at the hands of an American expatriate who everyone knew simply as J.B. Reputed around town as either a flamboyant, highly entertaining character or a hard-drinking rogue, depending on who you talk to, J.B. brought the bar to great fame with his sardonic stories, late-night rock and roll parties and endless supply of rum and ice cubes (the latter being a luxury around these parts). Alas, in 1991, J.B. picked up and left one day, but only after selling out to two teenage girls from Canada whose RV had broken down in his parking lot. The girls ran J.B.'s for four years, learned plenty about the bar and restaurant business, became young women and opened Cheers right up the road. (J.B.'s is now run by local Belizeans.) Now the dueling pit stops compete for the trickling of traffic in this part of the world—and are doing a bang-up business with locals and travelers alike.

LODGING   If you'd literally like to sleep under the stars, bunk down at **Monkey Bay Wildlife Sanctuary** (Mile Post 31, Western Highway; budget; 8-23180, fax: 8-23361). A dozen or so thatched camping platforms are scattered among the scrub savanna, including some with little thatched roofs (but no walls, so pray it doesn't rain) for those who didn't bring a tent. Bunk rooms (very basic), cold showers and meals are available at a main house run by sanctuary director Matt Miller, an American raising his family in Belize. Rates, as you might expect, are rock-bottom.

Few places come so strange and unexpected as **Jaguar Paw Jungle Resort** (Mile Post 37, Western Highway, then seven miles west; air-conditioning; very expensive; 81-3023, fax: 81-3024, or 800-335-8645 in the United States). For there, rising out of dense rainforest, is an imitation Maya temple, something very Disney in design, a towering block of concrete with faux Maya hieroglyphs attached to the outside walls. Inside is a voluminous space, a lobby and eatery and mirrored bar flooded with air-conditioning and the blinking of a TV screen compliments of a satellite dish. Americans Cy and Donna Young designed the temple and its attendant 16 rooms in zinc-roofed cabanas. When they opened Jaguar Paw in 1996, they installed air-conditioning in all the buildings and an oval swimming pool out back, and posted some of Belize's highest lodging rates. Every guest room is themed, quite contrived, from the Asian room with a black lacquer chest and a silk kimono on the wall to the American room with cranberry and hunter green walls and a mahogany four-poster bed. There's terrific river caving nearby, and you can cruise in a small boat or an inner tube through a honeycomb of caves. Or, join an all-day hike into numerous underground caverns. A full breakfast included in the rate; lunch and dinner is served à la carte in the lodge restaurant.

RESTAURANTS   Near the Belize Zoo and Monkey Bay Wildlife Sanctuary are two places to quench your thirst for a beer and for jungle pageantry. **Cheers** (Mile Post 31¼, Western Highway; budget; 14-9311) is basically a big concrete breezeway with a tin roof, wood rafters, potted orchids dangling from the eaves and Alabama or Bob Dylan on the stereo—take your pick. Order a Belikin beer and a burrito or burger. The tacos, fryjacks and pork chops are good, too. For breakfast, you can have banana pancakes or scrambled-egg burritos. The menu at **J.B.'s** (Mile Post 32, Western Highway; budget; 14-8098) is similarly simple, tasty and easy on the wallet. Choose from the Belize basics: burgers, fried chicken or stew chicken with rice and beans and sometimes cow foot soup.

GETTING THERE: I highly recommend that you drive a rental car here, but Batty Brothers, Novelos and Z-Line buses also service the area regularly from Belize City.

BELMOPAN

Belmopan became the capital of Belize in 1961, when Hurricane Hattie devastated Belize City, the then-capital. Though the government was moved, residents were slow to follow, preferring to live in Belize City even though they worked in Belmopan. In fact, the town was so desolate at night it was called the "City of Sadness." But Belmopan is slowly attracting new residents, and today it is home to 5000.

It takes about five minutes to see the entire city, built in a contemporary Maya style but resembling an aseptic cluster of cinderblock buildings corralled by chainlink. There is no real reason to linger here as Belmopan is not particularly attractive, and lately has been plagued by petty thieves and other undesirables. One Maya gem you might want to see is the **Archaeology Department** (8-22106), where a clammy underground vault houses an ever-changing collection of ancient relics uncovered in the past two decades. Tours are offered Monday, Wednesday and Friday from 1:30 to 4:00 p.m.; reservations are required and must be made by calling at least two days in advance. There is a small fee for the tour. Don't bother visiting from late September through November, when the relics go on tour around the country.

Just outside Belmopan, at the intersection of the Western Highway and the Hummingbird Highway, **Guanacaste National Park** (admission) offers a splendid walk in the forest. Packed into these 50 acres of cool, damp woods are colossal trees that make you feel like you're wandering past nature's own highrises. A guide from the visitors center will join you (don't explore unaccompanied, as muggings have been a problem) and describe the abundance of life that exists along the leafy trails. Among the more interesting: armadillo houses, termite nests and logs lined with bulldog bats, who feed on fish as well as lizards and small mammals. Birders will be happy to know that blue-crowned motmots, collared aracaris, green-breasted mangos and other extraordinary, elusive birds are permanent residents here. There's also the imposing 300-foot-tall guanacaste tree, which the park is named for, laden with over 35 species of air plants, many as big as normal trees. If you're lucky, the guide will pluck a pod from a cohune palm and break it open so you can taste the coconutty flavor. Bring your swimsuit for a dip in the clear, fast-flowing Belize River, which cuts right through the park.

LODGING   If you're looking for a Belizean ranch experience, I highly recommend ✪ **Warrie Head Ranch and Lodge** (Western Highway, six miles west of Belmopan; ceiling fans; expensive; 2-77257, fax: 2-75213 in Belize City). Named for the spine-covered warrie, a type of wild boar that lives in surrounding forests, the ranch is draped across 137 pastoral acres, with grassy knolls, clear creeks and tropical fruit trees. Warrie Head Ranch offers ten cozy rooms decorated with Belizean tile floors, knotty pine walls and jalousie windows. A library exudes real warmth with its wildlife photos, board games and books on Belize. While you are here, you will be very lucky to meet Lydia, the lodge's virtuoso host and cook, who rustles up giant meals of steak, chicken and fresh vegetables (for vegetarians).

Despite its countrified name, the **Bullfrog Inn** (25 Half Moon Avenue; air-conditioning; moderate; 8-22111, fax: 8-23155) is in the capital of Belmopan. The grounds are lush and filled with singing birds, but the rooms, though clean, carpeted and cooled by air conditioners, are rather featureless. On the positive side, restaurant is one of the best in town.

Considered the business traveler's choice, the **Belmopan Convention Hotel** (corner of Bliss Parade and Constitution Drive, Belmopan; fans; air-conditioning; cable TV; moderate; 8-22340, fax: 8-22130) is a gracious hacienda-style hostelry with a swimming pool. But don't expect Holiday Inn–style rooms; these are funky, featuring bright orange carpet, orange-striped bedspreads and hand-me-down furniture. Oh well, this *is* Belize!

RESTAURANTS   Checkered tablecloths, arched porticoes and fresh flowers lend real charm to the **Bullfrog Inn** (25 Half Moon Avenue, Belmopan; moderate; 8-22111). The most popular eatery in town, with politicians and visiting VIPs often gracing its tables, it has an open-air terrace that faces a tropical garden. Steaks, chicken, fish and hamburgers are standard fare, and there's an attached cocktail bar.

Across from the Belmopan bus station, the **Caladium Restaurant** (Market Square; budget; 8-22754) features a chalkboard menu of home-cooked fare. Fried fish or chicken, pork chops, T-bone steaks and thick, frothy milkshakes are local favorites. Daily specials might include curried mutton, Spanish meatloaf, fish or chicken boil ups and leg of lamb.

SHOPPING   The **Market Square** in downtown is comprised of stalls where vendors sell everything from copycat designer jewelry and radios to watermelons and chickens. Even if you don't buy, it's fun to watch. Open most days.

GETTING THERE: You'll have no problem driving to Belmopan from Belize City on the Western Highway. Or, take a Batty Brothers, Novelos or Z-Line bus from Belize City.

CAYO COUNTRY

South of Belmopan, the **Hummingbird Highway** is a part-paved, part-pot-holed path that resembles a collapsing sidewalk through the jungle. Bounding along in a beat-up jeep, with the feverish forest air pouring in through chattering windows, one expects to encounter a strange beast or an even stranger person. Instead, barefoot children dart out of the jungle clutching cups of corn kernels, so freshly cut that its sweet juice smell fills the air. If you ask where they are going, they will tell you to *madre*, so she can make her tortillas.

Even if you don't see the children, you will eventually spot the tiny signs for the **Blue Hole and St. Herman's Cave National Park** (on the Hummingbird Highway, 11 miles south of Belmopan; admission). The latter is Belize's "other" Blue Hole, a pool of sapphire water as clear as air, with schools of fish scooting in every direction, buried deep in the rainforest. Sunlight filters through the treetops, changing the water into greens and blues and every shade in between. Swimming is excellent here. From this cool, enchanted spot, fern-lined trails lead off into a honeycomb of caves that last for miles. The caves are pitch-black and desolated, so bring a couple of flashlights, good walking shoes and a companion.

Twenty miles farther south, take the turnoff for Saint Martins Village. After about two miles on a gravel road, you will land at the crest of a vivid lake that glows phosphorescent blue and green. The lake is the reason **Five Blues Lake National Park** was christened on Earth Day 1992. Spanning 850 forested acres, it features a labyrinth of hiking trails and a small shelter where you can enjoy a picnic.

Back on the Western Highway, just west of Belmopan, take the turnoff for **Spanish Lookout** and you will soon feel as if you've left Belize. There, stretching to the edge of the horizon, is a scene right out of Pennsylvania's Dutch Country: folded green hills, wind-tickled fields of corn, and straw-hatted Mennonite farmers in horse-drawn buggies. Blond, freckle-faced Mennonite children race down the dirt roads and through the corn fields, and windmills churn against a bright blue country sky.

The Mennonites, who trace their roots to 16th-century Switzerland and Germany, began immigrating to Belize in the 1800s. Since then, they have slowly turned the unforgiving limestone ground into fruitful soil, and are now considered Belize's most prolific farmers. The remote Spanish Lookout is one of their largest greenbelts. If you drive there, take a truck. The road is very rutted and covered with rocks, and delivers a real beating to your vehicle.

From here to the Guatemala border, the Western Highway rises and falls through pine-clad mountain ridges and rocky pasturelands speckled with

Keel-billed toucan

modest villages. This is the heart of **Cayo Country**, a region once rich with logging and chicle farming. Today, it boasts citrus groves and cattle ranches and an ever increasing ecotourism trade. The pulse of Cayo, as it's called around Belize, is **San Ignacio**, located 20 miles west of Belmopan. Draped along the banks of the Macal River and ringed with hills, San Ignacio is filled with restaurants, shops, businesses and nearly 9000 people who keep the town bubbling along. San Ignacio has long attracted a vast spectrum of humanity, from Maya and *Mestizos* to Guatemalan refugees, Lebanese entrepreneurs, Mennonite farmers, and adventure-seeking Americans and Europeans. Watching the various walks of life and listening to jungle tales told around town, one gets the distinct feeling that something exciting is about to happen.

After a stroll in San Ignacio, you may want to have a look at the minor ruins of **Cahal Pech** (Buena Vista Road; take the trail leading away from Cahal Pech Disco; admission). Its name means "Place of the Ticks" and its first impression is not impressive, but if you wander the forested grounds you'll find the Preclassic city quite extensive. A guide will be happy to show you around the seven courtyards and 34 structures, including several temples, two ball courts and a sweathouse, sprinkled across two acres. The largest ceremonial structure is 77 feet high, with sharply tiered steps running up its face. Sadly, several buildings have been layered with concrete to slow down erosion.

San Ignacio is the headquarters for booking tours to surrounding Maya ruins and various sights, and for arranging horseback riding and hiking in the hills. It is also the place to arrange a canoe trip or taxi ride to **Ix Chel Tropical Research Centre** and the **Rainforest Medicine Trail** (check with Eva's restaurant, 22 Burns Avenue, San Ignacio; 92-2267; admission). On the crest of a hill, amid five cleared acres of high bush country, the farm is owned by Americans Rosita Arvigo and Gregory Shropshire. The couple call it Ix Chel, after the Maya goddess of healing and of rainbows. On many summer afternoons, after the rain-gorged clouds have unleashed their showers on the forest, rainbows arch across the hilltop farm.

For several years, Arvigo and Shropshire have been collecting and researching the jungle vegetation that lies at their back door. So far, the husband-and-wife team have collected more than 750 plant species, which are being catalogued by the New York Botanical Garden. The garden, along with the National Institute of Health, Metropolitan Life Insurance and other organizations, have provided grants for research at the farm. Already, the world's jungles have produced treatments for ovarian cancer (a substance called taxol, derived from the yew tree) and Hodgkin's disease (substances from the periwinkle). It is hoped that the forest holds cures for other cancers and for AIDS. The couple's latest research is aimed at cultivating medicinal plants that can become cash crops for local farmers.

The **Rainforest Medicine Trail**, formerly called the Panti Maya Trail, which begins near the couple's house, helps visitors learn about their research here. You can take a self-guided tour from 7 a.m. to 5 p.m. Guided tours are available for groups by appointment only (call Eva's at 92-2267). With his descriptions of jungle healing secrets, a bush guide makes the trail come to life. Sunlight and dewy rain filters through the jungle ceiling as he reveals such cures as cowfoot, cocol mecca, negrita, grapevine and bullhoof vine—foliage that to the untrained eye seems no different than any other forest specimen. Bullhoof, he says, will stanch internal bleeding, and grapevine conceals a fountain of fresh water. For more than an hour he goes on like this, explaining mysteries and relating healing stories that make life here seem even more mysterious.

A few miles south of San Ignacio lies a picturesque farm village called **San Antonio**. The way there is on a bumpy dirt road that leaps and dives among hills cascading with cohune palms and jungly pasture, a roller coaster ride through neotropical scenery with a slim possibility of meeting another vehicle. Once you arrive, you are met by freshly painted farmhouses, horses grazing on velvet green knolls, a teeny clapboard barber shop, and a one-room schoolhouse that throws its door and windows open to the warmth of day.

Not far from the school, at the **Tanah Mayan Art Museum** (for information, call 92-3310 in San Ignacio; admission), you will be met by one or more of the five smiling, engaging Garcia Sisters. Sylvia, Carmelita, Aurora, Piedad and Maria will greet you in their *huipiles*, beautiful embroidered dresses traditional of their Yucatecan Maya heritage. They will take you through the many artifacts and artworks of their warmly arranged museum, from the welk shell jewelry, cedar violin and slate carvings to the 100-year-old butak chair handcarved from local Santa Maria wood by their great-great-grandfather. They will show you the cedar baby tub, carved from a single log with a machete and an axe, that their great-grandparents were bathed in, and that their grandparents bathed *them* in. And they will tell you the story of how their museum came to be.

"In the early 1980s, their father, a village farmer, met a little piece of black stone while working in the field," explains Piedad. It was so smooth and glossy he brought it home, and Aurora instinctively started carving it. When she was done, she had lured from the stone the image of a whale she had seen in a dream. Local villagers pronounced it a grand omen, saying that God had given them the stone to bring back the Maya art and culture that is so quickly disappearing today. Soon Aurora was carving more slate and needed a place to display and sell it. In 1985, in a loosely thrown up wood building, the sisters opened the Tanah Museum.

Since then, the museum has more than tripled in size, and carries many local artworks and handicrafts. Among the exhibits is Aurora's original whale, and though it reveals obvious talent, it is neither as detailed or compelling as the images she has gone on to resurrect from local slate. Younger sister Maria has also proven to have a knack for the ancient Maya art. The talent, Piedad says, is no doubt traceable to their *padre*, who, before he met that little black stone, used to carve limestone bowls and trade them to the neighbors for chickens.

LODGING   There's not a whole lot going on between Belmopan and San Ignacio, unless you detour off the Western Highway to **Pook's Hill** (Mile Post 52½, Western Highway, then five miles south on dirt roads; expensive; 81-2017, fax: 82-2948). Here, around a small Maya plaza of soft green lawns, is a sprinkling of stucco cabins crowned with palm thatching and simply decorated with Belizean hardwood and woven Guatemala fabrics. The lodge sits within a 300-acre reserve in the foothills of the Maya Mountains, and with superior opportunities for hiking and birding, river tubing, mountain biking and horseback riding. Rates include breakfast; lunch and dinner available.

✪ **Caesar's Place** (Mile Post 64, Western Highway; ceiling fans; moderate; 92-2341, fax: 92-3449), a roadside scattering of buildings and bougainvillea, is a friendly place to stop for a cold Belikin, hot home cooking or a room for the night. Four large rooms feature cedar paneling, Mexican tile floors and private baths with hot water. If you happen to be traveling by RV (unlikely, but possible!), Caesar's is one of the few places in Belize with full hookups. Out back, you can take a dip in Barton Creek.

On 70 acres along the Western Highway, **Grove Resort** (Mile Post 62, Western Highway; fans; air-conditioning; expensive to very expensive; 92-2421) offers American-style lodging in three pink apartment-like buildings. Every room is a suite, surprisingly spacious, with two double beds, a living room and refrigerator. Even more unexpected are the swimming pool lined with travelers palms, the grass tennis court, the thatched-roof gym and the various spa treatments (choose from a massage, facial, manicure, or herbal or seaweed body wrap). You can walk to several unexcavated Mayan ruins, or drive to nearby Spanish Lookout.

In Cayo, the **San Ignacio Hotel** (18 Buena Vista Road, San Ignacio; rooms have either ceiling fans or air-conditioning; moderate to expensive; 92-2034, fax: 92-2134) is as close as you get to a real hotel. Its hillside venue offers lovely vistas across Cayo and the Macal River, and there's a pretty swimming pool decorated with tropical planters and wrought-iron furniture, where one could easily lose an afternoon sampling Belizean rum (the margaritas are memorable, as well). Rooms are spacious and contemporary, adorned with Honduran mahogany furniture and offering private balconies.

Just uphill from the San Ignacio Hotel (though, strangely, sharing the same address), the **Piache Hotel** (18 Buena Vista Road, San Ignacio; ceiling fans; some rooms with air-conditioning; budget; 92-2032) is the thrifty traveler's choice. The grounds, sprinkled with plants potted in an assortment of tin cans, tubs and tires, reflect the style of a friendly eccentric. That would be Godsman Ellis, a gregarious Garifuna who can tell you much about San Ignacio and about Belize, preferably at his thatched cabana bar. Just off the bar, in a cinderblock building, are ten extremely basic but basically clean rooms, with rummage-sale furnishings and curtained bathroom doors. Some rooms here have air conditioners that more or less work.

At ✪ **Mida's Resort** (Branch Mouth Road, one-quarter of a mile north of San Ignacio; fans; budget; 92-3172 or 92-2101, fax: 92-3845), you can pitch a tent or string a hammock between the trees and sleep under the stars. Most people, however, prefer to stay in one of the five duplex cabanas, even if they are somewhat primitive with their cement walls and open windows. The setting is homey and pure country, five riverside acres of former pastureland owned by Englishman Mike Preston and his wife, Maria Preston, who was born in San Ignacio (Maria's father's cows grazed on the property until a 1990 flood wiped out most of the vegetation). Among their many ecotourism projects, the couple and their two sons are working to restore the land.

Popular with backpackers, hikers and naturalists, ✪ **Maya Mountain Lodge** (on Cristo Rey Road, three-quarters of a mile from the Western Highway, near San Ignacio; fans; moderate; 92-2164, fax: 92-2029, or 800-344-6292 in the United States) is an ecotourism retreat set along a verdant green hillside with tropical gardens and chirping cicadas. There are eight comfortable cottages, as well as six very basic rooms with vinyl floors, plywood walls and private curtained bathrooms (two have private baths down the hall). The real highlight is the lovely indoor-outdoor dining room, with a mango tree growing right through the middle. An extensive schedule of day trips and cultural programs is offered here, including the ever-popular "Belize Night" held every Friday during the winter and featuring a presentation on local topics.

Rubble from Maya ruins sprinkle the grounds at the remote **Clarissa Falls Cabins** (off the Western Highway, about three miles from San Ignacio; private and shared baths; budget; 92-3916). Like glorified camping, the eleven basic cottages have concrete floors and bamboo walls. Three have a shared bath, and all have hot water. There's also a dorm-style room with hammocks and folding beds where you can sleep for cheap, or you can pitch a tent along the water. The lodge resides in a most coveted spot along a bubbling creek, where iguanas and bromeliads decorate the trees. A thatched-roof restaurant serves tasty Belizean food.

In a stunning hillside setting overlooking the Macal River, ✪ **Chaa Creek** (on the Macal River, about eight miles outside San Ignacio; expensive to very expensive; 92-2037, fax: 92-2501) gives the feeling of being pampered— in the jungle. Unsurpassed for service and deep woods surroundings, its adobe cabanas are warm and inviting, with chestnut-colored Mexican tile floors, mahogany beds, Guatemalan blankets and thatched roofs soaring above the trees. By far the most coveted room is "The Tower," a voluminous 12-sided cabana propped high atop a water tower and affording views of the mountains and jungle. None of the cabanas have electricity or screens on the windows, but not to worry: there are few mosquitoes, only dazzling butterflies that float in one window and out the other. A Butterfly House, built for the scientist who started Chaa Creek's butterfly-breeding center, now accommodates guests with solar electricity and a kitchen. During the day, you can visit Chaa Creek's Natural History Centre, with exhibits on local culture and ecosystems and archaeology, then learn about the elusive, fabulously colored blue morpho butterfly, also called Belizean Blues, at the lodge's Blue Morpho Butterfly Breeding Centre. Other possible daytime pursuits: swimming and canoeing the Macal River, hiking the jungle, and exploring caves, waterfalls and Maya ruins near and far. Around dinnertime, you'll be welcomed by the owners, a gregarious couple named Mick and Lucy Fleming (he's English, she's American) who are well-known around Belize. The indoor-outdoor dining room is a romantic affair offering tasty, locally grown cuisine. Before dinner, everyone gathers on the birdwatching deck, near the elegant wood bar, to trade "You wouldn't believe it. . ." stories of the day.

Up river

~~Downriver~~ from Chaa Creek is ✪ **duPlooy's** (about ten miles outside San Ignacio; private and shared bath; ceiling fans; budget for basic rooms with shared bath to very expensive for newish bungalows; 92-3101, fax: 92-3301). Though not as fancy as its neighbor, duPlooy's offers the same feeling of rural peacefulness. Accommodations range from rooms with stone floors, private baths and screened porches to basic rooms with a shared bath in a pink guest lodge. Three pretty bungalows, opened in 1995, come with coffee makers and mini-refrigerators. Co-owner Ken duPlooy, originally from Zimbabwe, is an avid birder who will point out the many species camouflaged in the foliage.

Easy access makes ✪ **Windy Hill Cottages** (Western Highway, about one mile west of San Ignacio; ceiling fans; moderate; 92-2017, fax: 92-3080) a good choice for accommodations. It's one of the few country lodges that doesn't require a marathon trek down a rocky road, and it's the only one with a swimming pool—but don't expect the Taj Mahal. What you can expect are picturesque, comfortable surroundings and congenial, knowledgeable innkeepers who tend to your every need. Lourdes Hales, a registered nurse and native of San Ignacio, and her husband, Bob Hales, a 25-year resident of Belize, will also introduce you to local sites and customs and history. Each of the 25 rooms, spread among the hilltop cabins, has a veranda for enjoying hillside views. Six rooms are especially good for wheelchair visitors. There's an informal dining room, a bar, and even a thatched-roof game room with a pool table.

Across from Windy Hill and equally as convenient to Cayo sites are the six log cabins of **Log Cab-inns** (Western Highway, about one mile west of San Ignacio; TVs; moderate; 9-23367). Fashioned of peeled mahogany poles, they sit on a hill amid a grove of orange, papaya and custard apple trees. The floors are concrete but impeccably clean, the private baths outfitted with hot showers and the TVs tuning into a couple of fuzzy stations (then, who needs TV when you have the ruins and the rainforest?). Summer and fall, rates are budget.

A newly built road offers access to the ✪ **Black Rock Jungle River Lodge** (on the Macal River, upstream from San Ignacio; private and shared baths; moderate; for reservations, call 92-2341, fax: 92-3449), but the going may be rough and in rainy season access may require a 20-minute hike or horseback ride through damp, deep woods filled with birdsong. At the trek's end is a sheer limestone cliff with a swirling river and black boulders at its feet, and six fancy slate-and-thatch cabins perched near its edge. Banana plants engulf the cabins and 250 acres of private forest surround it. Water from the river is pumped up for drinking, bathing and cooking, and rays from the sun are used to make all the lodge's electricity. Tasty meals (extra charge) are prepared on an open hearth by a friendly staff. Among the many activities here: horseback riding, hiking, exploring nearby Flour Camp caves and birding, as well as swimming, canoeing and tubing on the Macal River. A great spot, for sure.

RESTAURANTS   A combination supermarket, gas station and restaurant, **Three Flags** (Mile Post 59, Western Highway, Unitedville; budget; 92-3456) offers a respite from Western Highway driving. The fare is basic but filling: burgers, sandwiches, hot dogs, and rice and beans for lunch; pork chops, fish filets, seafood and chicken platters for dinner.

Some people claim you haven't been to Cayo if you haven't been to **Eva's** (22 Burns Avenue, San Ignacio; budget; 92-2267). The central nerve of jungle comings and goings, Eva's is where you go to book tours, meet fellow Americans, buy postcards, and hear various tales that get taller as the night (and the beer) wears on. The food is strictly a side attraction, but it's cheap and not half bad. Among the choices are chicken curry, stew chicken, rice and beans, tamales and hamburgers.

San Ignacio's new hipster hangout, **Sandcastle Bar & Grill** (Savannah Street; budget to moderate; 92-3213) is open to the out-of-doors, with sand floors and views of chickens running around the neighbor's backyard. Omelettes, pancakes, beans and tortillas are breakfast choices. Lunch and dinner feature fish (snapper, shark steaks), fried chicken, pork chops and Mexican dishes. Wash it all down with a seaweed drink (think eggnog flavor)—everyone else does.

Upstairs Pollito (8 Hudson Street, San Ignacio; budget; 92-2019) easily has the best Belizean food in town. For a few bucks you get liberal portions of stew chicken, pork or beef, beans and rice and tortillas, a tall, cool cock-tail (recommended: vodka and Squirt) and little white fans humming over-head. Street noise seeps through jalousie windows and the corner TV is tuned to some talk show, like Maury Povich interviewing a man so gigantic he had to be cut from his house.

Martha's Kitchen (10 West Street, San Ignacio; budget; 92-3647), clean, airy and colorful, serves three meals a day at a few tables outside. Or you can order takeout (recommended: pizza, spaghetti and, if you're famished, the seared steak). Don't mind the other comings and goings here: Martha's is also an arts-and-crafts store, a laundromat and a guest house.

In San Ignacio, there are two possibilities for Far Eastern fare. You'll easily spot **Serendib** (27 Burns Avenue; budget to moderate; 92-2302) by its yel-low clapboard storefront. Inside are wood-paneled walls and whirring ceiling fans, and a menu of fried rice, chow mein, Sri Lankan curries and shrimp, as well as burgers and salads. More run-down, but still praised around town, is **Maxim's** (23 Far West Street; budget; 92-2283). In a tiny, dark cinder-block building decorated with wildlife murals, it serves sweet and sour dishes, chop suey, curries, fresh fish and burgers.

SHOPPING   Prices are kind of high but the selection is good at **Caesar's Place** (Mile Post 60, Western Highway; 92-2341), a boutique of local art-work, jungle healing potions, T-shirts and other high-quality Belizean gifts.

San Ignacio has a handful of interesting shops. If you're in need of inex-pensive tennis shoes or leather sandals, duck into **K. K. Store** (23 Burns Avenue; 92-34180). At **Arts & Crafts of Central America** (24 Burns Ave-nue; 92-2253), there's a good selection of Guatemalan woven rugs and blan-kets and handcrafted jewelry.

Caesar's Place Gift Shop (Burns Avenue, San Ignacio; 92-23770) is a sis-ter store of the one near Belmopan, carrying high-quality, made-in-Belize items such as carved-wood sugar bowls, pens and masks, bamboo flutes and vibrant sarongs.

NIGHTLIFE   The live-music jams at **Caeser's Place** (Mile Post 60, Western Highway; 92-2341) garden bar are big local events. The schedule and talent depends on who's passing through Belize, so call ahead for the lowdown.

In downtown San Ignacio, the **Blue Angel Club** (Hudson Street; 92-2431) is a second-floor roost with an enormous wood dancefloor outlined in chain-link fence. On weekends bands churn out reggae and soul music and locals pour in. Cover.

A giant longhouse offering fantastic views across Cayo, **Cahal Pech Disco** (Buena Vista Road, San Ignacio; 92-3380) is named for the nearby Maya ruins. Easily the most popular nightspot in Western Belize, on weekends it pulses to reggae and punta rock, compliments of top-notch local bands. Cover.

GETTING THERE: I recommend driving a rental car to San Ignacio, though regular bus service is available from Belize City on either Batty Brothers or Novelos.

MOUNTAIN PINE RIDGE AND CARACOL

South from San Antonio, the dirt roller coaster ride called the Chiquibul Road transforms into a clay trail that plunges into an enchanted forest known as **Mountain Pine Ridge** (from the Western Highway, take the turnoff at Mile Post 65 at the town of Georgeville). Were it not for the pockets of cohune jungle and broadleaf forest, you'd think that you had been transported from the jungle to the Great Smoky Mountains. Only these mountains are marbled with greens of every tropical shade and creased with rivers as clear as air. Chilly streams swirl around polished black boulders glinting in the sun, then disappear into networks of caves that have no end. Hardwood trees drip with ferns and giant bromeliads and orchids, perfuming the cool breeze that trickles through the leaves. Gone is the oppressive jungle humidity one has come to expect in Belize; here in Pine Ridge, as it's called locally, bonfires and fireplaces are the companions of evening.

Trails of clay, grassy dirt and limestone are the parkways of Pine Ridge. The trails are often muddy and flooded in the summer rainy season, so it's best to travel them any other time. In some places along the trails, leaves, vines and trees suck up every inch of space, though even here one can spot the toucans that decorate the treetops and the blue and orange butterflies that dance in and out of shadows. Ocellated turkeys dash in and out of the forest, and a brocket deer, frozen in the bush, aims his charcoal saucer eyes at a visitor. Green parrots poke their heads out of holes in a cohune palm, nests conveniently carved by a woodpecker. Allspice trees provide showers of pungent leaves; pluck one and smell it, and be reminded of pumpkin pie and holidays. Belizeans, however, are reminded of the spicy coconut milk their mothers gave them.

Much of Pine Ridge lies within the **Mountain Pine Ridge Forest Reserve**, which means logging is legal but regulated to allow the felling of only certain trees. In recent centuries, widespread logging stole plenty of the primary forest, though abandoned logging camps and sawmills are slowly being swallowed by the vegetation they tried to destroy. Headquarters for the reserve is in the village of **Augustine**, where tiny white tin-roofed houses gather beneath cathedrals of slash pine trees. Here, an old frame building set in the woods acts as the **Forestry Department station** (for information, call the main forestry office in Belmopan, 8-22082 or 8-22079), which can direct you to various sites in the area.

One you won't want to miss is **Río Frio Cave** (about a mile west of Augustine), reached by a pebbled path that ambles down from the road into a dark den of trees. It is not a cave in the normal sense, but an overwhelming tunnel of stone that arches to the heavens, with a mouth that shelters a white sand beach dotted with boulders the size of houses. Water rushes in one end of the cave and out the other, coursing the half-mile length of this stone vault. Dim light filters through the cave, illuminating razor-sharp stalactites and walls smoothed by eons of water. One-hundred-foot-long vines dangle, confetti-like, from the ceiling. As you leave Belize's largest known river cave, notice the steps angling into the cave's mouth: They are stone keepsakes from the nearby ancient city of Caracol.

There is nothing dark or mysterious about **Río On Pools** (about two miles north of Augustine), just a sense of not being able to get enough of the view. Like a great basin of Alka Seltzer, it is a hillside panorama of marbled brown rocks washed by fizzing water traveling in every direction and framed in giant slash pine trees. Where the rocks corral the water are mini-swimming pools, with water that's invitingly cool and clean. The best swimming is reached at the very top; the best views are toward the bottom.

Farther north and east lies Belize's most famous waterfall, **Hidden Valley Falls**, also called the Thousand Foot Falls because it thunders down 1000 feet from a granite ledge, disappearing into the misty jungle below. The falls are not viewed from close up, but from an overlook across a great ravine enveloped in a panorama of delicious green mountains and mystic haze that heightens as the sun takes leave. Here, on a platform that begins to jut into the ravine, with the wind whispering through pine needles, you can fixate on the scenery: mistletoe curled atop a slash pine tree, an orange-breasted falcon perched on a dead limb, visual lines between the broadleaf jungle and pine forest etched across the mountains. To make the views last, have a picnic on the nearby covered tables.

Not far from the overlook is a small tin-roofed frame building with a sign that says **Hidden Valley Institute for Environmental Studies**. Inside, it has the beginnings of a forest lab, with shelves lined with specimen bottles. The institute is the hopeful creation of a Floridian named J.C. "Bull" Headley, who owns the 18,500-acre Hidden Valley Reserve, located within the Pine Ridge Reserve. The Hidden Valley property includes the Thousand Foot Falls as well as the Hidden Valley Inn, which publishes a map to the myriads of lesser known overlooks and sites in the area, most open only to guests of the inn.

CARACOL   South of here, the cool Pine Ridge slowly slips into a deep, dense forest called the **Chiquibul Wilderness**. Here, set atop the Vaca Plateau in the foothills of the Maya Mountains, is the place everyone is talking about. **Caracol** (admission), it seems, was a supreme Maya city, surpassing even the mighty Tikal. It says as much on a marker, discovered on a Caracol ball court, that proclaims the victory of the Lord Water of Caracol over the warlords of Tikal. The year was 562 A.D., and Caracol reigned sovereign for the next century.

Caracol slept, consumed by jungle, until 1937, when it was discovered by a mahogany logger named Rosa Mai. Mai reported his find to the Belizean government, which dispatched then-Archaeology Commissioner A.H. Anderson.

During a two-week visit in 1938, Anderson logged numerous structures, altars and massive intricate stelae. He also bestowed the name Caracol, meaning "snail," for a road that coils through the hilly terrain, though it could just as well have been named for the mounds of snail shells found here.

Rumors of Caracol's fabulous stelae spread, but it wasn't until the early 1950s that epigrapher Linton Satterthwaite went in search of the great stone monuments. He did indeed find them, and carted some back to the University of Pennsylvania. During the next 30 years, various recovery teams visited Caracol, but they only stayed long enough to extract more of the beautiful stelae. Finally, in 1985, two archaeologists from the University of Central Florida launched a full-scale excavation. What Drs. Diane and Arlen Chase found—and are still finding—is a glorious city and culture that is reshaping current thinking about ancient Maya existence.

Caracol, it seems, had a big middle class. In fact, most of its 150,000-plus residents—three-quarters of Belize's current population—were probably middle class, enjoying all the wealth and perks historians had thought were reserved for nobility. Throughout the metropolis are elite neighborhoods whose homes are spacious and elegantly arranged, with bedrooms boasting large plaster benches—in effect, king-size beds. The extraordinary causeways that run out from the city center would have afforded scenic views

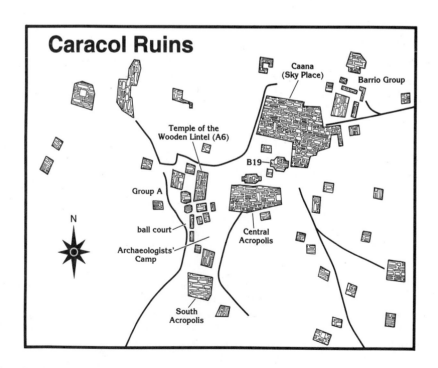

Caracol Ruins

Caana
(Sky Place)

Barrio Group

Temple of the
Wooden Lintel (A6)

B19

Group A

N

ball court

Central
Acropolis

Archaeologists'
Camp

South
Acropolis

of Caracol's splendorous buildings—not something city planners would have designed for a population of peasants. And though the Maya supposedly entombed only rulers and priests, many of Caracol's tombs held middle-class families and their painted vessels, gems and other valuables.

Indeed, Caracol's myriad tombs tell much about the city, and perhaps about Maya life. As of mid-1995, more than 120 tombs had been discovered—a staggering number, considerably more than have been found at any other Maya site. Caracol's "tomb culture" suggests that ordinary citizens buried their dead in specially made chambers in their homes, not in outlying cemeteries as previously believed. The Chases speculate that the dead may have even played a role in rituals conducted by their living descendants.

Two of the most exciting tomb finds, however, did not reveal middle-class members. Rather, the chambers uncovered by the Chases in 1992 held a king and a woman, likely his wife, and a royal family of four. The king's tomb, which dates to around 480 A.D., was embellished with 17 elaborately painted vessels, obsidian earflares, and jade and shell necklaces (though only fragments of these remain). In the second tomb, the floor was dusted with jade flakes. There were two men here, including one wearing a necklace of human teeth, a woman, and a fourth person of unknown sex. There was also a painted text indicating the tomb was built in 582 A.D., 100 years before it was sealed.

Arriving in the jungle mantle of Caracol today, it is difficult to appreciate the true scope of this Classic city. But as the Chases and their excavation team continue to peel back thousands of years of nature's shroud, they are discovering a place of staggering size, brilliant design and stylish architecture. At least 36,000 structures are spread across 166 square miles, making Caracol 865 percent more dense than the great Tikal. Work here could well continue for many decades; the Chases say that "by the year 2003, we don't even see ourselves out of the major plazas."

Much of their work, which includes "stabilizing" or securing the structures, is concentrated in the city's nucleus, where they have discovered stucco and plaster palaces, pyramids and temples that were painted dazzling shades of red and blue, and even red and white stripes. Those that weren't painted were silvery white, their marbleized limestone catching sunrays by day and moonlight by night. Among the grand buildings are several low-lying structures that were perhaps ancient fast-food stands.

From the administrative hub, causeways from 9 to 30 feet wide fan out like the spokes of a wheel, reaching up to six miles all around into Caracol's sprawling suburbia. These were not only footpaths but crucial routes for transporting food and water throughout the region. Where some of the causeways culminate are large plazas whose designs suggest markets and way stations for crops and merchandise. The crops likely came from Caracol's vast agricultural fields, evidenced by thousands of terraces found by the Chases. The terraces indicate not subsistence farming but cash crops—further proof of a sophisticated middle class.

To irrigate the fields and provide drinking water for residents, Maya engineers created a complex reservoir system that funneled water to crops and homes. It was a necessary system, since, strangely, the Maya had chosen to build their city far from a good water source. Now, nearly 2000 years later, that same reservoir provides bathing water for Caracol's current residents—the excavation team that includes the Chases, University of Central Florida undergraduates, postgraduate supervisors and about 45 Belizean bushmen, some of whom are descendants of those ancient Maya.

Actually, the entire team is only in residence from mid-February through the end of May each year (minus a break for Easter week), and this is absolutely the best time to visit Caracol. Not only can you see how archaeologists live (in meager huts next to banana groves) and work (in musty, dusty excavation pits), but you can tour an ancient city in the throes of modern discovery. Everyone who comes to Caracol is assigned a Belizean caretaker as a guide; visitors are not allowed to wander the site alone—a necessary rule, considering the extent of ongoing excavation and preservation.

Before you come, you must obtain a visitor's permit, available from the Forestry Department Station in Augustine, 30 miles north of Caracol, or from the Department of Archaeology in Belmopan (8-22106). The Belmopan office can also provide current road conditions; roads sometimes flood in the rainy season and are closed for up to 24 hours. This is a minor inconvenience, considering Caracol only became accessible year-round in early 1993. Before that, most of Caracol's few visitors came on horseback. The first two months the new roads opened, however, more than 2000 visitors streamed in—and nearly 18,000 visitors are expected during 1995.

The Caracol tour begins in the epicenter. Here looms the lofty **Caana**, Belize's tallest manmade structure, emerging 139 feet from the floor of **Plaza B** and crowned by three temples, several pyramids and a courtyard. It is also known as **Sky Place** and **Sky Palace**, the latter being bestowed by students, who love to sleep atop its summit on full moon nights. Caana is so stupendous that its temples are not fully visible from the plaza floor. But ascend its steep steps and you will discover many quadrants and rooms and sleeping benches. One of the chambers, nicknamed the "dwarf room," has inexplicable two-foot-high doorways and teeny benches.

At the top of Caana is a massive plaza and Caana's highest point, **Structure B19**. Here is where you should take time to look down on the jungle, whose ten-story trees are dwarfed by this proud view. Then stroll next door to **Temple B20**, where looters tunneled into three tombs, taking whatever valuables were there and destroying a painted text on a plastered wall. The Chases spent most of their first season, in 1985, cleaning up the damage and salvaging broken vessels and bones. One of Caana's pyramids, **Structure B18**, reveals a well-preserved staircase flanked by a stone mask. Between structures **B18** and **B19** are remnants of a decorative baseboard, painted such a deep red that the color remains almost as vivid today.

Situated conveniently near the great Caana is the elite **Barrio Group**. Like an uptown Manhattan, the posh residential area enjoyed easy access to Caracol's epicenter, or downtown. Likewise, the **South Acropolis**, across the city center, was an upscale area right next to the reservoir. Several tombs were uncovered among these homes, including a vertical vault harboring a woman and a man. The capstone, or tomb lid, was not painted red as traditional for Caracol nobility, indicating the couple may have been buried in their own house.

The South Acropolis residents no doubt watched a lot of *pok-ta-pok*, or Maya ballgames, in the neighboring **ball court**. They also likely witnessed the recording of their ruler's victory over the lords of Tikal. The triumphant battle between Caracol's Lord Water and his former Tikal overlord is recorded on a **ball court marker** that today is sheltered by a piece of aluminum. Several years ago, the marker was, incredibly, crushed by logging trucks. Thus, its 1400-year-old features are, unfortunately, very vague. The best way to admire its hieroglyphs is with a flashlight at night.

Across the epicenter, in **Group A**, some of Caracol's most influential figures lived, conducted business, and were eventually buried. Nine stelae and six altars were found here, as well as numerous burials that belonged to the elite. In **Structure A3**, the Chases discovered an important tomb containing eight pottery vessels, 13 quail skeletons, and the badly decomposed body of an adult. Glyphs on the tomb's capstones record a date of approximately 695 A.D. and describe a person of royal lineage.

Presiding over Group A is the **Temple of the Wooden Lintel**, or **Structure A6**, which, amazingly, has its original sapote wood door lintels preserved in a side room. Steep short steps run down the temple's face, but a determined person will want to scale them to explore the temple's myriads of floors and rooms. In the core of this building, researchers found an incredible 9000 pieces of jadeite, and a spectacular jadeite mask in a stone box. The box held more: 684 grams of liquid mercury—nearly half of all the mercury recovered by researchers throughout the Maya Kingdom. In this area, too, was an urn filled with a cache of mysteries: stingray spines, sharks' teeth, fish vertebrae, pumpkin seeds, pine needles, seaweed and even a beehive that has survived, virtually intact, all these centuries.

There is much more to see and learn at Caracol, even as researchers make new discoveries every day. And now that the roads are open year-round, researchers expect this extraordinary place to become Belize's premier inland destination. With that in mind, the Chases have rallied the Belize government to hire eight wardens—not easy in a country too poor to excavate the ruins in the first place.

XUNANTUNICH   From Caracol back to San Ignacio is about four hours of rough and tumble roads. You'll be so glad when you feel the smoothness of the Western Highway again, you'll want to stop off for a drink (highly recommended: the poolside terrace at the San Ignacio Hotel). Afterward, head west on the Western Highway to the village of San José Succotz, where you can take the hand-cranked car ferry across the gurgling Mopan River (notice the women washing their clothes). From here, a dirt road leads to **Xunantunich** (admission). One of the few Maya cities built atop a hill, Xunantunich (Shoo-NA-tu-NISH) is a stirring place looming along a limestone ridge in the Belize River Valley. Its name means "Stone Woman," a modern-day moniker alluding not only to this rocky plateau but to the erotic female images that could be conjured from the sleek, shapely temples.

Xunantunich flourished 1000 years ago, during the Classic Period. More than a century ago, amateur archaeologist Dr. Thomas Gann first explored the site, but did no excavations until he returned in 1924. At that time, he uncovered caches of burial items as well as hieroglyphs that were circling a main altar. He took them with him, and their whereabouts are a mystery today.

Over the years, excavations at Xunantunich have been piecemeal. In 1938, British archaeologist Eric S. Thompson unearthed a residential group, while in 1949, then-Archaeology Commissioner A.H. Anderson discovered the

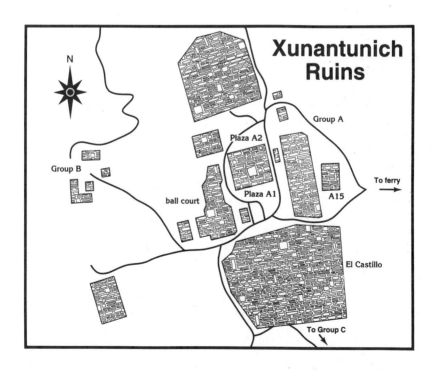

remnants of a stucco frieze. In 1952, an amateur British archaeologist named Michael Stewart discovered burials and offerings. Seven years later, a Cambridge University researcher named Euan Mackie uncovered evidence in one of the temples that Xunantunich had been wrenched by an earthquake in about 900 A.D. It was at least one possible explanation for why the city was abandoned at this same time.

During the 1970s, various teams worked to excavate and preserve Xunantunich's greatest structures. Today the site is small but immensely scenic, a one-mile oasis of emerald grasses speckled with cohune palms and limestone outcroppings. The city's buildings encase three plazas fashioned in north–south design and its outskirts are sprinkled with house mounds. The structures go from grand to comfortable to tiny, no doubt accommodating a spectrum of Maya classes.

Attention is naturally focused on where the elite spent their time. That would be **Group A**, where several temples gather around two grassy plazas. Dominating **Plazas A1** and **A2**—and all of Xunantunich—is 130-foot **El Castillo**, a terraced palace with a toothy contour and a skirt of velvety green grass. In Belize, it is second only in height to another great Maya palace, Caana, in the nearby city-state of Caracol. Climb the face of El Castillo and—when you've recovered from the overwhelming view of the countryside—notice the platform topped with two temples. The temples are famous for their elaborate bone-colored friezes, including an astronomical frieze and a frieze portraying a headless man. The palace's exposed blue-and-white limestone, glinting in the sunlight, takes on haunting shapes.

Like many Maya temples, Castillo is actually a series of buildings superimposed upon each other over the centuries. You can see evidence of earlier levels and layers everywhere; notice the wide terrace, about 35 feet up the north side, that at one point had buildings lining its edges. And if you look closely at the two upper temples, one resting upon the other, you'll see that the Maya originally covered the lower temple to make a foundation for the higher one. Only now, after archaeologists have cleared away debris and centuries of vegetation, is their construction so obvious.

Smaller temples congregate around Plaza A, one of the most interesting being **Structure A15**, which has a stone bench. Just off Plaza A is a small **ball court**, which now resembles a grassy alley. Nearby, the structures around **Group B** are thought to be upper- and middle-class homes, hinting that Xunantunich was once occupied by a cultured, elite society.

The ruins are an excellent place to have lunch, but bring your own. The closest refreshments are in San José Succotz, back across the Mopan River.

West from Xunantunich on the Western Highway, the last place before Guatemala is **Benque Viejo**. The small border town is a peaceful place with two-story clapboard homes painted in crayon colors, wash strung across the porches, and chicken-wire fences (and chickens) running all over the place.

There are no real sites here, other than the friendly residents, *Mestizos* and Mopan Maya, who tip their hats to you as you stroll down the dusty streets.

After Benque Viejo, you can turn back into the familiar terrain of Belize or make the adventurer's choice and cross into Guatemala. What awaits beyond the border is some of Mesoamerica's most spectacular rainforests and truly its most sensational Maya city. The 2500-year-old kingdom of Tikal still rules the vast jungles of northern Guatemala, known as the Petén, drawing more than 100,000 visitors each year. Tikal is only about 40 miles from the Belize/Guatemala border, but it's one long hellacious ride down a body-battering dirt road, with possibilities (albeit slim) of bandits hiding in the roadside bush. The border crossing, however, is not so much a test of courage as of patience.

On the Belize side, you will surrender your tourist card, have your passport stamped and pass through with relative ease. On the Guatemala side, at Melchor de Mencos, you must show your passport and visa and, depending on the time of day and mood of the border officials, pay a small fee, or *propina*. Several officials may also have to "review" your documents before allowing you to pass.

Despite ongoing political conflicts within Guatemala and its tenuous relationship with Belize, it's unlikely you'll encounter problems at the border or while traveling in Guatemala, especially in the Petén, where the government is focusing its tourism efforts. For more on visiting Guatemala, see Chapter Eleven.

LODGING   Since the early 1990s, several lodges have opened in Mountain Pine Ridge Forest Reserve, offering travelers easier access to this vast wilderness and to the exciting Maya city of Caracol.

Cool Shade Resort (Mile Post 2, Mountain Pine Ridge Road; ceiling fans; moderate; 92-2146, fax: 2-230263) isn't shady at all. It's set up high on a hill, mountains hovering all around, citrus groves patterned across the valley, butterflies swarming the hillsides—very pleasant. The main lodge of the 5000-acre farm estate is a wood-floored ranch house with a handful of simple but comfortable rooms, their plank walls freshly painted, their windows or porches inviting with superb views. A separate cabin has palm bark on the outside, a balcony made of twigs and a banana tree outside the door. Meals are served family-style in the big handsome dining room.

Eight miles from the Western Highway on Mountain Pine Ridge Road, you'll find the picturesque, 152-acre spread of **Mountain Equestrian Trails** (Mile Post 8, Mountain Pine Ridge Road, Central Farm; expensive; 92-3310, fax: 82-3361, or 800-838-3918 in the United States). American expatriates Marguerite and Jim Bevis and their four children welcome travelers to their quarterhorse ranch set amid pine forest. Four pleasant stucco-and-wood cabanas with private baths and hot water (but no electricity) offer a comfortable way to sleep in the woods, and there's a cantina serving meals and drinks. Families love it here; kids enjoy the trail rides through the jungle, with visits to beautiful rivers and falls and secret limestone caves. The Bevis' daughters can babysit for kids who want to hang around the ranch. Day tours to area ruins, including Caracol, are also available. A full breakfast is included.

If you want to feel as if you've retreated to some secret mountain hideaway, stay at ✪ **Hidden Valley Inn** (an hour from the Western Highway, take the turnoff at Georgeville; very expensive; for reservations, call 8-23320 in Belmopan, fax: 8-23334, or 800-334-7942 in the United States). Here, a cluster of lovely stucco cabanas huddle under sky-reaching pine trees surrounded by cushiony trails of pine needles and brilliant impatiens that grow like weeds. Inside, Mexican tile floors, dhurrie rugs and high angled ceilings create visual warmth, while wood-burning fireplaces provide physical warmth on nippy winter nights. Cocktails and tasty meals are served in a big elegant ranch house that feels like something out of the American Southwest. But you'll know it's not when you hear what sounds like a Chihuahua yapping—only to learn it's a barred forest falcon calling to its mate. The inn's property spans 18,500 acres and includes the scenic **Lake Lollyfolly** and **Bull's Point**, which looks across a shimmering green valley, and **Butterfly Falls**, a forested haunt where butterflies float across a creek and travel up a waterfall. There's also **King Vulture Falls**, where a mountain is etched with trenches of waterfalls ruled by King Vultures. To see the throngs of eerie black creatures, you'll need strong binoculars (preferably 80 power) or a telescope. Rates include breakfast and dinner.

Around the corner, the less fancy ✪ **Pine Ridge Lodge** (expensive; 92-3310 in Belize or 216-781-6888, or 800-316-0706 in the United States) offers seven wooded cottages ranging from basic to quite comfortable. The "For-

Ocellated turkey

est" and "Mayan" cottages are simply decorated, open and airy, but opt for the secluded, spacious "Riverview" cottage with a screened porch along a scenic creek. There's no electricity (kerosene lamps provide light), but there is hot water and the cook manages to turn out good food with a gas stove and generator-powered refrigerator.

Upon arriving at ✪ **Blancaneaux Lodge** (Mountain Pine Ridge, an hour from the Western Highway; private and shared baths; expensive to very expensive; 92-3878, fax 92-3919), one senses the place is vastly different from any other in Belize, having tremendous warmth and flair in its design, and yet set so far up here in the jungle mountain wilderness. Planters gush with exquisite flowers and frilly ivy masks a stone fireplace. A river churns down below a hillside decorated with flamboyant foliage—red scepters of ginger, purple sprays of orchids. A curved dining room is suspended above the forest, and the lodge's cabanas, villas and rooms are adorned in a sensual Mayan style. It all reflects the tastes of Francis Ford Coppola and his wife, Eleanor, who own the lodge. In 1981, the famed movie producer and director fell in love with Belize and bought the lodge—the oldest jungle lodge in Belize—and this exquisite piece of secluded forest. Belize, being Belize, didn't pay much attention back then, nor when Coppola opened the lodge in early 1993.

Coppola's special touches don't end in the kitchen or in the lodge surroundings. He installed his own hydroelectric plant using water from the river that flows just beneath the lodge. He has a private airstrip that eliminates the four-hour drive from Belize City (though chartered flights are expensive—about US$360 round-trip, minimum three passengers). And he opened seven cabanas, five villas, and two large rooms (the latter share a bath). The all-wood cabanas seem built into the trees, their roomy screened porches places to relax and take in the surrounding forest (and while you're at it, uncork a bottle of Niebaum-Coppola Rubicon from Coppola's own Napa Valley Winery.

A little past Blancaneaux you'll find the desirable **Five Sisters Lodge** (fans; moderate; 91-2005, fax: 92-3081), named for the five waterfalls that gush through the property. A stairway wends down to the falls, three natural pools and a palapa bar that sits on an island in the Privassion River. Choose from seven rooms in a main building (two with decks hung over the falls) or ten thatch-roof cabanas sprinkled among the grounds. The cabanas are a bit more expensive, but you get the extra privacy, a screened deck and a hammock where you can relax and listen to the falls. Reasonably priced Belizean meals are served in the dining rooms.

RESTAURANTS   When famed director Francis Ford Coppola opened **Blancaneaux Lodge** (Mountain Pine Ridge, about one hour from the Western Highway; expensive; reservations required by calling 92-3878) in 1993, he flew an espresso maker and pizza oven over from Italy. News of the two then-unheard-of-in-Belize items spread across the country, and requests for a seat at Coppola's table began pouring in (espresso makers have since, naturally, become more heard of). He is happy to oblige, provided guests make reservations. The menu, of course, leans toward Italian, which the lodge's Belizean chef has become adept at preparing. For lunch, there are calzones and specialty pizzas; for dinner, the five-course menu focuses on pasta, smoked meats and local seafood. Dishes to try: spaghetti carbonara, gnocchi with real ragu and Mrs. Scorcese's Chicken—"intense lemon chicken taught to me by Marty's mother," Coppola writes on the menu. Everything is superb.

GETTING THERE: There is no bus service to Mountain Pine Ridge. However, it is quite easy to find your way in a rental car to the Mountain Pine Ridge lodges (which I did solo), and certainly possible to drive all the way to Caracol (though I hired a driver). Because of its extremely remote locale down miles of unmarked dirt jungle roads, I recommend hiring a driver to take you into Caracol your first time; there's no need to hire a tour guide, since guides are provided at the ruins. All area lodges, including those in San Ignacio, will arrange a driver.

You can easily drive to Xunantunich and to Benque Viejo, though you can't take the car across the Guatemala border. There's no bus service to Xunantunich, but you can take a Batty Brothers or Novelos bus to Benque Viejo from San Ignacio.

CHAN CHICH

If you drive to **Chan Chich**, you will think you've accidentally exited the earth into some planetary jungle, like when *Star Trek*'s Captain Kirk gets unexpectedly beamed to a strange Eden. The extraordinary lodge and Maya ruin is flung way out in Belize's northwestern hinterlands, almost to Guatemala, nowhere near civilization, and at least a four-hour drive from Belize City in the dry season. Forget the rainy season—all the roads are washed out.

But most people who visit Chan Chich do it in a small charter plane, flying low over a wheat-colored plateau that explodes into emerald jungle, then nosing down into a pinpoint clearing called **Gallon Jug**. An old logging camp turned farm center, the Jug is owned by Belizean entrepreneur Barry Bowen, whose beverage company makes Belize's own Belikin Beer, and who in 1984 bought 125,000 surrounding acres and made them a nature reserve.

What Bowen and his crew found when they first arrived were lots of marijuana fields, numerous Maya temples that had been looted, and leftovers from poachers who were hunting with abandon. Indeed, under a single tree, in a bloody, feathery heap, were the bodies of 24 ocellated turkeys. Bowen's solution: build a lodge that would break even, but whose primary goal was to protect the forest by having year-round visitors. In 1988, he opened 12 hardwood cabanas, constructed entirely from local materials and set in the plaza of an unexcavated Maya ruin. The ocellated turkeys found today at Chan Chich preen around the grounds, fearing only rejection by a mate.

With virgin rainforest running for miles in every direction, the lodge offers visitors a window on the wildlife of Belize. Howler and spider monkeys navigate the trees overhead, while toucans nest near your room. Nighttime brings the chilling roars of howler monkeys; come dawn, you will think you awoke in nature's own amphitheater, flooded with a symphony of purrs, screeches, whishes, rattles and even pop-pop-pops. After a day or so, you learn the rhythms of the jungle, and they become your own.

In fact, because it is cushioned by protected lands—to the west lies the 1.7-million-acre Maya Biosphere Reserve; to the south, 200,000 acres owned by Programme for Belize—Chan Chich enjoys a spectacular abundance of wildlife. Birders, naturalists and lovers of archaeology are among the lodge's most devoted clientele, though its secrets are lately being divulged among mainstream travelers.

Lest you think building a lodge on a Maya ruin is sacrilege, Bowen points out that since he opened, problems with looting and marijuana growing have ceased. He has his opponents, but Bowen is proving himself an ecotourism advocate, taking care to protect the ruins while guests enjoy them and refusing to interfere with wild life (even bird feeders are not allowed).

LODGING   For the ultimate Belize jungle experience, spend the night in a 1700-year-old Maya city. It's possible at ❂ **Chan Chich Lodge** (ceiling fans; very expensive; for reservations, call 2-75634 or 2-34419, fax: 2-76961, or 800-343-8009 in the United States), whose lovely thatched cabanas rest atop a Classic plaza encased in ancient temples and tombs.

But living in this jungle doesn't mean roughing it. Chan Chich's 12 cabanas are attractive and entirely comfortable with their hot showers, downy linens and spacious quarters. Fashioned from gleaming local woods and crowned with soaring thatched roofs, the cabanas feature louvered windows and big screens parked near the ceiling for maximum coolness. Spacious wrap-around verandas are ideal for wildlife watching and for admiring the lodge's luxuriant landscaping. There's a restaurant where everyone meets for outstanding meals, as well as a bar where nightly stories sound like something out of turn-of-the-century Africa. Here's where you'll get to know Chan Chich caretakers Tom and Josie Harding, former Californians who are responsible for this extremely well-run facility.

Guests are provided maps of the many trails that radiate out from the lodge, or they can purchase the invaluable *Exploring the Rainforest, Chan Chich Lodge* guide by Carolyn M. Miller and Bruce W. Miller. Local guides, who are not only knowledgeable but really love the jungle, conduct tours of the trails and ruins, including burial chambers painted with friezes, several times daily and on some nights. Horseback riding, canoeing and local sightseeing excursions are available, as well.

During holidays and peak seasons (December through April), book at least several weeks in advance.

GETTING THERE: Because of its extreme remoteness, Chan Chich provides charter flights in small planes from Belize City to the nearby outpost of Gallon Jug—a fantastic way to see the wilds of northern Belize.

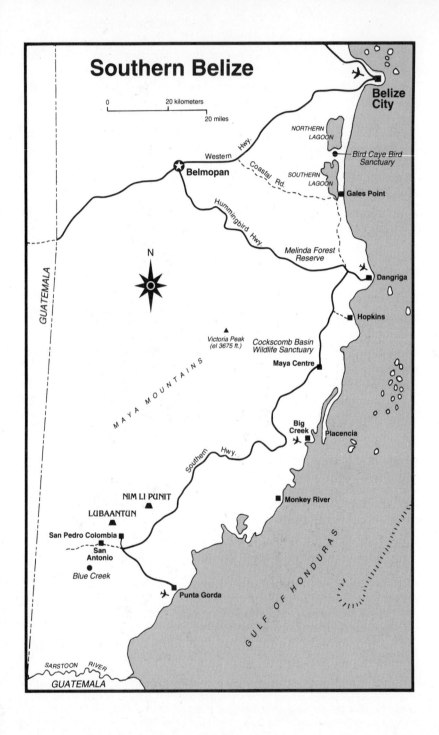

Southern Belize

0   20 kilometers

20 miles

Belize City

NORTHERN LAGOON

Western Hwy.

Coastal Rd.

Bird Caye Bird Sanctuary

★ **Belmopan**

SOUTHERN LAGOON

Gales Point

Hummingbird Hwy.

Melinda Forest Reserve

N

Dangriga

GUATEMALA

Hopkins

▲
Victoria Peak (el 3675 ft.)

Cockscomb Basin Wildlife Sanctuary

Maya Centre

M A Y A   M O U N T A I N S

Big Creek **Placencia**

Southern Hwy.

Monkey River

NIM LI PUNIT ▲

LUBAANTUN ▲

San Pedro Colombia ■

San Antonio ●

Blue Creek

Punta Gorda

G U L F   O F   H O N D U R A S

SARSTOON   RIVER

GUATEMALA

TEN

Southern Belize

The least populated, least visited and most rainy region of the country, southern Belize takes in the chunk of land south of Belize City to the Guatemala border. There are only three real towns—Dangriga, Placencia and Punta Gorda—all nestling against the Caribbean Sea, with primitive coastal villages scattered in between.

Inland is a different story. Here are the Maya lowlands and their foothills, looming as a deep, dark, forbidding chasm of rainforest punctured by jagged peaks of limestone and drop-off granite walls. Rising above all other peaks is Victoria Peak, Belize's highest at 3675 feet, whose "great cone of solid rock (shoots) perpendicularly skyward, seeming to float on the very roof of the forest," or so it was described by a member of the 1927 Grant Expedition, which, like many other teams over the years, failed to reach the summit. Thirty-nine years earlier, a team organized by British Honduras Governor Roger T. Goldsworthy did scale the peak and named it Victoria. Team member J. Bellamy, in a report to the Royal Geographical Society, said the whole area was "enveloped in a cloud of mystery."

"Karstic" is what geologists call the porous rock jungle of southern Belize, where bottomless fissures have been chiseled by eons of incessant rain. In the deepest recesses, the landscape is so dense and threatening, it is thought to be unexplored by humans, at least in modern times. Maya ruins are still being discovered, some of which have not seen humans in more than a thousand years. Those areas that have been explored exact respect from their explorers, for here are more poisonous snakes than anywhere else in Belize, and more drug runners. Abandoned logging camps dot inland rivers, their names—"Go to Hell" and *Sale Si Puedes* (Leave While You Can)—reminding one of the tenuous thread of life in these jungles.

Visitors to southern Belize shouldn't venture into these risky wilds, even with a bush guide. During more than ten years of research in southern Belize, one American archaeologist has dodged bandits' bullets and worked in areas that were "loaded with poisonous snakes." Chances are good you, too, would cross paths with a deadly snake, drug runner or looter, or with the Royal Highland Fusileers who patrol these frontier forests. The latter would ask for your government permits (several are needed to travel these jungle reserves) and purpose for being there ("simply having a look around" is *not* good enough).

However, there is much to see in less remote areas (which, incidentally, will seem *very* remote to many people), and you can take forays to several forested Maya ruins and a dense wildlife sanctuary. The worn, washboard Southern Highway provides access to these sights, though its poor condition prevents most people from venturing all 202 miles from Belize City to Punta Gorda, the end of the line in southern Belize. In fact, the trip is considered a measure of prowess, and if you want to earn a bit of Belizean admiration, wait until a night when the group rum bottle is near empty and announce that you drove "all the way to P.G.," the nickname for Punta Gorda.

Of course, *not* going all the way to Punta Gorda is one way to experience the Southern Highway and not get too physically and mentally mangled. Dangriga, the first major town, is only about a three-hour drive in the dry season; four to five hours in the rainy season. The next big stop, Placencia, is another hour and a half in a rattling car with dust and dirt flying behind you. But it's great adventure, and the tight web of jungle that clutches much of the road makes for a thrilling backdrop.

If you're pressed for time and energy, the best way to visit this region is to fly. Local airlines offer service to airstrips in Dangriga, Placencia and Punta Gorda. (Note the emphasis on *airstrips*. The closest thing to an airport is a palm tree and grass worn down by passengers waiting with their luggage.) Flying is not only much faster and also quite scenic, it costs the same as renting a car. Plus, you get to ride in a small tinny plane that feels like an old jalopy with wheels, usually piloted by a polite, clean-cut fellow fresh out of flying school (beverage service is *not* available, in case you had any doubts).

DANGRIGA

The largest town in southern Belize, **Dangriga**, with its downtown hubbub and harborfront vistas, feels like a miniature Belize City. It's not particularly scenic, just smaller and therefore less crowded and dirty. A walkable grid of paved and dirt streets is lined with clapboard hovels and businesses, highlighted by the Burger King (no relation to the one you're thinking of); the Sunrise and Starlight Chinese restaurants (just two of many); and Pepito's Store, which sells breadfruit on Breadfruit Road.

But beneath the drab, simple facade is a strong people with a rich, mysterious, tightly protected culture. More than three-quarters of Dangriga's 8000 residents are Garifunas (pronounced Ga-RIF-unas), whose ancestors came to Belize in the 1800s from the Caribbean island of St. Vincent. Two hundred years earlier, a ship carrying West African slaves ran aground in St. Vincent. No one's sure whether the survivors became slaves or citizens on the island, but what is certain is that they eventually intermarried with the native Caribs and created the Garifuna. Freedom was the foundation of their culture, and it caused them to rebel against British colonization of St. Vincent in the 19th century and flee to Central America.

Freedom is still integral to Garifuna existence today, specifically the freedom to practice their centuries-old farming and cooking methods, their painting, woodworking and music, and their enigmatic religion. Only in recent years have visitors to Dangriga been invited to observe some of the Garifuna ways.

One place to learn about both Garifuna art and the art of cooking is at the **home of Austin Rodriguez** (32 Tubroose Street; 5-22308; call ahead for an appointment). Amidst a gathering of clapboard shacks with chickens pecking around the dirt floors, Rodriguez fashions drums from mahogany, cedar and maple woods, stretching deerskin across the tops. The self-taught drummaker and Dangriga native has been carving congo and other drums for more than 30 years. His customers span several continents, and his drums have been played in many a *dugu*, the all-important Garifuna ceremony and feast for reconciling with dead ancestors.

While Rodriguez makes drums, the women and children of his extended family are usually busy making cassava bread. You can witness various stages of this day-long process, which includes peeling dozens of the white glistening root vegetables, feeding them into an electric masher (they were all mashed by hand until a few years ago), then stuffing the mashed mixture into a woala. Named for the big local snake, the woala is a six-foot-long rattan strainer that, when hung from a tree by several sturdy women, causes cassava juice to drain into buckets. After several hours, the juice is taken away to harden overnight (unhardened, it is poisonous), after which it will transform into starch. Meanwhile, the mashed and juiced cassava root is baked into a thin, white flatbread called *ariba*. To unaccustomed taste buds, it has about as much flavor as a paper towel, which is sad considering the amount of work involved. But to locals, a fresh-baked batch of *ariba* is a treasured thing, and those who receive it are very lucky indeed.

Nowhere is this cassava tradition better captured than on the canvases of **Benjamin Nicholas**, whose colorful and compelling portrayals of local life have gained national and international attention. "These are the people in my head. I've been painting them every day, nonstop, all my life," Nicholas will explain if you drop by his house and studio at 25 Howard Street (before you go, call 5-22785 for an appointment). In his mid-60s, the pensive man with a pushbroom mustache and pointy goatee fills his days and his canvases in a dim, concrete-floored room that looks out to sea through barred windows. His paintings, many unfinished, surround him with scenes of somber-eyed

Garifuna women toiling over their cassava, and of happy children playing by the sea.

Artist **Mercy Sabal** (55 Citron Street; 5-22651; call in advance for an appointment) preserves her native culture not with a brush and oils but with flowing quilts embroidered with vivid pictorials. One series, "Woman of the Soil," portrays her Garifuna sisters sweating in the fields as they dig up cassava and other vegetables—still part of their daily routine. Another shows them gathering coconuts and firewood and balancing *fania* baskets on their heads. For those wondering about a Garifuna woman's role in society, Sabal (and many others) will point out that she shoulders not only the household chores but is also responsible for gathering food, delivering babies, treating the sick and making clothes for her extended family.

From Dangriga, there are numerous possibilities for day trips, including nearby islands such as **Tobacco Caye** and **South Water Caye** for snorkeling and picnicking, and **Man-of-War Caye** for watching the frigate birds and brown boobies that swarm the island. Or you can head inland.

If you head north for six miles down a bumpy clay marl road, past hillsides masked in citrus and banana groves and vultures perched atop spindly trees, you will discover a real out-of-the-way but very important place. Here, from a humble little building surrounded by weeds comes millions of bottles of Marie Sharp's Hot Sauce. *The* hot pepper sauce of Belize, gracing the top of nearly every restaurant and home cook's table, it is made with habañero peppers, the world's hottest chile peppers, measuring between 200,000 and 300,000 on the Scoville Chart, the Richter scale of chile peppers (jalapeños measure 5000). This tiny "factory" and the surrounding 400 acres are called **Melinda Farm** (call 5-22080 for directions and an appointment), and is the birthplace of Marie Sharp's Hot Sauce, formerly called Melinda's Hot Pepper Sauce.

There are many stories surrounding this pepper sauce, one being that it was named for a woman called Melinda, which it is not. Rather, it is named after the Melinda Forest Reserve within which it lies. Another misnomer is that the sauce is made from peppers grown on Melinda Farm, when, in fact, the soil here is not suited for habañeros but for citrus. Farms in the surrounding Stann Creek Valley provide all those peppers for Marie Sharp's Hot Sauce.

Melinda Farm is owned by Marie and Jerry Sharp, who called their sauce Melinda's until they had a falling out with their United States bottlers and distributors (distant relatives in New Orleans), who purportedly put the Melinda label on inferior sauces made in other countries. Now the only bonafide Melinda sauce is that labeled Marie Sharp's (bottles in the U.S. still say Melinda's, but owning one in Belize is tantamount to treason).

Depending on the time of day and year, you can walk around the factory and watch the Belizean women giggling in their baker's hats while they stir up a batch of the tasty sauce. Amazingly, every batch goes into a 60-gallon trough with only three spigots, which fill 1536 bottles in just 90 minutes. During an average eight-hour day, close to 8000 bottles are filled. And that's just the hot pepper sauce. This tiny factory turns out many other unusual, delicious concoctions, including mango chutney spiked with ginger and brown sugar, guava, papaya and banana jams, and a hot pickle relish called *curtido*. If you're wondering what all those good smells are in each vat, food chemist and quality control manager Ivan Joseph can tell you the *basic* ingredients—detailed recipes are, of course, top-secret.

Joseph will take you outside the factory and show you a habañero plant (there is a small experimental field here), its satiny red lanterns dangling from a leafy bush. He will also take you through groves of citrus and papaya, and the tiny cemetery wherein resides the Burns Family, who originally owned the farm.

North from the farm about 12 miles, at the tip of a skinny peninsula that pokes into the wide Southern Lagoon, is a locked-in-time fishing village called **Gales Point**. You'll find only one lodge and about 300 people here but many more manatees, who are drawn to the warmth and safety of the lagoon. You can hire a boat (just ask around the village) to take you "manatee watching" through the picturesque Southern Lagoon and up into the Northern Lagoon, with a stop at the **Bird Caye Bird Sanctuary** for glimpses of ibis, herons and egrets.

After exploring the area north of Dangriga, head south, preferably on a different day, since the roads are rough and by now will seem endless. The first southern stop is **Hopkins**, a Garifuna fishing village where 20th-century life has just begun to trickle in. It's best to arrive by boat; it's not only faster and less stressful on the body but affords a striking view of the village as you approach the gathering of seaside stilt huts framed by the luscious green Maya Mountains.

Though electricity reached Hopkins in 1994, Garifuna families still cling to the traditions of their ancestors, shunning the trappings of modern life. In fact, before villagers opened several very primitive lodges, the only visitors were infrequent drifters who themselves knew little of the outside world. No matter who seems to wander into their sheltered outpost, the villagers are more than friendly, inviting you to dine in their homes (for a small fee, of course) and learn about their way of life. That might include accompanying a fisherman in a dugout canoe or joining a punta rock party with its feverish beat and fast, sexy dancing. Or, you can explore local waters on your own with a kayak, available for rent at the village docks.

South of Hopkins, a grinding ride down the clay washboard Southern Highway will bring you to **Maya Centre**. This is the gateway to the **Cockscomb Basin Wildlife Sanctuary** and home to an ever-expanding group of Mopan Maya, many of whom gave up their homes and *milpa* farms to make way for the sanctuary. If you patronize the village's one-room **crafts center**, which carries attractive slate carvings and woven baskets, you will be fueling the local economy with tourist dollars and therefore reducing the need for poaching and looting.

From Maya Centre, it's six miles into the jungle before you reach the sanctuary's **Visitors Center**, where there are picnic tables, primitive camping huts and trailheads that disappear into surrounding forest. There's also brief information on Cockscomb and its beginnings, though if you really want the big picture, read Alan Rabinowitz's book *Jaguar*. The fast-moving adventure recounts Rabinowitz's field research in Cockscomb during 1983–84, trapping, tagging and tracking jaguars, living with Maya villagers, surviving a plane crash, battling poachers and arrogant, wealthy American hunters flying down for a quick kill, enduring various jungle parasites and ailments, and dodging drug dealers and snakes (though one of his Maya assistants, while chasing a jaguar, was bitten by a fer-de-lance and subsequently died).

Most of the jaguars Rabinowitz tracked died as well, either by poachers, injuries obtained during capture, or reasons unknown. But the New York zoologist did prove one thing: That despite considerable poaching and wrecking of the forests for farmland, the jaguar still has a chance in Cockscomb, and indeed in Belize itself. Compared to Belize, most other Central and South American habitats are rapidly dwindling. Even in Costa Rica, Rabinowitz found "only a few places. . .where jaguars might still roam in their natural state."

In late 1984, after much work and support by the Belize Audubon Society, the Forestry Department and local Maya families, Cockscomb was declared

Jaguar

a National Forest Reserve where hunting was banned. In subsequent years, it was upgraded to a sanctuary to protect all animal and plant life, and now logging is banned. Today, it is the world's only jaguar preserve, boasting the densest population of jaguars ever recorded. It lies in a 100,000-acre bowl of forest, ringed on three sides by ridges and mountains, including Victoria Peak, which appears as a shard of rock looming in the distance.

A honeycomb of trails coils through portions of the sanctuary, offering hikes ranging from one hour to several days. Many of the trails are former logging roads carved as recently as the early 1980s. The jaguars and other cats of Cockscomb, including pumas, ocelots, jaguarundis and margays, use these roads to travel and stalk their prey. However, it's doubtful you'll see a jaguar unless it's dark, since it is a nocturnal beast and, despite its ferocious reputation, avoids prey larger than itself, specifically people. The other cats are just as elusive, preferring to watch *you* from their safe hiding place in the bush. It *is* likely that you'll encounter the jaguar's telltale signs—feces and scratch marks—and then you will know he or she is not far away.

Many other Cockscomb inhabitants are less shy about showing themselves. More than 290 species of birds light up the trees with song and color, including keel-billed toucans, scarlet macaws, great curassows and king vultures. You may also encounter a boa constrictor or red-eyed tree frog, or even a tapir (mountain cow), a creature who loves the dense, dewy foliage kept cool by triple canopies of trees.

Along the **Curassow Trail**, phosphorescent butterflies float across footpaths carpeted with silky ferns, and vines seem to drop out of the sky. Palm fronds stretch three stories high, and fungi grow as big and brilliant as lacquered seashells. A trail of pebbles beckons down to a swimming hole with water so clear you can drop a coin 25 feet to the bottom and tell if it lands heads or tails. Overhead, waterfalls plunge down from the boulders.

Scattered throughout the basin are the ruins of ceremonial centers and house mounds that belonged to the ancient Maya, perhaps the first humans to call Cockscomb home. But far greater than these small reminders are **four Maya sites**—discovered in 1993—entombed deep in the perilous rocky rainforests southwest of Cockscomb. After ten years of research in southern Belize, including excavations at Lubaantun and Nim Li Punit near Punta Gorda, archaeologist Peter S. Dunham found the sites in terrain so dense and precipitous it was thought no humans could have survived there. But the Maya not only survived, they created thriving communities more than a thousand years ago on what Dunham believes may be "the only volcanic and metamorphic deposits of their kind in the Maya area." For this land of 1000-foot limestone cliffs and hammocks seething with fer-de-lance snakes is also super-rich in minerals, which likely drew the Maya. Dunham, assistant professor of anthropology at Cleveland State University, suspects the Maya were mining hematite for red ochre, pyrite for mirrors, granite for grinding stone and other minerals that "underwrote the Maya economy."

Although each of these ancient communities had a "downtown" area with pyramids, there are no grand buildings to indicate a "New York" or an "L.A." "This is like finding a Denver mining town or a Houston oil town," explains Dunham. The archaeologist and his team of five students, a biologist and a geologist located the sites on tips from hunters. After setting up camp, the Royal Highland Fusileers who patrol the jungles brought the team supplies, and hence they named one of the communities RHF. They call the other three Tiampiha, the Yucatec Maya word for "between two waters;" Tzimin Che, which is Mopan Maya for tapir; and Ekxux, Mopan Maya for the rare red extremely poisonous fer-de-lances who live at the site.

Dunham's research here will continue for years, though it is unlikely that the sites will ever by accessible to the public. He cautions anyone who even thinks of visiting: "Don't do it. The area is very rugged and very dangerous, full of looters and drug runners. I've been shot at."

Tours to the Cockscomb sanctuary, however, are highly recommended and can be arranged in Dangriga through **Pelican Beach Resort** (north end of town, near the airstrip; 5-22044). Or, from the southern town of Placencia, contact **Junior Burgess** (6-23139), one of the best bush guides in Belize. Cockscomb is about half-way between Dangriga and Placencia. For information on camping in Cockscomb, contact the Belize Audubon Society at 2-77369 in Belize City or write to the sanctuary at P.O. Box 90, Dangriga, Belize.

LODGING   As befitting a last frontier, the lodging in southern Belize is low on comfort, high on funkiness—and character, if you're lucky. Elegance exists only in the seaside sense, and only in Placencia at a place called Rum Point Inn (see Placencia Lodging section later in this chapter).

You can drive to **Manatee Lodge** (Coastal Road, Gales Point; ceiling fans; very expensive; for reservations: 8-23320, fax: 8-23334, or 904-222-2333, 800-334-7942 in the United States), wending 25 miles south of Belize City along solid dirt roads through plantations and foothills of the Maya Mountains. Or, you can board a small boat and glide through silent mangrove canals and jungly lagoons. The two-story, white clapboard lodge sits on the Southern Lagoon, on a peninsula that elbows out into the breezes. Fishers are the most frequent guests, using their days to stalk tarpon and snook, though naturalists and other solitude lovers will enjoy the deep seclusion. Each of the eight roomy rooms has a private bath with hot water and comes with a canoe. Meals are included in the rate.

In Dangriga, the best place on the sea is the ✪ **Pelican Beach Resort** (north end of town; ceiling fans; some rooms with phone; cable TV; expensive; 5-22044, fax: 5-22570), where several old houses are strung together beneath the palm trees. Checking into one of the spacious, timeworn rooms is like climbing into an old bathrobe: vinyl-covered floors creak beneath your feet, a stuffed vinyl chair invites you to rest your body, and a rare-in-Belize bathtub lets you soak off the film of the jungle. Constant sea breezes and strong ceiling fans keep things cool, so you only miss the air-conditioning on hot summer nights. Resort owners Therese and Tony Rath are members of the Belize Audubon Society and are well-known conservation pioneers around Belize. Tony's wildlife photos grace the walls of the lobby and dining room, the latter being the best restaurant in town.

Dangriga's most modern digs are at the **Bonefish Hotel** (15 Mahogany Street; air-conditioning; fans; moderate to expensive; 5-22165, fax: 5-22296), a two-story cinderblock building washed in seafoam green and situated across from the sea. A 1993 remodeling gave the place an airy ambience, and most of the rooms are brightly painted and spacious. The views aren't great but there is cool air-conditioning (go for it—it's *hot* in Dangriga!) and big bathrooms with new tubs. The lobby is small and fashioned like a comfortable living room, and there's a cozy dining room where home cooking is the order of the day.

In the primitive village of Hopkins, several ultrabasic spots open their doors, the best being **Sandy Beach Lodge** (seaside on the south end of the village; private and shared baths; budget; for reservations call 5-22033). It's run by the Hopkins Women's Cooperative, the only women's cooperative in Belize, and it features 22 rooms, some with shared baths, but all basically clean. Best of all, the gregarious women who run this place are great cooks!

A mile south of Hopkins, on one of the prettiest patches of white sand in all of Belize, rest the seven thatch-roof cabanas of ☉ **Jaguar Reef Lodge** (ceiling fans; very expensive; 92-3452, or 800-633-4734 in the United States). Opened in late 1994, the warm and stylish retreat is no backwoods lodge: rich tile floors, native Belizean hardwood, big cathedral ceilings and spacious decks adorn the duplex suites, a total of 14 rooms. Owners Bruce Foerster, Neil Rogers (of International Expeditions fame) and others spent US$1.2 million on this ecotraveler's haven. A portion of the profits go to conservation organizations. Ideally situated, the lodge is only 15 minutes from reef or rainforest. Seven-day trips are offered ranging from hikes to Mayan ruins in the jungle to kayaking down freshwater creeks (the price of these day trips are extra). If you would rather relax at the lodge you could always play volleyball or enjoy a full-body massage. The Cockscomb Basin Wildlife Sanctuary, home to many jaguars, is only 30 minutes away by car.

RESTAURANTS   Listen to the waves roll ashore at the **Pelican Beach Resort** (north end of town, Dangriga; moderate; 5-22044), where an entirely pleasant dining room is decorated with wavy Belizean tiles, louvered windows and pink linens. There are usually three choices for dinner, including some type of steak, chicken and grilled catch of the day. Side dishes of baked plantains and tomato pasta are just as delicious.

Chinese restaurants seem as plentiful as palm trees in Dangriga. My favorite is the **Sunrise** (96 Commerce Street; budget; 5-22482), where the dining room is neat as a pin. Besides chop suey and curries, you can order fried conch or fried chicken, and choose from more than ten soups, including lobster noodle and chicken and shrimp.

There are only three tables and a television that blares all day in Creole and Spanish, but the food is tasty and plentiful at **Ritchie's Dinette** (84 Commerce Street, Dangriga; budget; 5-22112). The blackboard menu is short and simple: saucy stew chicken, beef or fish, with a side of rice and beans.

Owner/cook/waitress Pola serves up tasty Garifuna fare at her namesake eatery, **Pola's Kitchen** (25A Tubroose Street, Dangriga; budget; 5-22675). Open for breakfast, lunch and dinner, the dining room is decorated with photos of famous African-Americans such as Malcolm X and Rosa Parks.

For hearty, homestyle food in a casual dining room with one big vinyl-covered table, stop by the **Bonefish Hotel** (15 Mahogany Street, Dangriga; moderate; 5-22165). Depending on what the cook's cooking, you may have pork chops, fried chicken or T-bone steak, accompanied by potatoes, rice, whipped cassava with coconut milk (a Garifuna specialty), and a green salad. For breakfast, there are eggs and bacon and pancakes.

NIGHTLIFE   In Dangriga, **The Malibu** and **The Round House** (north end of town, across from the Pelican Beach Resort; 5-22487) are twin thatched-roof buildings that sit along the sea, only yards apart, offering rum drinks and the best punta rock concerts around.

GETTING THERE: Maya Airways offers the most frequent service to Dangriga from Belize City and other points around Belize. However, you can also catch a flight from Belize City to Dangriga on Tropic Airways. Bus service from Belize City to Dangriga is offered by Z-Line.

If you're flying in, as the toucan flies, Dangriga is 37 miles south of Belize City. But as you and your car travel, it is either 77 miles or 107, depending on the time of year. In the dry season, you can take the shorter route: the Western Highway from Belize City to Mile Post 31, then south on the new dirt Coastal Highway to Gales Point and then Dangriga. In the rainy season, you'll have to follow the Western Highway all the way to the Hummingbird Highway near Belmopan, then turn south for four hours of potholed trails that most resemble the site of a recent bomb explosion. The jungle scenes, however, are like something out of a banana republic postcard, and there are places where you can swim in clear pools and explore cool caves clouded with mist.

PLACENCIA

Many travelers find Placencia the most desirable place in southern Belize. Its sands are whiter and deeper than most cayes' sand, and its seaside resorts are instantly captivating. True to its name, the area forms a peninsula where a lagoon meets the Caribbean Sea. The peninsula's northern end is a wild and windswept coast with occasional resorts. The southern end is a jumble of weathered stilt buildings perched in the sand and edged by a concrete sidewalk. There are many palm trees, but no road. Could this be the town? Remembering you are in Belize, you realize that, of course, it is!

Spend a few hours in Placencia Village, and you'll meet half the town (the other half comes out at night, when seaside watering holes are alive with music and rum). Young Anglos adore it here, and give the sleepy village a bohemian edge. Though still remote and primitive, Placencia has gained a reputation as a savvy ecotourism destination. Surrounding jungles welcome exploration and dazzling, little-explored offshore reefs beckon to divers.

The fastest developing area on the peninsula lies about two miles north of Placencia Village in a place called **Seine Bight**. Only about 650 people reside in this traditional Garifuna village, but lodges, resorts and eateries are quickly fastening themselves to the seaside, most owned and run by Americans, and soon visitors may themselves number in the hundreds.

For now, though, daily Seine Bight activities follow the old-time Garifuna culture. The women gather to wash clothes, tend to the children, make cassava bread and catch up on village gossip, while the men fish, play dominoes and do their own socializing, usually with the help of some cold Belikins. And because the women have their own Garifuna dialect, the gap between the sexes seems even wider—though most everyone is receptive to visitors, especially those interested in their intriguing way of life.

LODGING   Along the sea in Placencia Village, five charming cabanas rest right in the sand at **RanGuana Lodge** (fans; moderate to expensive; 6-23112). Brightly painted on the outside, the interiors feature wood walls and barrel ceilings, bathtubs and coffeemakers. Ask for a cabana facing the sea.

Near the tip of Placencia's point, a scattering of mobile homes and cabanas have been freshened up and planted in the sand. Odd as they may seem, the six mobile homes at **Sonny's Resort** (ceiling fans; some mini-refrigerators; moderate; 6-23103, fax: 2-32819) are not bad considering the amount of space and the screened porch, though for a slightly higher price you can have a fancier cabana with a mini-refrigerator, coffeemaker and ceiling fan.

Deb and Dave's Last Resort (Placencia Village; shared bath; fans; budget; 6-23207) isn't exactly a resort, but it's definitely one of the best deals in town. The four bright guest rooms have wooden floors, front doors that open onto a deck and garden, and either one double bed or two singles. All share a large modern bathroom. From Deb and Dave's, it's an easy, breezy walk into town and to the beach.

The **Barracuda and Jaguar Inn** (Placencia Village; ceiling fans; moderate; 6-23330, fax: 6-23250) offers lodging in four cabanas of natural hardwood, with tin roofs, louvered windows, and private baths. From your screened front porch you can look out onto a lily pond and tropical garden—creations of owners Wende and Anton, who traveled across Belize gathering plants and flowers. The couple serves breakfast, lunch and dinner in a thatched-roof room open to the out-of-doors, and offer area tours.

A trio of chocolate-brown buildings along the sea signify you've reached **Kitty's Place** (one-and-a-half miles north of Placencia Village; private and shared baths; ceiling and table fans; some kitchens; moderate to expensive; 6-22027). It's a comfortably worn spot with warmth and character, thanks to American owner Kitty Fox. Choose from apartment-style rooms with private bath and kitchen or smaller quarters with shared bath. There's also a good restaurant and little bar here.

Foremost among area resorts, and one of my very favorite Belize lodges, is ❂ **Rum Point Inn** (two miles north of Placencia Village; very expensive; 6-23239, fax: 6-23240, or 800-747-1381 in the United States). At the inn, located near the Placencia airstrip, you'll meet delightful owners George and Corol Bevier, former Americans who are Belize aficionados. Their vast library, one of Belize's best, has volumes on local ancient history, flora and fauna, land and sea—enough to occupy you for days. George, a retired medical entomologist, has recorded the daily weather for 20 years, only to report there are no weather patterns in Belize! The inn consists of ten unusual sculpted domes right on the beach and eight newish family-style rooms set among gardens. The domes have ceilings that are high and round and give the feeling of being in a rotunda. All the accommodations are decorated with Guatemalan textile–covered chairs and comfortable beds. Meals are served family style, with lively conversation on ecotourism. Numerous day trips are offered here, including dive excursions through the lodge's dive shop, and there are bicycles, sailboats, and kayaks available for play.

Asia meets Belize at the **Hotel Seine Bight** (Seine Bight Village; expensive to very expensive; 6-23536), with its dining room accessed by a Japanese footbridge and the main room's great rotunda wearing an enormous cone-shaped, thatched roof. There are two guest rooms, each dramatically painted in red and black and covered in vines. The restaurant fare ranges from lasagna to Tandoori chicken, and is excellent.

The twelve rooms at the **Nautical Inn** (Seine Bight Village; have phones and air-conditioning; 62-3595, fax: 62-3594, or 800-688-0377 in the United States) reside in five octagonal buildings, painted gray and arranged around a small palm-studded beach. It's an easygoing place with lots of daytime possibilities: beach volleyball, bicycling, motor scootering, canoeing, sailing, and diving or snorkeling from the inn's motor boat. The "Oar House" is the venue for meals and cocktails, as well as the short-notice parties the congenial owners are famous for.

The name **French Quarter Belize** (Seine Bight Village; fans; very expensive; for reservations, call 6-23562 in Placencia, or 800-641-6665 in the United States) suggests a Nawlins connection, but think Caribbean Sea: The five stilt cabanas sit squarely on the water, drinking in stunning views and welcome winds. Inside are stylish rooms done in Guatemalan textiles, hand-crafted Mennonite furnishings and paintings by the locally famous artist Lo-la. All have a queen-size bed and futon. There's a dining room where you can take your meals, or, if you'd rather eat in town, the inn rents scooters and bicycles (rental charge) to take you there.

Toward the north end of the peninsula, **Singing Sands Inn** (four miles north of Placencia Village; expensive; 6-22243, or 800-617-2637 in the United States) is as pretty as can be. Landscaped with luxuriant flowers, the inn features a tropical restaurant and a thatched-roof bar that's popular with the locals. Six cabanas line the beach, each with attractive wood furniture, wood paneling and porch overlooking the sea. Coral heads right off the beach offer good, easy snorkeling. A quiet, relaxing place.

RESTAURANTS   In Placencia Village, locals and visitors gather to test their skills at pool at **The Corner Pocket** (moderate; 6-23175). The big, weath-ered clapboard building rests right on the sea, and also serves steaks and pork chops.

Chili's (Placencia Village; near the gas station) is nothing more than a wooden stand at the end of the road, near a gas station. But it serves great coffee and French toast, and the conch fritters aren't half bad either.

The **Flamboyant** (Placencia Village; budget; 6-23322) does indeed rest be-side a flamboyant tree, which in summer wears a fabulous plume of red. Dine under the tree—some of the coolest shade in town and, hence, a big hangout—or inside the impeccably clean restaurant where ceiling fans circulate the warm air. Come for breakfast, lunch or dinner, the latter featuring the requisite rice and beans and gamey offerings such as deer meat with stew beans.

Some of Placencia's best Belizean home cooking happens at **Brenda's Place** (south end of Placencia Village; budget; 6-23137). The breakfast, lunch and dinner menus change daily, depending on local offerings and Brenda's mood. But count on Caribbean-style seafood, chicken and steaks served on plates that runneth over. Brenda's pies are legendary. (The popularity of these offerings propelled Brenda's one-time roadside food stand into an es-tablished restaurant.)

The kitchen at **The Galley** (Placencia Village; moderate to expensive; 6-23133) is considered one of Placencia's best. The cook and bartender have been around more than 13 years and know quality. Culinary prospects range from conch stew, fried chicken and steamed fish to stir-fried vegetables and the ever-popular Creole shrimp and lobster. Musical accompaniment is top-notch jazz, compliments of a CD player. Placencia's first official smoothies (they call them milkshakes here) were served at The Galley. Be sure to try one; choices include soursop, mango, banana, pineapple and seaweed.

The creative couple who owns Barracuda and Jaguar Inn have opened **Pick-led Parrot Bar and Grill** (Placencia Village; budget to moderate; 6-23330) with smashing success. Built close to the beach, but not directly on it, the venue is perfectly Placencian: a thatched-roof hut set in the path of perpetual sea breezes. The focus is fresh seafood, seconded by homemade pastas. If you're in town on a Friday, stop by for the Pickled Parrot pizza party.

SHOPPING   A few funky shops in Placencia Village are worth a stop. A metallurgist from New York turns out unusual, high-quality silver jewelry at the **Sierra Design Studio** (in front of the elementary school). T-shirts, shorts, disposable cameras, film and various other touristry—what more could you expect from a store named **Things 'n Other Things** (next to The Galley restaurant; 6-23305). Local handiworks are mainstays at **Made in Belize** where shelves display crafts, jewelry and hand-painted T-shirts. **Miss Lizzies** (upstairs from Jamie's Restaurant) offers a mixed bag of homemade preserves, crochet, wine and used books. The local grocery, **Wallen's Market** (near the soccer field; 6-23128) stocks household items as well as postcards. Not much larger than a walk-in closet, **Orange Peel** (next to Wallen's Market; 6-23184) is the place for Belizean woodcarvings and T-shirts.

In Seine Bight, you should look for Lola, Placencia's best-known and best-loved artist, working in the front room of her house. The colorfully painted sign out front simply proclaims, **Lola's Art**. Here you can buy one of the self-taught artist's vibrant paintings, handicrafts made of coconuts and wood, dolls or notecards.

The T-shirts, cotton dresses and other last-minute items at **Rum Point Inn's** gift shop (two miles north of Placencia Village; 6-23239) are attractive and well designed.

NIGHTLIFE   It's never a bad time for a drink or a friendly game of pool at the **Corner Pocket** (seafront, Placencia Village; 6-23175). Boisterous and seaworn, it's always crowded.

Everyone's talking about **Cozy Corner Bar & Disco** (Placencia Village), a shuttered white house where you can dance and meet fellow travelers. Wednesday nights feature famous "chicken drops" (guess what the chickens drop).

The bar at **Tentacles** (on the water, south end of Placencia Village) is fine for a drink *before* the disco. The crustacean-shaped building looks like it's crawling out to sea.

The adjacent **Dockside** (Placencia Village; 6-23333) is perfectly Belizean: a thatch-roof bar propped on a dock over the sea, its sides open to the big blue sky. You'll almost always find folks gathered around the TV, some lounging in hammocks. It doesn't really matter what's on—it's one of the few TVs in town.

GETTING THERE: Maya Airways offers regular flights from Belize City to the Placencia airstrip, usually with a stop in Dangriga along the way. Tropic Air also services Placencia airport. Bus service from Belize City to Placencia is available on the Z-Line.

By car or bus, Placencia is about an hour and a half to two hours south of Dangriga on the Southern Highway, a dirt road that's usually in fair condition. In the rainy season, portions of the road may be closed, so check road conditions in advance.

PUNTA GORDA

On the Southern Highway, about 25 miles north of Punta Gorda, you'll see a sign for **Nim Li Punit**. This Late Classic site lacks the scope and architectural intrigue of Lubaantun, but boasts at least 25 intricately sculpted stelae. One measures more than 30 feet, making it one of the tallest along the Maya Route. Nim Li Punit means "Big Hat," likely referring to its location along a ridge overlooking coastal plains.

Perhaps no town in Belize is quite so edge-of-the-world as **Punta Gorda**. Just before the Guatemala border, it's about as south as you can get on the Southern Highway. Given the sad state of the road, it's understandable that few Belizeans ever travel to P.G. (as Punta Gorda is known in Belize), though they spend a lot of time talking about it. Indeed, there's a certain mystique about this place where Garifunas still practice sacred ceremonies, pounding on drums, shuffling their feet and calling to dead ancestors. But only rarely are outsiders permitted to witness these impassioned rituals.

What visitors to Punta Gorda will see is a quirky outpost where chickens sprint across the streets and filmy store windows advertise five-gallon buckets of pigs' tails. There are a handful of Americans here who will tell you that life in this banana republic is a big adventure, fraught with occasional bouts of malaria or dengue fever, cars breaking down and not being fixed (getting a simple part can take weeks), and pesky plane crashes. To really "get away from it all," they take a skiff to nearby deserted Moho Caye, sit on the beach, and drink a beer.

Punta Gorda itself is pretty much "away from it all," and there's not much to do in town. However, the lush jungles outside town harbor several sightseeing treasures. Tours to these areas can be arranged through the **Toledo Visitors Information Center** (Front Street at the wharf; 7-22470) or **Requena's Charter Service** (12 Front Street).

Heading west from Punta Gorda, a dirt road climbs through dense rainforest, skirting Maya villages where cacao beans are drying next to thatched huts. In the village of **San Antonio**, the **San Luis Rey Church** was built in 1954 with stones from surrounding Maya ruins. No doubt some came from **Lubaantun** (five miles west of San Antonio, just past the village of San Pedro Colombia), a Late Classic ceremonial center hidden in undergrowth. This isolated ruin sees few visitors, but those lucky enough to come will find Santiago Coc, the Maya caretaker who gives enthusiastic tours. Coc should know the area; in 1970, he assisted archaeologist Norman Hammond, then a doctoral student at Cambridge, with excavations.

Lubaantun means "Place of Fallen Stones," and that's just what it looks like. Within a mile of cleared jungle are mound upon mound of stones, some masked in fungi and others sprouting big trees. Eleven major buildings are set in five plazas, built atop a ridge similar to western Belize's Xunantunich. But unlike any other Maya site, the structures here were built without any mortar. Instead, each stone was painstakingly cut to fit another—yet the only tools found were pieces of flint. Archaeologists also found grinding stones for corn and an open chamber with a human jawbone and 1000 mollusk shells, though their purpose is unknown.

But the most astonishing find was a crystal skull, perfectly carved from a single cube of rock crystal. Void of tool marks, its construction seems impossible. In 1926, Canadian Anna Mitchel-Hedges discovered the skull in a temple vault and took it to Canada, where it resides today. Belizeans, rightfully perturbed, believe the skull should be returned to Belize.

A little farther down the dirt road, a path winds through cool jungle to **Blue Creek**. There's no sign for this marvelous swimming hole and local secret. A tangle of vines sway overhead, and schools of fish dart through the lucid water. Water gushes down from the jungle hills, creating many small falls. A quarter-mile farther on the trail are several caves and a wood shed for camping.

Back on the dirt road, and heading east, a sign on an abandoned, weed-choked clunker advertises **Dem Dats Doin** (admission; for information, call 7-22470). It's owned by a Hawaiian couple who call their spread a "Self-Sufficient Integrated Farm System." A guided tour introduces you to their "biogas digester," which uses pig manure to create methane gas to run their lights and refrigerator. The manure also fertilizes their gardens, which provide food (the pigs are for sale, by the way). You'll see a "solar oven," a foil-lined box that even bakes cakes, and vials where jungle plants are being converted to perfumes, rums and oils. If this weren't Belize, it would seem a very strange place!

Once you've seen the jungle side of Punta Gorda, you can head out to sea. Day trips to the **Snake Cayes** and **Moho Caye** (for information, visit the Toledo Visitors Information Center, Front Street at the wharf; 7-22470) offer snorkeling and fly-fishing in pristine, remote waters. One of the most exciting excursions from Punta Gorda is a three-day trip down the **Río Dulce** to **Livingston, Guatemala** (also arranged through the visitors center). **Requena's Charter Service** (12 Front Street) offers scheduled trips to Puerto Barrios, Guatemala, on Monday, Wednesday and Saturday, and charters on other days. For more on visiting Guatemala, see Chapter Eleven.

LODGING   Punta Gorda has many older, sad-looking lodges whose rooms are sporadically occupied. Which means if you don't mind slumming it, you can stay here for low budget prices, especially if the hotel is empty and you wrangle a good deal (like from US$15 to $20).

No doubt the best deal for an ecotourist is to stay outside Punta Gorda in a remote Maya village. As part of an experimental ecotourism program, several Maya and Garifuna villages are welcoming visitors. In one of the best programs, called the **Maya Guest House Program**, travelers spend one or more days with the residents of Laguna Village, San Miguel, Santa Cruz or one of the other villages tucked in the rainforest outside Punta Gorda. During a stay, guests can help village women grind corn for tortillas, watch basket weaving and pottery making, help the men cut sugar cane and explore a local cave that has 1000-year-old Maya paintings. At night, there's barefoot dancing around a bonfire.

Accommodations are in bunkhouses with concrete floors or in one-room thatched huts with concrete floors and bunk beds, a slight step up from the villagers' own mud-floored huts strung with hammocks. Some accommodations are separate for men and women. There's also a separate building with a shower and outhouse. Guests get a basket with their eating utensils, which they carry to various homes for meals, as local families share the responsibility for feeding visitors.

In case you're wondering about a language barrier, many villagers speak English, including giggling children who become elated at the sight of a visitor. Profits from the program help fund village schools, waste disposal and homestead farming, an alternative to slash-and-burn methods. Very expensive rates include transportation to the village, all meals and two tours. For information and reservations, contact Reyes Chun at the **Toledo Ecotourism Association** (65 Front Street, Punta Gorda; 7-22119).

West of Punta Gorda, located deep in the cloud forests of southern Belize, **Fallen Stones Butterfly Ranch and Jungle Lodge** (Punta Gorda; expensive; phone/fax: 72-2176) sits on a Maya mountaintop, its ten thatched-roof cabanas set in a small clearing and connected by stone paths. The forest extends out, greenery stretching forever, and there are distant views of emerald valleys and jungle-masked hills. Blue morpho butterflies prowl the grounds, little streaks of fluorescent indigo igniting the forest air, and hummingbirds dart among the flowers. Hiking here is exceptional; sign up for the three-hour guided hike that wends through thick bush to the Río Grande River, where canoes await to take you to the primitive Maya village of San Pedro, Columbia. A shorter hike is to the Maya ruins of Lubaantun, only a few miles away, or to nearby natural hot springs for a warm, cleansing dip. Other pursuits: river rafting, or simply sitting by the lodge's swimming pool, listening to the burr of the jungle. Rates include breakfast.

If you do stay in Punta Gorda, you'll find just one first-rate establishment, which opened in 1992. The **Traveller's Inn** (José Maria Nunez Street, near the bus station; air-conditioning; satellite TV; expensive; 7-22568) offers roomy rooms, adorned with thick mauve carpets, vertical blinds and shiny wood dressers and armoires. There's also satellite television—generally unheard of in Punta Gorda.

Best of the low-end lodges, **Nature's Way Guest House** (65 Front Street, Punta Gorda; shared bath; budget; 7-22119) gives the impression it's been here a very long time. Engulfed in flowering plants and vines, the funky seaside building has concrete floors of varying colors and a number of stoops and terraces. The rooms are one step up from a youth hostel, and have shared baths. The owners are an American-Belizean couple who also offer local tours.

The 11 rooms at the cinderblock **Miramar Hotel** (95 Front Street, Punta Gorda; budget for rooms without air-conditioning; expensive for rooms with it; some rooms with TV; 7-22033) seem respectable enough, with their newish vinyl floors, tidy bathrooms and eccentric decor of paneled walls, butterfly-patterned shower curtains and terrycloth bedspreads. The concrete porches have views ranging from good to forget-it, and some rooms even have televisions, which you'll need to drown out the noise from the Chinese restaurant downstairs.

The **Saint Charles Inn** (23 King Street, Punta Gorda; ceiling and wall fans; satellite TV; budget; 7-22149) has rooms that are less run-down than most in its price range. There are 13 units in all, spread between two buildings facing a grassy courtyard. All have private baths with hot water, pretty linoleum floors and walls painted a soothing cream.

RESTAURANTS   If someone listed a couple of restaurants in Punta Gorda—say, the Morning Glory Café and the Miramar—you might begin to think you have culinary prospects, that this is what you have been waiting for in Belize. But these thoughts should be put to rest, since P.G. is not a culinary kind of place, but a town of stifling, bare-bones eateries serving strangely cooked food.

The single bright speck on the P.G. restaurant horizon can be found at **Traveller's Inn** (José Maria Nunez Street; moderate; 7-22568), a bright little motel near the bus station. Crisp linens and fresh flowers top the tables, and an air conditioner chases away the sweltering heat. Tender grilled steaks, saucy chicken and fresh seafood are the bill of fare, and the accompanying vegetables and salads are crisp and full of flavor.

For breakfast, the **Morning Glory Café** (59 Front Street, Punta Gorda; budget; no phone) serves fairly dependable fare if it decides to open. Eggs, bacon and papaya juice can be had for less than US$2. Later in the day, you can order fried chicken or fish, hamburgers or hot dogs, or smoked pork chops that have quite a good reputation around P.G. The venue isn't glorious, just a bottom floor of a well-worn building, with spidery plants covering the windows.

The menu's definitely not limited at the **Miramar** (95 Front Street, Punta Gorda; moderate; 7-22033), where you can order anything from beefsteak, pork chops and sweet-and-sour pork to baked pigeon, fried rice and seashell soup. P.G.'s best-known Asian restaurant comes with air-conditioning and a vagabond motif of colored beads, tourist photos of China and folding metal chairs.

SHOPPING   Your only real shopping possibility is the Guatemalan market in downtown Punta Gorda. However, the clothing, radios, and beach towels sold in the market are better purchased across the border (see Chapter Eleven for more information).

GETTING THERE: By far the easiest way to reach Punta Gorda is by plane. Maya Airways has the most frequent service from Belize City, typically with stops in Dangriga and Placencia on the way down. The trip by bus from Belize City, aboard the Z-Line, is a rough-and-tumble ten hours and borderline masochistic, especially considering the price of a round-trip air ticket from Belize City is only US$50.

By car, Punta Gorda is another three to four hours south of Placencia, or nine to ten hours south of Belize City. No doubt about it—take the plane.

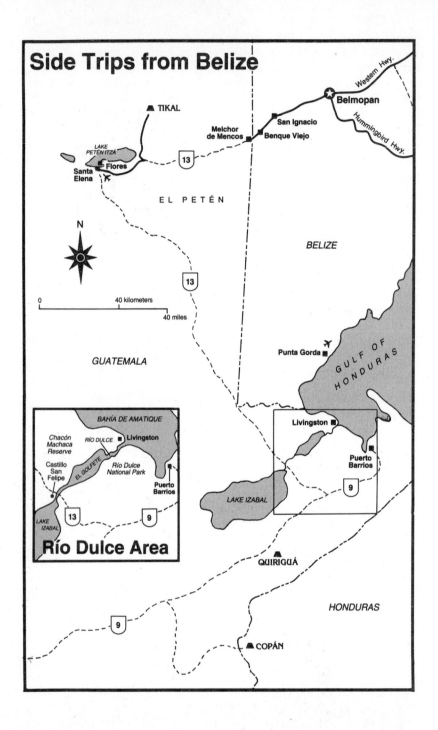

ELEVEN

Side Trips from Belize

If you choose to venture beyond the western back of Belize, you'll find a badly beaten dirt road that punches into the ever-darkening well of Guatemala's vast northern jungle known as El Petén, past great guanacaste trees filled with the chatter of monkeys and sapodilla trees scarred by the machetes of *chicleros*, to Tikal, the most splendid of all cities in the Maya world. The lofty kingdom of Tikal rears up from the depths of North America's largest rainforest like some ferocious giant, its proud pyramids appearing to float above the dark green ceiling of the jungle. Anyone seeing Tikal for the first, or even the fifth, time will realize it is one of the true wonders of the world. No other Maya ruin boasts such majestic architecture and a setting that captures the imagination and won't let go. And if you want to experience primeval rainforest up close, Tikal is one of the best places on earth to do it.

On the southern fringes of Belize lies the threshold to a vastly different Guatemala, a paradox of paradisiac rivers and rainforests and villages virtually unchanged for 200 years, backing up to vast banana plantations, hot and dirty ports and squatters shacks—the fruits of 20th-century enterprise. From the locked-in-time Río Dulce and village of Livingston, not far from the Belize coast, through the magical Río Dulce National Park and mammoth Lake Izabal to the tough-and-tumble town of Puerto Barrios, this is a land of contrasts, and of extremely rewarding adventures.

Farther south into Guatemala, the little-known Maya city of Quiriguá beckons to those who would explore its grand plaza and storied stelae enveloped by banana plantations, and nearly obliterated by big banana business earlier this century. Quiriguá's rival, the fabulous Copán, looms four hours south off the beaten path, down a long, muscle-wrenching dirt road and across the Honduras border. It is so remote that fewer travelers go there than to the other great Maya sites, yet the unique stone sculptures of Copán are so striking—indeed, haunting—that visitors rank the city as one of the most thrilling destinations of Central America.

177

Whether you choose to take this southern side trip from Belize or the western foray into Tikal—or, best of all, both—you should allow several days in each region. For there is so much to see and absorb and ponder, and distances are deceivingly long, though travelers to these areas agree unanimously that they are well worth the effort.

WESTERN SIDE TRIPS

TIKAL NATIONAL PARK AND EL PETÉN   Tikal was the greatest capital of the ancient Maya world. Founded as early as 600 B.C., it reached a peak population of about 50,000 a thousand years later and was one of the two largest cities in the Western Hemisphere during the Classic Period, along with Teotíhuacan in central Mexico. Tikal was situated in the exact center of the Maya land, and had close cultural ties to all parts of the region. Many experts believe the knowledge and ideas that shaped the classic Maya civilization originated in Tikal around 250 A.D., and the abandonment of Tikal around 900 A.D. coincided with the collapse of high Maya civilization everywhere.

One aspect of Tikal's magic is that it is so hard to reach. What was once the wealthy and populous centerpiece of the ancient Maya world is now a remote frontier backwater surrounded by millions of acres of almost impenetrable rainforest called **El Petén**. There is no easy way to get there overland. But it is much faster to go there from Belize than from southern Guatemala. One reason is that more than a decade ago, Guatemala's military government at the time received international aid to widen and pave the road from southern Guatemala to El Petén, but the funds were diverted by corrupt leaders and the road never got built. More recently, in connection with the present Guatemalan government's agreement to set aside a large part of the Petén rainforest as a UNESCO Man and Biosphere Reserve, the World Bank pledged new funding to improve the road and stimulate tourism in El Petén—but the money will not be released until Guatemala convinces the bank that it will take all necessary measures to protect the Petén rainforest from pioneers flocking there to build new settlements and destroy the forest.

However, the road to Tikal from Benque Viejo, Belize, near the Guatemala border, is only about 40 miles. Still, it is a badly beaten dirt trail that promises a two-hour, battering, bone-jarring test of endurance for all who venture upon it. Plus, the hassle and delay of crossing the border, along with occasional reports of bandit activity along this road, make it a trip that's certainly not for the faint-hearted.

The easiest way to get to Tikal is by plane, a surprisingly short hop—only 45 minutes—from Belize City. Once you're in the plane, you'll be rewarded with a rich tapestry of smooth plateaus and dense rainforest. Notice the difference between the forests in Belize and Guatemala; in Belize, there are but a few tiny pockets of *milpa* farming, but flying over the Petén, you can

see vividly the deforestation that is taking place in this environmentally delicate region. Thick rainforest still blankets the ridgelines and hilltops, but
each valley is cleared for crops and livestock as fast as a narrow dirt jeep
road can penetrate it.

Passenger planes land at the airport near **Santa Elena** on the south shore
of Lake Petén Itzá, about an hour's trip by shuttle bus from Tikal National
Park. Most of the Petén's 25,000 residents live in Santa Elena and the contiguous town of San Benito. Together, the two towns form a frontier boom-
town sprawl laced with open sewers and rattling with gas-powered electrical
generators. While a modest tourist trade provides income for some area residents, more of them harvest renewable forest products such as chicle gum
and pepsin leaves or join crews for oil exploration, the newest threat to the
rainforest.

The capital of El Petén, **Flores** (population 1500) is built on a small island
in the lake and is reached by a long earthen causeway from Santa Elena.
A quintessentially quaint little town with an Old World feel to its tangled,
claustrophobic streets, Flores is built on the site of Tayasal, the last ancient
Maya stronghold to fall to the Spanish Empire. Tayasal was visited by Hernán
Cortés, conqueror of Mexico, in 1525, but endured unmolested for nearly
two centuries before a military expedition captured and razed it in 1697.

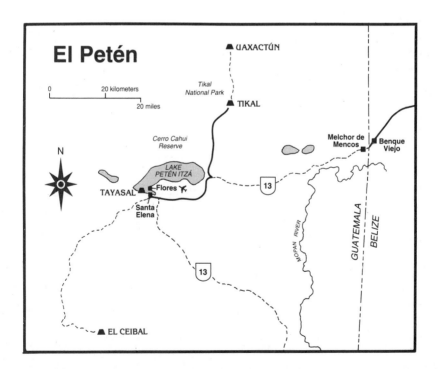

You can walk all over town in less than an hour. The La Ruta Maya Conservation Foundation and George Washington University's Institute of Urban Development Research have developed plans that would encourage the cultivation of Flores as a tourist center complete with houseboat tourist accommodations on Lake Petén Itzá, a regional museum in the abandoned prison building facing the hilltop town square, and even a sewage treatment plant. All this is years in the future, though. For now, Flores is one of Central America's more low-key and isolated frontier towns.

Ask at any restaurant or hotel in the Flores-Santa Elena area and they can probably put you in touch with a guide who will take you on an inexpensive three-hour boat tour of the islands near Flores. Stops on the tour include a group of small temple mounds—all that remains of the old Maya fortress city of **Tayasal**—as well as a spot called **La Garrucha**, where you can climb a tall tower, hang from a cable and zip above the water to land on another island nearby, then climb another tower there and zip back. The final stop on most boat tours is **Petencito** (admission), a zoo occupied exclusively by animals native to the Petén rainforest, including many rare or elusive species—jaguars, cougars, marmosets, tepezcuintles—that visitors are unlikely to spot in the wild. If you thought the cable slide at La Garrucha was fun, give the very scary 300-foot concrete water slide at Petencito a try!

The 38-mile stretch of wide blacktop highway that runs between Santa Elena and Tikal National Park is, incredibly, the only pavement in the northern half of Guatemala. For much of the distance, the road runs past a huge but not very active army base left over from Guatemala's long civil war, during which rebel guerrillas are said to have operated within the national park and throughout El Petén. Midway along the highway, at the eastern tip of Lake Petén Itzá near the intersection with the road from Belize, a dirt road turns off and follows the north shore of the lake all the way back to San Benito. A few miles from the main highway on the north shore road brings you to the **Cerro Cahui Reserve**, a 1600-acre reserve set aside to protect a last fragment of natural habitat for several endangered wetland species— the Petén turkey, the Petén crocodile and the tapir. Explore the network of trails through the luxuriant forest of the reserve. You'll spot bright tropical birds and maybe javelinas, armadillos and spider monkeys.

Tikal National Park (admission) is a different kind of experience from other major Maya ruins, in part because the archaeological site is so big. Most visitors find that trying to see everything at Tikal in a single day is too exhausting and that three days is just about right to fully appreciate the park.

There are two museums near the entrance to the ruins area. The **Tikal Museum**, located near the Jungle Lodge, contains many of the best small artifacts that have been found among the ruins, including pottery painted with elaborate scenes of ancient Maya life and polished bones etched with pictures of gods, demons and warriors. The highlight of the museum is a replica of the tomb of Lord Ah Cacau, the greatest ruler of Tikal, containing his bones, eight pounds of jade jewelry, incense pots and other treasures positioned as archaeologists originally discovered them in a vault below the Temple of the Great Jaguar. On the other side of the parking lot, a fairly new building houses the **visitors center and Stelae Museum**. Although the Petén rainforest seems far removed from the industrial world, within the past few decades acid rain has seriously damaged many stelae, making it necessary to move the best ones indoors for protection. Outside the visitors center is a huge model, about one thousand square feet, showing what Tikal looked like 1100 years ago.

From the parking lot near the hotels and museums, a rocky causeway, or pedestrians-only road, built by the ancient Maya and restored by modern archaeologists, cuts through the dense forest for nearly a mile to the central Plaza Mayor, the heart of ancient Tikal. From there, a triangular loop trail takes you through the Mundo Perdido complex, to lofty Templo IV, then to clusters of nondescript structures, called simply Complex M, Complex P, Group H and Complex Q, before returning to the Plaza Mayor. A separate trail leads to the solitary Temple of the Inscriptions. Park rangers have placed small concrete water basins beside the causeways at several points to attract monkeys and birds. A full circuit of the main ruins involves a hot, fairly strenuous hike of some six miles through the rainforest.

At the center of the Tikal ruins area is the meticulously restored group of buildings flanking the four sides of the two-acre **Plaza Mayor** (Great Plaza). Now covered with neatly mown grass, the whole square was paved with stucco in ancient times and resurfaced about once every century-and-a-half. The plaza was in use as early as 150 B.C. The first layer of pavement has been dated to about 100 A.D. and the final layer to 700 A.D.—a generation before any of the temples that now surround the plaza were completed. All of the structures at Tikal were painted bright red, with colorful bas-relief murals on the huge roof combs.

Along the north side of the plaza stand two rows of tombstone-shaped **stelae** with round altars in front of them. Other, similar stelae are set near the stairways of the various structures around the plaza. Most of the stelae are carved with the images of Tikal's noblemen in ceremonial garb with elaborate plumed headdresses, and many have hieroglyphs carved along the sides. As you explore outlying parts of the ruins, you will see dozens of massive stone stelae like these scattered throughout the forest. On some, the relief carving has been obliterated by time; others were quarried but never carved or erected, or smashed on purpose as the leaders they glorified fell into disrepute; and the best-preserved still invite us to wonder about the meanings of the messages so painstakingly inscribed and dispatched across the centuries to us, the people of the future. The oldest dated stela at Tikal was erected in 292 A.D., and the most recent in 771 A.D.

At the east and west ends of the plaza stand two of the extremely tall, stepped pyramids unique to Tikal. On the east end, **Temple I**, sometimes called the Temple of the Great Jaguar, is the taller. Towering 170 feet high with its lofty, crumbling roof comb, it is one of the few pyramids in the Maya world that the public is not allowed to climb. A sign on a chain across the narrow stairway says that it is closed temporarily for restoration, but tour guides claim that it has been closed indefinitely since a tourist fell down the steep stairs to his death in the early 1980s. The tomb of Ah Cacau, the most important of ancient Tikal's leaders, was discovered at the foot of this pyramid. He reigned during the early part of the 8th century A.D., and his name translates as "Lord Chocolate." His remains, along with artifacts from his tomb including priceless jade jewelry, can be seen in a replica of the burial vault at the Tikal Museum. Just to the south of Temple I is the main **ball court**, surprisingly small for such an important ceremonial center as Tikal.

Directly across the plaza, on the west side, is **Temple II**, also known as the Temple of the Masks. It is squat and wider than Temple I, with three levels to Temple I's nine. The top level's broad walkway around all sides of the temple offers good views of the Plaza Mayor, the acropolises and the surrounding forest canopy. Temples I and II were built at the same time and are thought to represent the male and female principles. Carvings on the lintels and walls of the temple chambers on top suggest to some archaeologists that Temple II was a burial pyramid for the wife of Ah Cacau, who was buried under Temple I. This is mere theory, however, as her tomb has not been found.

While the **North Acropolis** may lack the dramatic architecture of the pyramids, it is by far the more interesting structure to explore. It is a broad mound with a number of separate temples, apparently dedicated to different gods, and a tricky labyrinth of stairways and passages to reach them. Eight temples made up the acropolis in the 8th century, when Tikal's great pyramids were built. Archaeological digs have revealed that the mound on which the temples stand contains older temples built upon the ruins of yet older ones, dating back to 400 B.C. One excavation of the facade of a buried temple contains a huge stucco mask, taller than a person, of a fierce-eyed rain god with a bulbous, warty nose, perfectly preserved by earth and rubble while the stucco sculptures on the exposed buildings of Tikal were being obliterated by the rainforest climate. To the right of the giant mask, a dark, vaulted passageway leads into the pyramid. Feel your way through the darkness to the end, then strike a match and you'll find yourself face-to-face with another gargantuan god mask.

The **Central Acropolis** sprawls across four acres. It is believed to have been the royal palace of Tikal, a complex of spacious multistory residences built around six separate courtyards. Only the front part of the palace, facing the plaza, has been completely excavated; the back part blends gracefully into the forest. The stupendous roof comb that breaks the skyline behind the Central Acropolis is the top of **Temple V**, the second-tallest pyramid at Tikal at 185 feet in height. Still unexcavated and shrouded by trees, it shows what all five of the great temple pyramids at Tikal must have looked like when early archaeologists came to explore and photograph the site at the end of the 19th century. A narrow foot trail from the east end of the Central Acropolis leads into the rainforest to Temple V, then returns to the main trail near Mundo Perdido.

The **Mundo Perdido** ("Lost World") complex, which lies southwest of the Plaza Mayor, presents a sharp contrast to the central ruins area. The massive **Main Pyramid** at the center of a group of 38 structures was built at least 500 years before the pyramids of the Plaza Mayor, suggesting that this area may have been the main ceremonial center for much of Tikal's history. Unlike the main plaza with its formal, landscaped feel, the Mundo Perdido complex has been excavated with an eye toward minimizing the impact on the surrounding forest, so the lower structures are nestled among the roots and trunks of forest giants. From the top of the great pyramid, you can see the summits of Temples I and II on the Plaza Mayor, just the roof combs rising face-to-face, sun-and-moon, he-and-she through the canopy of a rainforest that rolls unbroken, astonishing in its vastness, all the way to the distant horizon. East of the pyramid and north of a small plaza with seven

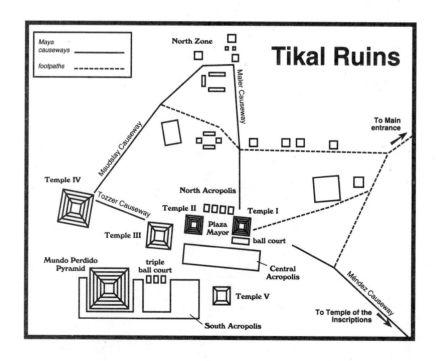

temples, is a **triple ball court** thought to be the only one of its kind in the Maya world.

At the westernmost end of the ruins area, **Temple IV**, known as the Temple of the Double-Headed Serpent, is the tallest manmade structure at Tikal. At 228 feet high, this pyramid was also the second-tallest structure in the ancient Maya world. It was believed to be the tallest until one pyramid at El Mirador, 42 miles straight-line distance to the north across the roadless depths of the Petén rainforest and presently inaccessible to sightseers, was measured at about a yard taller. Temple IV has been cleared but not ex-cavated, so instead of a very steep stairway to the top, there's a very steep foot trail. As you reach the summit, a metal ladder affixed to the temple wall lets you climb all the way up to the roof comb. Near Temple IV are a parking lot, reached by a road that circles around the archaeological zone, and a group picnic area, so it is common to find busloads of school children swarming up and down the pyramid.

On the other side of the main ruins area, the Méndez Causeway branches away from the main trail and leads in a straight line through the forest for half a mile to the **Temple of the Inscriptions**, a large, solitary temple on Tikal's outskirts. Covering the entire surface of the roof comb, you can still make out the only major hieroglyphic inscription found at Tikal. The temple is so far removed from the main ruins of Tikal that it was not discovered until 1951. Why this unusual and impressive temple should be set apart by

Spider monkeys

both distance and architecture from the rest of the city is unknown. The stela that stands in front of the temple was intentionally smashed, probably by the people of ancient Tikal.

Visitors are not allowed to spend the night in the ruins area. Rangers check to see that everybody is out before dark. They explain that jaguars and other dangerous beasts roam the forest at night, and if pressed ("But I thought jaguars were almost extinct. . . .") admit that it is other, supernatural beings that make the ruins a place to be avoided at night. Outsiders doubt it, they say, but everybody around there knows it is true.

No night watchman will stop you from walking to the ruins after midnight. Dawn as experienced from the ruins at Tikal is an ultimate travel experience, absolutely worth the inconvenience of rising before first light. Early-to-bed, early-to-rise is less of a hardship here than it would be most places because the electricity shuts off at 9:30 p.m. in the national park hotels.

A mist as thick as ocean fog shrouds Tikal in the hours before dawn. As the sun rises, the mist glows first pink and then golden. For a moment, you can glimpse the glory of Tikal in ancient times. Then the ancient temples, shadows at first, turn to stone as the mist burns away. The forest comes alive suddenly with the cries of monkeys and birds and the throbbing drone of insects, and the heat of the day begins. A dawn tour led by freelancing off-duty park rangers is well worth the small fee. The rangers, many of whom were born and raised on the edge of the Petén rainforest, are amazingly knowledgeable about the diversity of plant and animal species found in the park. You can also walk into the park on your own as early as you like, and young travelers staying at the campground organize informal 4:00 a.m. expeditions to the pyramids most mornings.

At any time of day you choose to walk among the various outlying ruins of Tikal, they quickly become a mere excuse for venturing deeper into the rainforest. At every turn, a smaller trail beckons you off into the deep jungle for a spontaneous visit to some half-buried temple or hidden forest glade. Monkeys create dins of excitement as you enter their territory. Colorful toucans scatter from the trees in front of you. The diversity of plant and animal life in the Petén jungle means that around every bend in the trail you discover something new—a tree full of orchids, a strange fruit, a kaleidoscopic butterfly swarm, a line of leaf cutter ants marching in single file for as far as you can see. The Petén rainforest supports the richest array of wildlife to be found anywhere on the North American continent.

Mammals that live in the Petén forest include several species of predatory cats—margays, jaguarundis, ocelots, cougars and jaguars—as well as other uncommon species such as anteaters, kinkajous and tapirs. Visitors are unlikely to see any of these rare, elusive animals in the wild, but there are other jungle creatures you can expect to see. Foremost among them are spider monkeys, easy to spot because of the rattling, crashing noises they make as they leap from branch to branch. Black howler monkeys, common in Belize and reportedly common throughout the Petén just a few years ago, are still spotted once in a while. Armadillos, tepezcuintles and coatimundis may be seen in the underbrush toward dusk, as are javelinas (called peccaries in Belize), a small piglike beast. Visitors often catch glimpses of silver foxes, known to the locals as "gatos de la selva" ("forest cats"), gliding through the ruins of Tikal. Other forest denizens include weasels, opossums, porcupines and deer.

The abundance of wildlife is particularly astonishing considering much of its habitat is almost certainly less than a thousand years old. Using satellite mapping to reveal the outlines of ancient farmers' fields, archaeologists have determined that virtually all the land within a 60-mile radius of Tikal had been cleared for cultivation 1100 years ago. Here, peasants grew maize, beans and tomatoes on small suburban farms, supplying food for themselves as well as the priests and rulers who lived in the great city center. After the abandonment of the city began, around 900 A.D., it is difficult to estimate how long it took for the lofty ceiba, mahogany and sapodilla trees to take root among the ruins. The jungle existed in something like its present form when Spanish conquistador Hernán Cortés visited the region in 1525.

Anywhere you go in the backcountry of Tikal National Park, you will find low mounds and tumbled-down stone walls that remain from those ancient homesteads—even in places that are almost inaccessible today. Archaeologists will probably never excavate all of the sites in the jungle of Tikal National Park, and visitors will always be able to wonder what undiscovered treasures may lie hidden there. Whenever you explore and wherever you wander, use good judgment. Jungle trails have a way of tempting people onward. Remember that there is a risk of getting lost in this terrain.

Despite its size, the 222-acre Tikal National Park protects less than two percent of El Petén, the largest contiguous expanse of rainforest on the North American continent. The northern third of the Petén rainforest—all the land north of Tikal to the northern, eastern and western borders of Guatemala, has been designated as the Maya Biosphere Reserve, a unit of the UNESCO Man and Biosphere program that protects inhabited wilderness areas, allowing some economic use of the forest in a buffer zone around a protected core area. The Maya Biosphere Reserve, encompassing an area of 5400 square miles, is one of the most ambitious efforts to save the rainforest anywhere in the world. La Ruta Maya Conservation Foundation, armed with a large grant from the MacArthur Foundation, hopes to go one step further, merging Guatemala's Maya Biosphere Reserve with Belize's Río Bravo Conservation Area and Mexico's Calakmul Biosphere Reserve to form the Maya Peace Park, a huge international park that would span the three nations' often-troubled borders and allow cooperative ecotourism development in the region.

At least 25 other major ceremonial centers have been found in the Maya Biosphere Reserve and another dozen along the Río Pasión in the southwestern part of the department of Petén. Of those in the biosphere reserve, most are accessible only by very primitive four-wheel-drive tracks that can only be used during the dry season, and several are in terrain so impassable that archaeologists can only reach them by helicopter. None are currently open to the public, though proponents of the Maya Peace Park plan hope that El Mirador, site of a large ceremonial center whose temples include the tallest known Maya pyramid, will someday be opened to tourists by shuttle bus or even monorail.

At present, the only ruin in the Maya Biosphere Reserve that casual visitors can get to from Tikal is **Uaxactún**, located 12 miles north of the Tikal ruins and just a short distance outside the north boundary of the national park. A newly improved road is passable by car during the dry season. For centuries, Uaxactún was a rival city to Tikal. Nothing about these partially excavated but unrestored ruins suggests that this ceremonial site even came close to achieving the grandeur of Tikal, but inscriptions on Tikal's temples and stelae reveal that the two cities fought bloody wars and that, at least once, the army of Uaxactún conquered Tikal. Backpackers may choose to hike from Tikal to Uaxactún. Camping equipment is a must, since even strong hikers find it impossible to walk there and back the same day.

One Maya ruin site that you may want to visit is **El Ceibal** (see "Getting There" section later in this chapter for details), noted by archaeologists as having the only circular temple in the entire Maya world. It also has 31 carved stone stelae, including one that certainly seems to depict a Maya warrior talking on the telephone! The stelae, altars and stone walls at El Ceibal are covered with a bright orange lichen, creating a dramatic contrast to the amazingly lush rainforest that constantly threatens to swallow the ancient city once more.

Several trails lead from the ruins into the surrounding protected rainforest of Ceibal National Park, the most likely place for visitors to the Petén to see rare howler monkeys. The forest here is also known for its abundant bird life, including parrots, macaws and toucans. One bird unique to the forest along the Río Pasión is the snail hawk, a small raptor that preys on tree snails.

LODGING   Staying at Tikal National Park is best because there is too much in the park to experience in a single day, and the shuttle trip between Flores/ Santa Elena and Tikal, an hour each way, costs more than a hotel room does. Staying in the park also lets you spend the night surrounded by the sounds of the jungle and visit the ruins in the eerie dawn mist.

There are three hotels in Tikal National Park, totaling 49 rooms between them. Because of development restrictions imposed by the Guatemalan government when the Maya Biosphere Reserve was created, no new hotels can be built. Sometimes, tour groups fill them to capacity and other times they are almost empty. You don't know until you go there, because it's not easy to make advance reservations and none of the hotels has a telephone. The men who drive shuttle vans between the airport at Santa Elena and the national park may know about room availability. Otherwise, the best plan for travelers arriving on the morning plane is just to go to the park by noon and see whether you can find lodging. If you can't get a room, you'll have time to return to Flores by midafternoon and find one there.

The most comfortable, and most interesting, place to stay inside the national park is the 22-room ✪ **Tikal Inn** (moderate; 502-9-26-0065; fax: 502-9-50-0065), a classic jungle lodge that consists of an attractively rustic main building, where you'll find the dining room, lobby and four rather elegantly decorated guest rooms with four-poster beds, as well as a row of thatched-roof cabanas along one side of a broad expanse of lawn with a swimming pool in the center and dense rainforest around the perimeter of the grounds. The cabanas have complete modern conveniences, including electric light from 6:00 p.m. to 9:30 p.m. and private bathrooms with running water that is warm late in the day. The hotel's mascot ocelot lives in a large enclosure in the jungle nearby, screams hauntingly in the night, and sometimes is let loose on the grounds to romp with cat-loving guests. Reservations can only be made by sending a letter to "Tikal Inn, Tikal, Petén, Guatemala" telling what dates you want, then sending payment in full after you receive confirmation. Modified American plan available.

The largest hotel at Tikal is the 32-room **Jungle Lodge** (moderate; send reservation requests to 29 Calle No. 18-01, Zona 12, Guatemala City or call 502-2-76-0294 in Guatemala City). It was originally built in the 1930s to house archaeological teams working at Tikal. A recent remodeling has converted the rustic old cabins into spacious, pleasant cabanas with tin roofs that are noisy in the rain and private baths with reliable hot water. The rates are higher than at the Tikal Inn.

The third option, the **Jaguar Inn** (moderate; 502-9-26-0002), next door to the Tikal Museum, has nine guest rooms in simple thatched-roof cottages with private baths. During the dry season, several large, furnished tents are also rented out as guest accommodations. The food here is not very good, so it is better to opt for a room only, without meals, and eat across the road at the campground.

The most luxurious accommodations in El Petén are at the **Hotel Camino Real Tikal** (El Remate; air-conditioning; satellite TV; very expensive; 502-9-500-207, fax: 502-2-500-222; for reservations call 502-2-334-633 in Guatemala City), outside the national park near the intersection where the road from Belize intersects the highway between Santa Elena and Tikal. All 120 rooms have private baths and satellite television complete with remote control—self-indulgent amenities in a region where most of the local people live without running water or indoor plumbing. Guest facilities include a swimming pool, a lakefront beach, tennis courts, restaurants, a bar and a disco.

Near Cerro Cahui, ✪ **El Gringo Perdido** (El Remate; shared bath; budget; 502-2-327-683) is a primitive jungle lodge with 12 four-bed cabins that share a restroom and shower facilities with eight low-budget camping *palapas* designed for hammocks. There is also an open-air dining *palapa* where budget-priced meals are served.

In Santa Elena, one of the better hotels is the ✪ **Hotel Maya Internacional** (moderate to expensive; 502-9-811-276; for reservations write 2 Avenida No. 7-78, Zona 10, Guatemala City, or call 36-39-09). This compound of 20 rustic rooms in duplex bungalows on stilts over Lake Petén Itzá used to be the top of the line in the Petén region, but has lost most of its formerly landscaped grounds to the rising water level of the lake over the past few years. Nature lovers can watch from the bungalow porch as multitudes of egrets, herons and other wading birds fish among the water lilies just a few feet away. Rooms have private baths. Be careful of the electric water-heating shower heads, common in hotels around Santa Elena and Flores, but said to be dangerous because of the possibility of electrocution.

One of the most pleasant hotels in the Santa Elena and Flores area, the **Hotel del Patio Tikal** (2 Calle at 8 Avenida, Santa Elena; air-conditioning; satellite TV; expensive; 502-9-500-104, fax: 502-9-501-229) offers 22 air-conditioned rooms with private baths around a parklike courtyard with a fountain.

At the other end of the lodging spectrum is the venerable **Hotel San Juan** (Santa Elena; private and shared baths; some with satellite TV; budget; 502-9-500-562, fax: 502-9-500-041). The hotel doubles as a bus terminal, where second-class buses from Río Dulce, Poptún, Sayaxché and Cobán come and go day and night, making the rooms on the hotel's street side very noisy. This is a long-established gathering place for adventurous travelers, and most local guides organize their tours from the lobby. The 55 rooms (37 with private bath but only a very limited supply of solar-heated water) are as plain as can be.

Of numerous small lodgings in the island town of Flores, the modern **Hotel Sabana** (moderate; phone/fax: 502-9-501-248) is a favorite simply because of the view. Unlike most of the other hotels, which are located near the causeway, this one is on the far side of the island overlooking the full expanse of Lake Petén Itzá. Of the 28 rooms, the ones at the back have the best lake views. The four-story hotel has nothing in the way of decor to spruce up its plain, concrete block architecture, but the grand panorama from the second-story patio makes up for it.

Opened in 1996, **Hotel Isla De Flores** (Flores, El Petén; air-conditioning; phones; TVs; budget to moderate; 502-926-0614 or 502-926-0617, fax: 502-476-0294) is a welcome place, with the overriding feeling of newness, its floors done in polished white tile and ceilings in light wood beams. All 18 rooms have comfortable beds and private baths, but ask for a room on the back, where you also get a splendid view of the lake.

RESTAURANTS   At Tikal, each of the hotels has its own small restaurant serving a set menu at set hours, with the price of breakfast and dinner included in the "modified American plan" room rate. The only alternatives are a series of *comedores* situated down the road from the campground, serving basic food at budget prices. The restaurant at the campground itself is the largest in the area and serves a low-priced selection of soups, sandwiches and spaghetti.

Flores has a number of rustic-but-nice restaurants that offer entrées of local game from the Petén rainforest, typically including alligator, venison, tepezcuintle, armadillo, wild turkey, pheasant and rabbit. This is the traditional food of the region, and travelers who feel queasy about dining on freshly killed jungle animals may have to subsist on fruit salads. More conventional meats such as chicken and pork are only found in the dining rooms of better hotels. The town's best restaurants are in a cluster along Calle Centroamérica, the main street one block north of the island end of the causeway.

The tastiest meals in Flores are found at **La Mesa de los Maya** (Calle Centroamérica; budget; 502-9-811-240). The servings are generous and the cuisine is out of this world. Handwoven tablecloths and wall hangings brighten the two cozy, plain-but-honest little dining rooms, as does the friendly pet toucan. There is a full bar on the premises, though a drink costs much more than a dinner does.

A block down the street, **Restaurant La Jungla** (Calle Centroamérica; budget; no phone) is overgrown with jungle plants like a fern bar run amok—strange but tolerable. What's not tolerable are the boa constrictor skins, jaguar heads, stuffed birds and other wall trophies that not only shriek of anti-ecotourism but make you feel as if your dinner entrée were watching over your shoulder. Beyond this, the food and service are okay.

Around the block, facing the waterfront about a block west of the causeway, **El Faisan** (Flores; budget; no phone) is another small restaurant and bar serving a similar selection of grilled wild animal meats. Rough wood paneling decorated from floor to ceiling with photos, drawings and maps of Tikal create an archaeology ambience that sets it apart from the other restaurants nearby. It is open later in the evening than most of the others, too.

SHOPPING   The souvenir industry in Flores and Tikal is in its infancy. A cluster of four shops near the Tikal Museum and the entrance to the ruins area has a high-priced selection of native *típica* clothing from other parts of Guatemala that is worth looking at only if you are not planning to visit the highlands on your trip. It also has lots and lots of Tikal T-shirts. Other makeshift shops along the narrow streets of Flores also stock limited selections of *típica*. The best souvenirs of Tikal are the videotapes with aerial footage of the rainforest and the ruins and an audio tape of jungle sounds recorded at Tikal.

GETTING THERE: The best way to travel overland to Tikal is with a tour arranged through one of the many lodges in Belize's Cayo District (see Chapter Nine). A package tour eliminates potential problems of going it on your own—changing buses at the border, being denied entry if you're in a rental car (which are rarely allowed across the border), being denied a tourist card (or having to pay a generous *mordida* for one), trusting taxi drivers to take you all the way to Tikal on the agreed fee, or dealing with Guatemala military officials (and rebel guerillas impersonating military officials) who may stop you en route to Tikal to check your passport. If you do decide to cross the border on your own, make sure you obtain a Guatemala visa in advance, either in the United States, Belize or Mexico.

By far the simplest way to get to Tikal is by plane, a surprisingly short hop—only 45 minutes—from Belize City to Flores. **Tropic Air** (2-45671 in Belize City or 800-422-3435 in the United States) offers two flights daily on most weekdays; the fare is only about US$121 round-trip. Be aware, however, that flights are often delayed or canceled altogether, especially if there aren't enough passengers, so stay flexible.

The biggest problem facing visitors who would like to explore more remote areas of El Petén is lack of transportation. Very few travelers come to Tikal in their own vehicles, and public transportation is quite limited. A few enterprising guides, who don't advertise but can be found by word of mouth through any hotel or restaurant operator or shuttle van driver, run tours from Flores and Tikal to other Maya ruins in the Petén—especially El Ceibal, which can also be reached by public transportation. The trip involves traveling 36 miles by car or bus on a good dirt road to the jungle village of Sayaxché and hiring a boat there to take you 11 miles down the Río Pasión to the ruins. The ruins can also be reached by a new four-wheel-drive track, but the jungle boat trip is more fun.

SOUTHERN SIDE TRIPS

RÍO DULCE AREA   From Punta Gorda in southern Belize, it's a short, scenic ride across the Gulf of Honduras to the Guatemala coast, stopping first at Puerto Barrios and then Livingston. To cross into this southern area of Guatemala, you will need only your passport and a visa, issued in advance from a Guatemalan consulate in the United States, Belize or Mexico. If you plan to continue on to Copán in Honduras—a highly recommended side trip—a passport will suffice.

One of Guatemala's most unusual little towns, **Livingston** is perched at the mouth of the Río Dulce, where the gorge spills into the Gulf of Honduras, an outcropping of a village in the southwesternmost corner of the Caribbean Sea. Isolated by unbridged river, roadless forest and the Belizean border just up the coast, Livingston is Guatemala's only Garifuna community. It's a small community of 3000 people, most of whom are multilingual, speaking Spanish and English as well as the African-based Garifuna patois.

Livingston's brightly painted wooden houses and storefronts run uphill from the docks along a single main street, which is paved, although there is not a single motor vehicle in town—a fact to which the town owes its timeless tropical charm. In a few hours, you can stroll every street in town, visit the simple Catholic church with its ebony-skinned Jesus and Virgin of Guadalupe, then walk over the hill and up the narrow, hard, brown beach where Livingston's dreadlocked youth can usually be found savoring reggae and ganja, to the far end, where a trail leads up to **Siete Altares**, a series of waterfalls and pools just right for bathing. *Note*: Hire a local to guide you there; a few tourists have been robbed at the falls.

Beyond that, there's not much for either visitors or locals to do in Livingston. For both, people-watching is a major pastime, and the most rewarding time to do it is on weekends, when settlers paddle to town from fishing camps up the coast and emerge from the jungle via foot trails to attend church services. No cars, no televisions, no soldiers or armed guards, and nothing to do at all. If you do spend a night or two, you may find Livingston one of the most relaxed and relaxing places on the continent.

Once you feel rejuvenated, you won't want to miss a trip up the **Río Dulce**. This truly rewarding excursion up the "Sweet River" will undoubtedly be one of the highlights of your southern side trip from Belize. You can hire a boat in Livingston to take you the 18 winding, hill-studded miles into the gorge and to the crossroads of Castillo San Felipe. (Conversely, you can cruise *down* river from Puerto Barrios to Livingston, after disembarking in Puerto Barrios from Punta Gorda, Belize). Paddling down the Río Dulce, spectacular scenery presents itself at virtually every turn, from the sheer silver cliffs that soar above the riverbanks to the colossal trees upholstered in emerald greenery. The remote tropical paradise feel of the Río Dulce is in part illusory, for just beyond the top rim of the gorge are endless banana fields and the shacks and villages of some of the poorest country people in Guatemala. Yet the river still allows glimpses of one of the last fragments of primeval America, much of it practically unchanged since the days of Columbus.

The river narrows abruptly into a steep canyon whose walls, dripping with lush vegetation, reach hundreds of feet above the water. Egrets peer from every tree, pelicans glide by just inches above the water, turtles sun themselves along the riverbank. Here and there a cluster of thatch-roofed huts nestles between the cliffs and the water. People who live along the Río Dulce—mothers with infants and bundles of groceries from Livingston, even unaccompanied young children—paddle their hand-hewn dugout canoes called *cayucas* up and down the river in a kind of uncomplicated purity that daydreams are made of.

After the steep canyon, the Río Dulce opens into a broad expanse of open water called **El Golfete**, where local fishermen cast their nests. Much of the north shore of El Golfete is protected as the **Chacón Machaca Reserve**, a wildlife sanctuary for the endangered West Indian Manatee. Guides claim that jaguars and tapirs also still roam the deep forest along the north shore.

Upriver from El Golfete is a scattering of expensive vacation homes and several marinas mostly full of American yachts and sailboats. Then there is **Lake Izabal**, the largest lake in Guatemala, stretching some 12 miles wide and 27 miles long. Its waters reach a depth of 60 feet. The lake's shoreline, dotted with more than a dozen fishing villages, is virtually inaccessible by land. The largest village, El Estor, can be reached by a grueling 84-mile unpaved road that leaves the highway midway between the Mario Dary Quetzal Reserve and Cobán, and takes all day to drive. The other villages can only be reached by boat. Fishing is the main pastime on the lake, and motor launches with pilot can be hired at the Castillo San Felipe bridge or any of the resort hotels nearby.

Presiding over the lake is **Castillo San Felipe** (admission), a small stone fort complete with lookout towers, a drawbridge and cannons on the ramparts. It was built in 1686 to guard the mouth of Lake Izabal from British privateers like Sir Francis Drake. The fort has a shady picnic area and a swimming beach.

LODGING   An anomalous 45-room resort hotel tucked off the main street about a block above the docks in Livingston, the **Hotel Tucán Dugú** (moderate to expensive; 502-9-481-588) offers bright, modern rooms and suites in a huge thatch-roofed building with a swimming pool. Prices are moderate

Tapir

for regular rooms in the main building and expensive for the more private bungalows along the walkway that leads down to the hotel's private beach.

Practically across the street from the Tucán Dugú, you'll find a completely different kind of Caribbean charm at the **Hotel Río Dulce** (shared bath; budget; 502-9-481-059), a plain but picture-perfect little blue two-story inn with a white picket fence, flower gardens, a big front porch perfectly situated for main-street people-watching, and basic rooms at a very low budget price. Youthful backpackers find their way here from all over the world.

The waterfront ✪ **Hotel La Casa Rosada** (Livingston; shared bath; budget; for reservations, call 510-525-4470, fax: 510-525-5427 in the United States) has ten thatch-roofed bungalows with handpainted Guatemalan furniture, and shared baths. Canoes are available to guests. The hotel serves a hearty breakfast, including the only freshly ground coffee in town.

At the upper end of the Río Dulce near the Castillo San Felipe Bridge, you'll find the ✪ **Hotel Catamaran** (moderate; 502-9-324-829), a complex of bungalows on an island downriver from the bridge. There is an inexpensive guarded parking lot under the bridge, and motor launches—often the same ones that go downriver to Livingston in the morning—wait nearby to take you across to the hotel. Guest accommodations, set along the shore and around grounds bursting with colorful flowers with a cage of parrots and a swimming pool in the middle, are rustic and simply furnished but quite large and airy, with private baths, screens to keep the mosquitoes out and balconies overlooking the water. The river gently lapping outside the window assures guests a sound night's sleep.

Another resort complex in the best sense of the word, the **Hotel Izabal Tropical** (ceiling fans; moderate; 502-9-478-401) is situated on the shore of Lake Izabal about two-and-a-half miles down a dirt road from Castillo San Felipe. Fourteen thatch-roofed bamboo-and-stucco guest cabanas are scattered across a hillside along the lake. Each has a private bathroom with shower. The hotel has both a children's and an adult's swimming pool and luxuriant gardens that blossom year-round. It also has its own dock, and you can usually find boats for hire there with or without a captain.

Campers will find their dream spot at ✪ **El Tortugal Resort** (budget; phone/fax: 502-9-323-352), a backpackers' retreat in a jungle setting a half-mile upriver from the San Felipe bridge. It offers swimming, windsurfing, and kayak and canoe rentals. Sites for tent and hammock camping are in the low-budget price range. A boat takes passengers there for a nominal fee, leaving on request between 8 a.m. and 5 p.m. from the Cafetería Emy near the bridge.

The eco-travelers haven called **Hacienda Tijax** (Río Dulce; budget to moderate; 502-333-5773) is on 500 acres of prime hiking and birdwatching terrain, though the accommodations are rustic. There are dormitory-style buildings, but go for a thatched-roof, open-air bungalow—at least you'll have some privacy. Bungalow beds are draped in mosquito nets, and there are private baths.

RESTAURANTS   Livingston has several modest restaurants that cater to the low-key lunchtime tourist trade, since the locals generally catch their own meals. The **Restaurante Tiburongato** (budget; no phone), a clean place with checkered plastic tablecloths and an open-air latticework facade that looks out on the town's main street, is typical. Menu items include ceviche and a local seafood stew called *tapado*, made with coconuts and plantains.

If you're spending the night in Livingston, your best dinner bet is the amazing **African Place** (moderate; no phone). Designed and built by an immigrant from Spain, it is an authentic Moorish-style stone castle in miniature, patterned after those of southern Spain, with archways, ornate tilework and wrought-iron grillwork accenting windows that peer out into the jungle. On the menu are wonderfully imaginative seafood dishes such as shrimp in garlic sauce and curried fish.

In the Río Dulce resort area around the bridge at Castillo San Felipe, the best meals are served in restaurants at the various hotels along the river. The **Hotel Catamaran** (moderate; 502-9-324-829) has a thatch-roofed open-air restaurant built out over the water. The menu includes most of the standard Guatemalan restaurant items—fruit salads, *desayuno chapín*, roast chicken, spaghetti, local fish—and you can watch the big luxury sailboats with American names glide past as you eat. Hours of service are limited. Accessible by a dirt road instead of by boat, the **Hotel Izabal Tropical** (moderate; 502-9-478-401) also has a restaurant built over the water, with a range of menu choices and prices similar to those at the Catamaran.

Budget-priced food stands clustered around the Castillo San Felipe bridge sell fish—most likely perch or tarpon—freshly caught from the lake, grilled with spices and served with tortillas and rice on the side. Try **Mary's** (budget; no phone), a tiny place at the end of a dock just east of the bridge.

Thin-crust pizzas baked with blue cheese, pork chops simmered until fork-tender, banana-rum crêpes for desert—such are the designs of a woman named Holly, owner and chef of **Hollymar's** (on the water at the Castillo San Felipe Bridge; budget; phone/fax: 502-369-2681). Breakfasts are equally tasty and inventive; try the fresh-baked cinnamon buns or yogurt with tropical fruit and granola. Built on the end of a pier, there is always a cool breeze wafting off the water at Hollymar's.

SHOPPING   Many of the storefronts that line the main street of Livingston offer various handcrafted goods. Prices are high for clothing brought in from other parts of Guatemala, but locally made gift items such as coconut carvings and Afro-Caribbean paintings may bring a smile to your face as they tug at your billfold.

A few roadside stalls near the Castillo San Felipe bridge offer limited selections of native *típica* clothing. A hut near the pool at the **Hotel Catamaran** houses a small gallery where members of a cooperative network of American artists—who live on boats nearby—show their work.

GETTING THERE: From Punta Gorda, in southern Belize, it's a short boat ride across the Gulf of Honduras to the Guatemala coast, stopping first at Puerto Barrios and then Livingston. You can catch a boat at the **Punta Gorda Wharf** (Front Street on the sea), where there is service twice a week, usually on Tuesday and Friday afternoons. Or, walk over to the **Toledo Visitors Information Center** (next to the wharf; 7-22470), which can arrange excursions ranging from one to several days, taking in Livingston and Guatemala's Río Dulce. **Requena's Charter Service** (12 Front Street, Punta Gorda) has scheduled service to Puerto Barrios on Monday, Wednesday and Saturday.

COPÁN   It's a long haul to Copán (admission) from the Río Dulce area. You can hire a taxi or join an overnight tour to Copán, but expect a six-hour journey. It is more than worth the trouble of getting there. Indeed, after visitors set eyes on Copán and its unique, haunting stone sculptures, most agree that it is one of the most exciting Maya sites of the world. You can still feel the magic that inspired American explorer John Lloyd Stephens to write in 1841, "The beauty of the sculpture, the solemn stillness of the woods, disturbed only by the scrambling of monkeys and the chattering of parrots, the desolation of the city, and the mystery that hung over it, all created an interest higher, if possible, than I had ever felt among the ruins of the Old World."

Copán lies just six-and-a-half miles across the Honduras border, so close it is often regarded as a Guatemala travel destination. The border crossing is a tiny place called El Florido. There are shuttle vans from the border that go both to the village of Copán Ruinas and to the ruins a half-mile away. As the number of visitors to Copán has multiplied, the town of Copán Ruinas, which owes its very existence to the ancient site nearby, has become such a delightful place—with bargain hotels, restaurants that serve good coffee, and not a soldier in sight—that even without the ruins it would be a fun, funky destination. The walk between the village and the ruins' visitors center, along a pretty forest trail that parallels the road, takes you past monumental statues of ancient kings en route to the main ceremonial center.

Set on the bank of the Río Copán (also called the Río Amarillo), ancient Copán dominated an extensive series of valleys upriver for more than three centuries. Though it is one of the most remote parts of Honduras today, the valleys and forests around Copán were densely populated in ancient times. The city itself had a population of about 10,000, and most of the jungle in the valley had been cleared for agriculture, as it is today. Surrounding the main archaeological site, the vegetation has grown back in a

wild tangle of hardwoods and vines, from which archaeologists have reclaimed the ancient city's central plazas. Beautifully carved stelae, which
may mark astronomical alignments, stand on several hilltops reached by
one-half-mile and one-mile foot trails from the main center, and if you take
time to walk or ride horseback up to one of them, particularly **Stela 12**,
you will be rewarded with a stupendous view of the ruins and the river valley
over which the lords of Copán reigned. Carved on Stela 12 is the most complete genealogy anywhere of a Maya royal family; but only a few dozen
people in the world know how to read the inscription.

The first thing you see as you arrive at the ruins after a stroll down the
road from town is the big **Copán Museum of Maya Sculpture** (included
in ruins admission), a white-and-red, two-level, 40,000-square-foot structure. The entrance to the museum is through a snake's-mouth doorway and
a serpentine tunnel. At the other end is a full-size replica of the Rosalila
Temple, painted in its original colors. The temple this is modeled on, which
was found buried within the larger Temple 16, is not open to the public.
The museum exhibits six other building facades among its 3000 pieces of
sculpture from Copán, some of which are copies of ones owned by other
museums around the world.

The first part of the Copán ruins you enter is a group of low, broad-stepped
pyramids and ceremonial platforms that surround two small plazas desig-

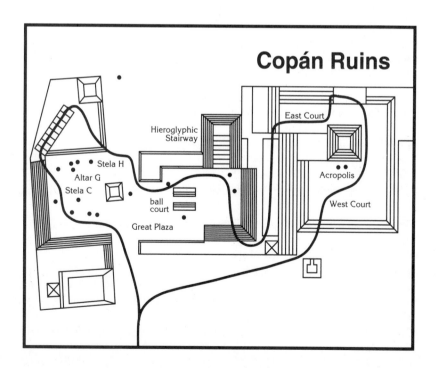

nated the **East Court** and the **West Court,** each with several pieces of less-than-awesome sculpture set in the stairways. Then, dramatically, you enter the **Great Plaza** of ancient Copán. Also known as the Plaza of Red Plaster, this broad ceremonial courtyard, now covered with lawn, was entirely paved during Copán's glory days. It contains the most remarkable sculptures found anywhere in the Maya world. While the major features of Copán—the great statues and the hieroglyphic stairway—are right on the plaza, the ancient city covered a large area and impressive stelae and unexcavated temple mounds can be found along a number of trails through the forest. These sites and trails are shown on a relief map in the visitors center.

Carved from massive blocks of a fine-textured stone called andesite, the stelae of Copán stand about ten feet tall. Unlike the relief stelae sculptures of human forms seen at other sites like Chichén Itzá, Palenque and Tikal, the stelae of Copán are carved almost completely in the round. There are a dozen stelae in the Great Plaza, all portraying rulers of Copán, and each statue is decorated with hieroglyphs that record the lineage, birth, marriage and death dates, and major accomplishments of the lord it represents. The headdresses, too, bear amazingly detailed ornamentation of stylized human and animal forms with symbolic meanings.

The stelae were originally painted bright red. **Stela C,** the only one in the plaza with faces on both sides, has fallen over and lain with one side protected from the weather for centuries, and so still shows traces of the paint. Each of the stelae has a cross-shaped underground vault at its base. Some of the vaults have been excavated to reveal objects such as knife blades, pottery, animal bones and even, in the vault below **Stela H,** pieces of gold imported from South America. The vaults are unique to Copán, and their exact meaning remains a mystery.

In front of several stelae are strange "zoomorphic" altars carved in highly stylized animal shapes (frogs, jaguars, giant snakes) and more fanciful forms patterned with hieroglyphs and sacred signs. The altars were used for religious offerings, including animal sacrifices. They may also have been used as thrones for priests. Near Stela H are two altars in the shape of plumed serpents, and a third showing men's faces peering from the open jaws of a two-headed snake. The two-headed snake, **Altar G,** bears the latest date hieroglyph found at Copán—800 A.D.

You can't miss the most spectacular structure in Copán, the **Hieroglyphic Stairway**. It's the one shaded by the huge tarp that was, unfortunately, erected too late to save much of the ancient Maya writing it contained from being erased by acid rain. Rising between two balustrades decorated with serpent motifs, the stairway is made from 2500 blocks of stone, each carved with hieroglyphs. The longest inscription found anywhere in the Maya world, it appears to be a comprehensive history of Copán up to the stairway's dedication date, 763 A.D. On this masterpiece, as John Lloyd Stephens mused a century and a half ago, the rulers of Copán "published a record of themselves, through which we might one day hold conference with a perished race." More than a few archaeologists have dedicated their whole lives to deciphering the message of the Hieroglyphic Stairway. Unfortunately, archaeologists reconstructed the stairway long before they knew how to read Maya hieroglyphs, so they had no way of putting them in correct sequence. Today, using computers to piece pictures of the stones together like a jigsaw puzzle, experts have translated roughly a third of it.

In 1989, members of the Copán Acropolis Archaeological Project tunneled 56 feet in from an entrance beside the Hieroglyphic Stairway to discover a large burial vault containing the remains of a noble personage believed to be a son of Copán's greatest king, Smoke-Imix, and brother of the next king, 18-Rabbit. Buried with him were some of the most exquisite jade carvings and jewelry that archaeologists have ever found at a Maya site.

Besides those in the new sculpture museum, other artifacts found during excavations of the ancient city are exhibited at the **Museo Regional de Arqueología**, facing the central plaza in the village of Copán Ruinas. In ancient times, the finest pottery in the Maya world—notably polychrome pieces decorated with elaborate ceremonial scenes—was made at Copán, and some of the best examples are on display in the museum along with tools, jade masks and jewelry. Some hieroglyph panels have been moved to the museums for protection from wear and erosion, while replicas have been installed at the ruins. Included among the exhibits are the complete contents of the tomb of a priest or sorcerer, found in a section of the archaeological zone now called **Las Sepulturas** ("The Tombs") and dated to about 450 A.D. Las Sepulturas, a small site that was once a ruling-class suburb of Copán, where a group of large stone houses has been restored, is located one-and-one-quarter mile past the main ruins on the same road.

Other points of interest around Copán Ruinas include **Agua Caliente** (admission), a cluster of thermal pools along the banks of a jungle river. To get there, follow the road that turns off the ruins road by the walled-in soccer field as it climbs into the hills north of town. The hot springs are a 45-minute drive into the hills. Minibuses go there and back from Copán Ruinas once or twice daily. At Santa Rita, a village 5 miles along the road past Copán, you can hike up the river to the **Cascada El Rubí**, a lovely secluded waterfall. About 12 miles past Copán is **Peña Quemada** (admission), a private rainforest reserve teeming with birds and also inhabited by rare howler monkeys; you can only visit with a guide.

LODGING   Spending the night on the Honduras side of the border affords you the opportunity to visit the ruins in the cool, misty hours just after dawn, when you may find that you have the mystery-laden site all to yourself. There are several small hotels in the village of Copán Ruinas. Travelers arriving by early afternoon usually have no problem finding a room. Streets in Copán Ruinas have no names or addresses, but nothing is farther than two blocks from the central plaza.

The best place in town is the 40-room **Hotel Marina Copán** (air-conditioning; cable TV; expensive; 504-983-070; fax: 504-573-076). It has a restaurant, a swimming pool, a private courtyard with benches under flowering shade trees, and usually tour buses parked in front. Rooms are spacious and attractive, with large dark wood desks and armoires.

Another clean, modern hotel, smaller and located just off the park, is the 12-room **Hotel Los Jaguares** (air-conditioning; phones; cable TV; moderate; 504-983-451). Surrounding a central courtyard, some rooms have private terraces.

One good bet is the 14-room **Hotel Maya Copán** (budget; no phone), on the town square. The hotel offers decent rooms with white walls and private baths separated from the main part of the room by low divider curtains. Rooms open onto a courtyard so overgrown with flora that guests feel like they are staying in the jungle, not in town. Some second-floor rooms also have views of the town plaza.

The **Hotel Los Gemelos** (shared baths; ceiling fans; budget; no phone), two blocks west of the plaza, offers simple rooms. There is a pleasant sitting area stocked with information on Honduras off a friendly little courtyard, and the low-budget price is right.

Down the road past the ruins, near the town of Santa Rita, the ✪ **Hacienda El Jaral** (ceiling fans; cable TV; moderate to expensive; 504-532-070; fax: 504-575-489) has 16 clean, modern rooms in a group of duplex cabins. The forested hillside setting makes an ideal base for exploring foot trails that run throughout the area. A lagoon on the resort property attracts birds— especially from October to May, when it is home to a flock of 3000 cattle egrets that migrate from the southern United States.

RESTAURANTS   There are more than a dozen restaurants and *comedores* in Copán Ruinas. The favorite of gringos in the know is the **Restaurante Bar Tunkul** (budget; no phone), an open-air place two blocks west of the plaza that serves giant burritos, garlic chicken, and excellent vegetarian plates as well as good coffee.

Across the street from the Tunkul, the **Restaurant La Llama del Bosque** (budget; no phone) bills itself as "Copán's original tourist restaurant," and judging from the stock of postcards and curios in the front part of the establishment, the claim is most likely accurate. The food is a mix of traditional Honduran dishes like *baleadas*, a local specialty, and various meats *parrilladas*.

Glifos (moderate to expensive), the restaurant inside the relatively fancy Hotel Marina, features a gringo-oriented menu featuring such selections as open-faced roast beef sandwiches, as well as daily gourmet specials. The setting is so nice you'll forget you're in Central America.

A more unusual choice for fine dining is **Los Gauchos** (moderate; no phone), a suburban-looking home on the edge of town that has been converted to a Uruguayan-style steakhouse where you can order up thick slabs of beef grilled over an open fire and served with cooked vegetables and spicy South American sauces and condiments. Seating on the long, narrow outdoor terrace provides a view of the neighboring farm pastures, cornfields and the mountains beyond.

GETTING THERE: From the Río Dulce area, you can hire a taxi or join an overnight tour to Copán, which lies just six-and-a-half miles across the Honduras border. The border crossing is a tiny place called El Florido. The border is open from 7:00 a.m. to 6:00 p.m. You must clear both Guatemalan and Honduran authorities each direction and pay fees in the US$5 to $10 range each time. Telling the border guards of both countries that you are only visiting the ruins saves time and trouble. The Honduran authorities will issue a frontier pass that eliminates the need to apply for a visa in advance. The Guatemalans will save your tourist card (the paper stapled to your passport), cancel the exit stamp when you return and let you back into the country on the same document, avoiding the technicality that would otherwise bar travelers without multiple-entry visas from reentering Guatemala for 72 hours. Minibuses putt back and forth frequently along the road from the border to both the ruins and the nearby village of Copán Ruinas.

RECOMMENDED READING

Baudez, Claude and Sydney Picasso. *Lost Cities of the Maya*. New York, Harry Abrams, 1992. An excellent account of recent discoveries and revelations in the Maya World.

Chaplin, Gordon. *Fever Coast Log*. New York, Simon & Shuster, 1992. A telling sailboat journey through the ports of Belize and Central America, related with biting wit and an eye for the offbeat.

Ellis, Zoila. *On Heroes, Lizards and Passion*. Benque Viejo del Carmen, Belize, Cubola Productions, 1988. A collection of seven short, warmly told stories by young Belizean writer Zoila Ellis.

Foster, Bryan. *The Baymen's Legacy*. Benque Viejo del Carmen, Belize, 1992. A history of Belize City, spanning the 18th to the 20th centuries, it's packed with interesting anecdotes.

Horwich, Robert H. and Jonathon Lyon. *A Belizean Rain Forest: The Community Baboon Sanctuary*. Gay Mills, Wisconsin, Orangutan Press, 1990. How a group of Belize farmers joined together to create one of the world's most unusual sanctuaries.

Kricher, John C. *A Neotropical Companion*. Princeton University Press, 1989. A fascinating and comprehensive handbook to the plants and animals of the rainforest.

Rabinowitz, Alan. *Jaguar: Struggle and Triumph in the Jungles of Belize*. New York, Doubleday, 1986. The highly entertaining story of a New York zoologist who befriended the local Maya and survived plane crashes, drug dealers and ruthless poachers in his quest to establish the world's only jaguar preserve. An excellent insight into Belize's Maya culture.

Rauscher, Freya. *Cruising Guide to Belize and Mexico's Caribbean Coast*. Westcott Cove Publishing Company, 1991. The most comprehensive guide to Belize's offshore, weaving navigation and description with local color and anecdotal history. Sailors will find it indispensable.

Schele, Linda and David Freidel. *A Forest of Kings: The Untold Story of the Ancient Maya*. William Morrow, 1990. The authors decode Maya hieroglyphs to unlock an astonishingly complex world of rulers and kingdoms. With detailed diagrams and splendid color photos.

Stephens, John L. *Incidents of Travel in Central America, Chiapas and Yucatan*. New York, Dover Publications, 1969 (two volumes). Originally published in 1841, this book covers Stephens' groundbreaking discoveries of the Maya world in Belize, Copán and Quiriguá.

Stephens, Katie. *Jungle Walk: Birds and Beasts of Belize*. Belize, Angelus Press, 1989. An amusing, informative guide to Belize's wild animals.

Wright, Ronald. *Time Among the Maya*. Weidenfeld & Nicolson, 1989. Told with passion, wit and cynicism, this follows the author's eventful journey through the Maya world.

Snakes of Belize. Belize City, Belize Audubon Society. A handy guide for anyone headed into the jungle.

GLOSSARY

CUISINE

ariba—Garifuna flatbread made with cassava

bamboo chicken—iguana

Belikin—Belize's ubiquitous national beer

boil up—a stew, usually made with fish

Caribbean Rum—Belize's best rum

cassava—ruddy white tuber and a staple of the Garifuna diet

ceviche—raw white fish cured in lime juice with diced onions, chilies, seasonings and tomatoes

fryjacks—ribbons of dough that are crisp-fried and showered with confectioners sugar

gibnut—a large, nocturnal rodent whose white meat is considered a delicacy (also called paca)

habañero—an extremely hot pepper, and the primary ingredient in Marie Sharp's Hot Pepper Sauce

heart of palm—tender, snow white core of the cohune palm, considered a delicacy since the time of the Maya

Marie Sharp's Hot Pepper Sauce—addictive habañero pepper sauce, brewed in southern Belize and found on most Belizean tables

stew—stewed as in stew chicken or stew beef

MISCELLANEOUS DEFINITIONS

baboon—black howler monkey

Belize breeze—marijuana

biosphere reserve—a nature preserve where human activity is controlled but not prohibited

biotope—areas within a biosphere reserve that have a uniform environment of plants and animals

brukdown—rhythmic island music, originating in 19th-century Belizean logging camps

cayo—Spanish for caye, or island. San Ignacio was named Cayo because from the air it appears as an island surrounded by rivers

chicle—the sap from the sapodilla tree, used during the early 1900s to make chewing gum

chiclero—Maya bush man who gathered *chicle*, mainly for the Wrigley's chewing gum and Life Savers companies *coatimundi*—also called a quash; a forest dweller, similar in appearance to a raccoon, that is easily spotted around Maya ruins and on back roads

dory—dugout canoe

garifuna—also *garinagu*; person of African and West Indian blood who immigrated from the island of St. Vincent

glyph—hieroglyph, as in those found in Maya cities

high bush—thick jungle

Kekchi—a distinct Belizean Maya group with its own Maya dialect

kinkajou—also called honey bear; a member of the raccoon family, with soft fur and a gregarious, endearing personality

Kukulcán—Maya sun god

Mestizo—person of mixed Spanish and Indian blood

milpa—corn field; often a slash-and-burn field

Mopan—a distinct Belizean Maya group with its own Maya dialect

peccary—a bristle-haired, snouted mammal that looks like a cross between a porcupine and a pig

pit-pan—wooden boat that plies the Belize rivers. Just 50 years ago, pit-pans were a primary transportation in Belize

pok-ta-pok—a basketball-style Maya sport using a small rubber ball

punta rock—Caribbean-style music that sounds part reggae, part disco and part rock-and-roll

sacbé—a Maya causeway that was paved with limestone in ancient times

sleeping policeman—speed bump

tapir—also called mountain cow, the shy, portly, long-snouted forest dweller is Belize's national animal

tayra—also called bushdog, it is a weasel-like animal that's extremely territorial

tiger—local term for jaguar

tiger cat—local word for ocelot; a "small tiger cat" is a margay

Yucatec—a distinct Belizean Maya group with its own Maya dialect

wee-wees—leaf-cutter ants

wowla or *woala*—boa constrictor

Index

Lodging Index

www. belizenet. com/lamanai.html

Dining Index

NOTES

Notes from the Publisher

An alert, adventurous reader is as important as a travel writer in keeping a guidebook up-to-date and accurate. So if you happen upon a great restaurant, discover a special locale or (heaven forbid) find an error in the text, we'd appreciate hearing from you. Just write to:

Ulysses Press
P.O. Box 3440
Berkeley, CA 94703

***

It is our desire as publishers to create guidebooks that are responsible as well as informative.

We hope that our guidebooks treat the people, country and land we visit with respect. We ask that our readers do the same. The hiker's motto, "Walk softly on the Earth," applies to travelers everywhere . . . in the desert, on the beach and in town.

You're already helping!

**Simply by purchasing the *The New Key to Belize*
you have helped preserve Belize's environment.**

Would you like to do more?

At Ulysses Press, we believe that ecotourism can have a positive impact on a region's environment and can actually help preserve its natural state. In line with this philosophy, we donate a percentage of the sales from all New Key guides to conservation organizations working in the destination country—in Belize our environmental partner is *The Belize Zoo & Tropical Education Center.*

Founded in 1983, *The Belize Zoo & Tropical Education Center* is one of the newest zoos in Central America, and one of the most progressive zoos in the world. The more than 100 species of animals are not kept in cages; instead they dwell in expansive patches of their natural forest habitat. Plus, none of the animals were captured to be placed in the zoo; they were all injured, abused or abandoned animals that the zoo rescued and rehabilitated, but that can not be returned to the wild.

Dedicated to bringing the native wildlife closer to the people of Belize, the zoo has an interactive education facility where thousands come to learn about the special natural resources of Belize and the importance of conserving and pre-serving them.

Ulysses Press encourages you to further support this organization. For more information or to make a donation contact:

The Belize Zoo & Tropical Education Center
P.O. Box 1787
Belize City, Belize, C.A.
Phone and Fax: 501-81-3004

HIDDEN GUIDES

Adventure travel or a relaxing vacation?—"Hidden" guidebooks are the only travel books in the business to provide detailed information on both. Aimed at environmentally aware travelers, our motto is "Adventure Travel Plus." These books combine details on unique hotels, restaurants and sightseeing with information on camping, sports and hiking for the outdoor enthusiast.

THE NEW KEY GUIDES

Based on the concept of ecotourism, The New Key Guides are dedicated to the preservation of Central America's rare and endangered species, architecture and archaeology. Filled with helpful tips, they give travelers everything they need to know about these exotic destinations.

ULTIMATE FAMILY GUIDES

These innovative guides present the best and most unique features of a family destination. Quality is the keynote. In addition to thoroughly covering each destination, they feature short articles and one-line "teasers" that are both fun and informative.

Ulysses Press books are available at bookstores everywhere. If any of the following titles are unavailable at your local bookstore, ask the bookseller to order them.

You can also order books directly from Ulysses Press
P.O. Box 3440, Berkeley, CA 94703
800-377-2542 or 510-601-8301
fax: 510-601-8307
e-mail: Ulypress@aol.com

Order Form

HIDDEN GUIDEBOOKS

____ Hidden Arizona, $13.95
____ Hidden Bahamas, $12.95
____ Hidden Baja, $14.95
____ Hidden Boston and Cape Cod, $11.95
____ Hidden Carolinas, $16.95
____ Hidden Coast of California, $16.95
____ Hidden Colorado, $13.95
____ Hidden Florida, $16.95
____ Hidden Florida Keys & Everglades, $10.95
____ Hidden Hawaii, $16.95
____ Hidden Idaho, $13.95
____ Hidden Maui, $12.95
____ Hidden Montana, $13.95

____ Hidden New England, $16.95
____ Hidden New Mexico, $13.95
____ Hidden Oahu, $12.95
____ Hidden Oregon, $13.95
____ Hidden Pacific Northwest, $16.95
____ Hidden Rockies, $16.95
____ Hidden San Francisco and
      Northern California, $15.95
____ Hidden Southern California, $16.95
____ Hidden Southwest, $16.95
____ Hidden Tahiti, $16.95
____ Hidden Tennessee, $15.95
____ Hidden Wyoming, $13.95

THE NEW KEY GUIDEBOOKS

____ The New Key to Belize, $14.95
____ The New Key to Cancún and
      the Yucatán, $14.95
____ The New Key to Costa Rica, $16.95

____ The New Key to Ecuador and
      the Galápagos, $16.95
____ The New Key to Guatemala, $14.95

ULTIMATE FAMILY GUIDEBOOKS

____ Disneyland and Beyond, $12.95

____ Disney World and Beyond, $13.95

Mark the book(s) you're ordering and enter the total cost here ➡ [   ]

California residents add 8% sales tax here ➡ [   ]

Shipping, check box for your preferred method and enter cost here ➡ [   ]

☐ BOOK RATE   **FREE! FREE! FREE!**

☐ PRIORITY MAIL $3.00 First book, $1.00/each additional book

☐ UPS 2-DAY AIR $7.00 First book, $1.00/each additional book

[   ]

Billing, enter total amount due here and check method of payment ➡

☐ CHECK   ☐ MONEY ORDER

☐ VISA/MASTERCARD _____ EXP. DATE _____

NAME _____ PHONE _____

ADDRESS _____

_____

CITY _____ STATE _____ ZIP_____

MONEY-BACK GUARANTEE ON DIRECT ORDERS PLACED THROUGH ULYSSES PRESS.

ABOUT THE AUTHOR

Stacy Ritz is the author of *Hidden Carolinas* and *Disney World and Beyond: The Ultimate Family Guidebook*. She also co-authored *Hidden Florida* and *Hidden New England*. Formerly a staff writer for *The Tampa Tribune*, she is a regular contributor to *Bride's* magazine and the *Fort Lauderdale Sun-Sentinel*, and has written for *Parents* magazine, the *Washington Post*, *Miami Herald*, *Orlando Sentinel*, *Caribbean Travel & Life* and *Detroit News*. She lives in the Florida Keys.

ABOUT THE ILLUSTRATOR

Glenn Kim is a freelance illustrator residing in San Francisco. His work appears in numerous Ulysses Press titles, including *Hidden Tahiti*, *Hidden Southwest* and *The New Key to Guatemala*. He has also done illustrations for the National Forest Service, several Bay Area magazines, book covers and greeting cards, as well as for advertising agencies.